"The media landscape continues to shift dramatically each year, and reliance on PR pros to deliver is significant. They're counted on to provide strong, compelling pitches to writers and editors who are extremely stretched; to provide effective spokespeople for interviews; to disseminate excellent photos and videos, and other dynamic content; and, to deliver ideas and accompanying materials aimed beyond print. This book explains how that happens."

Meghan Finn, *Chief Communications & Engagement Officer at Breast Cancer Research Foundation*

"Today writing is highly focused on 'owned PR.' For example, we are writing content for our own internal newsrooms and digital properties and writing posts for corporate or social channels. *Strategic Public Relations Writing* shows how that works."

Alfred D'Agostino, *Director, Corporate Affairs, Leadership Communications at PayPal*

D0882063

STRATEGIC PUBLIC RELATIONS WRITING

Putting strategy front and center, this public relations writing textbook coaches students to readiness for a career as an effective strategic communicator.

The book focuses on the strategic aspect of public relations writing that distinguishes it from other writing, such as journalistic or academic. It highlights the essential types of writing necessary for effective public relations in multiple media channels, demonstrated by contemporary cases direct from practitioners working today. Overviews of the various tactical formats that must be mastered for powerful, strategic public relations – ranging from social media posts and website updates to podcasts, speeches and infographics – prepare students to be effective and up-to-date professionals. Full of examples and exercises, the book's strength is in its practical utility for career preparation and success.

This text is suited to public relations writing courses at the undergraduate and postgraduate level, particularly those with a focus on strategy or that combine strategy and writing into one course.

Online resources include chapter outlines; a test bank; sample homework, paper and portfolio-building assignments; and lecture slides. They can be accessed at www.routledge.com/9781032163871.

Jim Eggensperger taught at Iona College, USA, for 18 years and is Adjunct Professor there in the Department of Mass Communication and Adjunct Professor in the College of Business and Communications at Brenau University, USA.

Jeanne M. Salvatore is Assistant Professor in the Advertising & Marketing Communications program in the School of Business & Technology at Fashion Institute of Technology in New York, USA, and Adjunct Professor in the Department of Media and Communications Arts at City College in New York, USA.

STRATEGIC PUBLIC RELATIONS WRITING

Proven Tactics and Techniques

Jim Eggensperger and Jeanne M. Salvatore

Routledge
Taylor & Francis Group

NEW YORK AND LONDON

First published 2022
by Routledge
605 Third Avenue, New York, NY 10158

and by Routledge
4 Park Square, Milton Park, Abingdon, Oxon, OX14 4RN

Routledge is an imprint of the Taylor & Francis Group, an informa business

Library of Congress Cataloging-in-Publication Data
Names: Eggensperger, Jim, author. | Salvatore, Jeanne, author.
Title: Strategic public relations writing : proven tactics and
    techniques / Jim Eggensperger and Jeanne Salvatore.
Description: New York, NY : Routledge, 2022. | Includes
    bibliographical references and index.
Identifiers: LCCN 2021060883 (print) | LCCN 2021060884 (ebook) |
    ISBN 9781032157313 (hardback) | ISBN 9781032163871
    (paperback) | ISBN 9781003248330 (ebook)
Subjects: LCSH: Public relations—Authorship. | Public relations.
Classification: LCC HD59 .E344 2022 (print) | LCC HD59 (ebook) |
    DDC 659.2072—dc23/eng/20220104
LC record available at https://lccn.loc.gov/2021060883
LC ebook record available at https://lccn.loc.gov/2021060884

ISBN: 978-1-032-15731-3 (hbk)
ISBN: 978-1-032-16387-1 (pbk)
ISBN: 978-1-003-24833-0 (ebk)

DOI: 10.4324/9781003248330

Typeset in Garamond
by Apex CoVantage, LLC

Access the Support Material: www.routledge.com/9781032163871

CONTENTS

FIGURES

PREFACE

Writing about writing in the digital age is a fraught endeavor and is complicated to a higher degree when the writing is about public relations and PR strategies.

The current textbook was not undertaken lightly. Both the authors had full plates and full lives, but they came together and concluded that the work would be valuable to students with career trajectories leading to professional communications.

We scanned the landscape and concluded that even books we had assigned in courses about PR writing did not meet our personal ideals and our professional and academic experience.

And so, the adventure was launched and resulted in what you are holding. It is the product of uncounted discussions, emails and texts with professional friends and academic colleagues and feedback from years of teaching the principles and techniques and mindset of producing effective public communications.

Jeanne and Jim worked together at Iona College in New Rochelle, New York, and stayed in touch over years and through job changes and geographic separation, linked by professional interest and dedication to the development of PR professionals.

That said, the book could not have been imagined, proposed and completed without the encouragement, interest and help of a great number of people.

Jeanne especially wants to thank her family and friends for their encouragement and support during a very busy writing schedule. She would also like to thank her students at The Fashion Institute of Technology and New York's City College, who were a constant source of inspiration for this book.

Jim could not have spent the time and thought without the active support and understanding of wife Lydia, sons JT and Ryan and their families, as well as a platoon of former students and colleagues.

New colleagues – Dr. Julia Clay at Brenau University in Gainesville, Georgia, in particular – have provided a comfortable and welcoming new academic home and lab for writing ideas and learning.

Jim Eggensperger, PhD
Brenau University
Jeanne M. Salvatore, MS, MA
New York Fashion Institute
December 2021

ACKNOWLEDGMENTS

We do want to thank, in no particular order, our friends and colleagues at Brenau University, The Fashion Institute of Technology and New York's City College in New York City, who cheered and nudged in the various stages that make up the book-writing and production processes.

Students and colleagues helped to formulate the ideas that make up the text and provided opportunities and insights that pointed to the need for a book that reflects strategic public relations writing and thinking as it stands in the third decade of the 21st century.

In particular, Jim is indebted to the following: Meghan Finn, an Iona College alum and big-hearted supporter; Supriya Anand, another Iona alum and senior digital marketing strategist at Amazon Web Services; Aaron Virola, vice president and general manager of AxiCom NY; Dwayne Doherty, an alum and senior vice president for PR at Rockefeller Group; Lauren Samaha, now with consumer public relations at Amazon; Johanna Younghans Baker, a senior editor at Michigan Medicine; and Al D'Agostino, director, corporate affairs and leadership communications at PayPal.

Jeanne would like to thank Sherry Goldman, president, Goldman Communications Group, for her insight and encouragement; Chris Vaccaro, senior media relations specialist, NOAA Communications; former co-worker Mike Barry, chief communications officer at the Insurance Information Institute; Grant Winter, a veteran journalist who works for the Black News Channel; Lea-Ann Germinder, president and founder, Germinder and Associates; Douglas Simon, chief executive officer, DS Simon Media; Leslie Gottlieb, president, LG Strategic Communications, and Dan Prince, president, Prince Communications.

It goes without saying that our publisher at Taylor and Francis, Felisa Salvago-Keyes, played an unmatched role in guiding and fostering the development of this text. We owe her a real debt of gratitude.

These lists show that we cannot take all or most of the credit for the contents, only responsibility for omissions, overlooks and shortcomings.

Jim Eggensperger and Jeanne M. Salvatore
Cumming, Georgia, and New York City
November 2021

NOTE TO PROFESSORS AND COLLEAGUES

Thank you for taking a look at *Strategic Public Relations Writing: Proven Tactics and Techniques*.

As seasoned, scarred practitioners who teach advanced PR students every semester, we wrote the book we would like to use – one that explains both how to create PR tactics as well as why they are being executed. The goal of this textbook is to propel students into meaningful careers, armed with the skills that employers will value and have told us that they want.

We think this book brings together thinking and writing approaches that have not been seen in a single textbook before. There are certainly textbooks that focus on how to draft PR tactics like press releases, media advisories and infographics. There are also textbooks on social media. And, of course, there are textbooks on public relations. However, as professors of communications, we could not find a single textbook that combines all of these topics. And that has current examples from executives and practitioners at major agencies and companies.

And there is the business part. As a former student who is a senior vice president at a major PR firm wrote:

> We want to see senior hires be able to convey strategic thinking through high-level writing and formats such as plan development, presentations, new business proposals. My day-to-day goes from pitching media to writing award acceptance remarks, internal organizational change emails, newsletters, reactive issues statements – the list goes on!

As former communications executives as well as college professors, we have drawn upon current PR practitioners for current cases that use the latest techniques to create tactics and even campaigns that have been successful – even winning awards – for their clients and organizations.

We believe wholeheartedly that live cases provide some of the best possible learning opportunities. Some of the cases have been written to disguise client or company names, but the reality shines through. Why do we focus on marketplace activities more than theories?

The world has shifted. And, even though the public relations field has always been very dynamic, PR professionals are seeing more change than ever. The profession is constantly evolving. From the SEC permitting release of news by Twitter to iPhone movies being sent to media outlets after being edited in the field, the ecosystem (as lots of students explain to us) has undergone tectonic shifts. In fact, students should expect that the public relations profession should radically change in the four years they spend in school.

The goal of this text is to prepare students not only for the profession of today but for the one of the future. Therefore, the value proposition of this text is for students to have a better grasp of understanding, describing and advising on strategy, organizational objectives and having a keen insight of the power of public relations to reach strategic goals.

"You have to understand upper management and be able to add value to the organization's decisions" is the kind of advice we have heard.

It is important to note that this book assumes that the student has the basic ability to write. This is not a textbook about how to write. We assume that students using this text will be ready for more strategic stuff, being persuasive and describing nuanced situations. PR writing is a very specific type of writing. And this book will provide ample opportunity to practice and hone the craft. It will also address PR editing and the evolution of language in society.

This textbook provides that point of view, starting with an overview of strategy as seen by CEOs and working through new approaches to familiar tactics – from news releases to press kits – that abide by the new velocity for information and the higher-level attitude and cognition demanded of PR pros.

Textbook Special Features

We have added some teaching tools that should help to make this new approach fit into your classroom. We have included one real-life success campaign planning outline that will show students step-by-step the thinking, decision-making, creative actions and goals for a 21st-century campaign. We also have developed a campaign planner, which can be used to create a semester-long series of connected assignments leading to a sample campaign.

We have added checklists for different tactics to show the critical steps and inclusions.

And we have added insight stories that demonstrate how high-level, long-range strategy can guide a PR and branding campaign according to some of the most successful PR people in the field.

And these examples will be updated periodically on the Taylor and Francis textbook site, so there will be contemporary links and examples that students can relate to.

As authors, we want you to succeed in the classroom and prepare the next generation of advanced PR professionals with practice-tested assignments.

1 INTRODUCTION
The Strategic PR Professional

Learning Goals for This Chapter

After reading this chapter, you should be able to:

- Describe strategic communications for organizations.
- Discuss the role of PR professionals in defining and describing strategy.
- Explain how strategy can be communicated to multiple audiences.
- Show knowledge of changes in speed, writing formats and audiences and how the changes have affected strategic public relations.

Strategic.

What does that word mean in the world of public relations? Or in the world at large?

In the worlds of business and other organizations, strategic thinking and strategy development are vital and highly valued. They are the focus of MBA courses, of academic journal articles and of yearly meetings in organizations of all types.

The Center for Management and Organization Effectiveness says it this way: "Strategic thinking is simply an intentional and rational thought process that focuses on the analysis of critical factors and variables that will influence the long-term success of a business, a team, or an individual." Go to www.cmoe.org to read more.

Being strategic – in thinking, acting and writing – is important for people making big decisions that may involve taking big risks. By the same token, thinking and acting strategically is critically important to public relations professionals who need to think much as executives – and at times even more. How does PR fit into that? PR has the job of turning high-level planning and occasionally very esoteric actions and concepts into stories that can be understood and appreciated by many different audiences or stakeholders – defined as people important to an organization's success.

Cision and PRWeek surveyed 560 senior-level PR or communications professionals in mid-2021. The respondents came from both agencies and in-house departments. The study revealed that the senior PR executives have concluded

that PR's end goal has to be far more strategic than simply getting blanket coverage. It has to be a means to a bigger business end. Almost eight in ten pros (79%) say

DOI: 10.4324/9781003248330-1

their PR campaigns focus on engaging the end user/target audience. Only 21% said it is about getting as many stories placed as possible.

To quote the Center for Management and Organization Effectiveness again: "Strategic thinking is the ability to anticipate, prepare and get positioned for the future. Strategic people think and act before they have to – before they are forced to take up a defensive or reactive position."

That almost sounds like the approach of a grandmaster of chess – anticipating moves and thinking steps ahead of the opponent.

Those big decisions vary widely. They can involve such actions as launching a revolutionary product or planning a hostile takeover of another company or moving corporate headquarters to another state. Strategy calls for people who think beyond the horizon, beyond the next quarter or even the next year – people who are comfortable with the future and with taking into consideration the many forces that face modern organizations.

The role of public relations has never been more vital for organizations than it is today, in the third decade of the 21st century. PR can influence events around the world, help organizations be effective and successful, and guide decision-makers to the best outcomes.

Supriya Anand, senior digital marketing strategist at Amazon Web Services, said this about the changing nature of PR and communications strategies:

In the last five years of my career, the companies I've worked for are looking for PR to build thought leadership, change perceptions or become market leaders in a particular category. Most of this is driven by competitive landscape, media coverage or consumer demands.

Therefore, there are new demands placed on marketing and PR professionals to continuously monitor what is being said about their company across the media landscape to assess opportunities and risks.

This textbook was written to guide higher-level students in public relations and related fields to understand some of the challenges of strategic thinking in organizations and how writing can support the development and implementation of strategies for organizations of all sizes and types.

Thinking strategically includes a broad range of activities and skills. It's recognizing major trends – seeing, for example, some of the impact that the transition to digital information can have on everything from movie watching to reminders from your home control device to bring home bread and milk. It's thinking far and wide, from across the street to over the horizon. It's understanding the inner workings of an organization and how they can be explained to audiences inside and outside.

Comprehending the actions of an organization can be difficult until you learn to think about being the boss. Then you have to balance competing demands for time, resources and people. You have to learn how to handle competing factions like sales versus manufacturing. And you have to understand how to sell or convince others that your ideas will work and are the best.

Larry Bossidy (Bossidy and Charan, 2009), the former chief executive officer of GE Credit Corp. and CEO of Allied Signal Corp., writes about running a business this way: "The leader must be in charge of getting things done by running the three core processes – picking other leaders, setting the strategic direction and conducting operations." That quote really gives you some insight as to what is important to the people at the top of an organization where you might work – whether a company that makes things for sale or a nonprofit that helps hundreds or thousands of people or a PR agency working for a variety of organizations.

Jack Welch, an almost legendary American businessman and Bossidy's boss at GE, wrote about strategy in his book *Jack: Straight from the Gut*, saying: "Business success is less a function of grandiose predictions than it is a result of being able to respond rapidly to real changes as they occur. That's why strategy has to be dynamic and anticipatory" (p. 390).

In short, PR people need to empathize with multiple audiences – some call them stakeholders – and to explain positions that may be very attractive or may be very unappealing.

Strategic PR pros have the job of turning high-level planning and at times very esoteric actions and concepts into stories and responding quickly in changing situations. It's writing on a deadline and creating word pictures that virtually anyone can understand.

This textbook resulted from years of thinking strategically and advising senior management about the best strategic options for the good of companies, nonprofits, associations and a wide variety of organizations.

It demonstrates strategic thinking by PR professionals in the fray today, some of whom work for major corporations and nonprofits. Others guide the communications fortunes of clients who range from hospitals to giant multinational consumer-products firms. You will find PR cases that range from travel promotion to fighting deadly diseases. And you will get to peek behind the curtain and see how these seasoned professionals managed situations strategically.

And you will be supported by checklists and detailed explanations of how to find and use strategic information. How to write for various situations. And get tips about what not to do.

For example, if you were working for a large pharmaceutical company which was developing a life-saving drug that showed some good promise, but had a couple of unexpected setbacks in the last phase of testing, how would you approach the explanation?

- Be defensive and say the company was doing its best?
- Be optimistic but empathetic and display human emotions and concern for any people hurt during the testing?
- Be remote from the personal issues and discuss the science of testing and the potential great things that could come out of the discoveries and mention that the company has spent billions of dollars on getting the new product to this stage and should be commended for its vision and courage?

Authors' note: The following description of a contemporary strategic PR strategy was written by an executive in a New York PR firm. It highlights the changing nature of PR, driven by digital technology and reduced media presence. The name of the author and the client identity have been removed at the request of the client.

The Shifting Landscape of PR Writing

Strategic writing has shifted tremendously in the world of public relations.

Driven mostly by the shrinking media landscape, we've moved from drafting two- or three-page press releases to drafting one-page blogs or announcements packed with visuals and content. All in an effort to better serve journalists who have limited time and attention spans.

What's more, the perspective and voice captured in writing has become more important than ever. Similar to the style of pitches and social posts, long-form writing (blogs and press releases) needs to be condensed and presented in the simplest way possible.

The new rules:

- Use fewer words than before.
- Be bold in the perspective.
- Use weekend language (no jargon).

Even when supporting some of the most complex ideas or concepts, using simple language can often make or break your ability to secure coverage and tell impactful stories. This becomes especially important when trying to break through or create white spaces for clients that enable them to articulate the value of new products or establish thought leadership perspectives.

For example, my client, a leader in the technology/PC sector, attends a high-profile trade show every year but recently was desperately looking for new ways to approach up-leveling their written content.

In years past, the client – as well as their competitors – would list speeds and feeds in their press releases with little to no focus on the customer benefit or value. We advised our client to rethink their storytelling approach by leading with the customer experience/value of their new products and back that up by only messaging their most differentiated features and specs.

For those journalists who wanted every last detail, we provided media with a link to a virtual press kit, giving them access to documents, materials and visuals that would go deep on each product. Separately, we also created a series of blog posts around big industry bets to further establish their thought leadership and provide media with enriched narratives that would layer additional context and color around our stories. In the end, the approach paid off, resulting in a YoY *(authors' note: year over year)* increase of tier one media coverage and message pull through.

The authors fervently hope that by the end of your course and with the aid of this text, you will have a deep understanding of the power and challenge of writing strategically for public relations and related communications disciplines.

Robert Dilenschneider, a revered thinker about public relations and former chairman of the communications firm Hill and Knowlton, wrote about this in 2010: "The public relations sector spills over into many specialized areas that require very specific and sophisticated communications skills."

The Arthur Page Society, an organization of top communications officers at major businesses, said this in its 2017 report titled "CEO View: Communications at the Center of the Enterprise":

> Total business knowledge is table stakes. In years past, CEOs have expressed hope that their CCO (chief communications officer) would know all about their enterprise's business in order to more strategically apply communications to advance its goals. Now, many CEOs require their CCO to be knowledgeable about the business – from strategy to operations – so they are able to provide strategic input on issues that span business functions. This is especially true at enterprises with communications departments that are well established and have a broad mandate. At these enterprises, CCOs are expected to have enough business background and insight to weigh in intelligently on areas well outside of their core communications competency, such as supply chain, finance, sales and beyond. You can read the Page Society report here: https://knowledge.page.org/report/the-ceo-view-communications-at-the-center-of-the-enterprise/

For most organizations, strategy underpins all functions. It starts with the vision and the mission, which are usually developed based on the origins of the enterprise – why it was started and how it has evolved over time. The categories of goals for modern organizations are virtually unlimited. The founder of Netflix, Inc., Reed Hastings, took the idea of having consumers order DVDs by mail to some investors in early 2000 and was laughed out of the room. But he and his partner thought they had an idea whose time had come. And within ten years, the primary competitor for Netflix was bankrupt and Netflix had gone public and had millions of customers, which it then moved to streaming.

In his book, *No Rules Rules: Netflix and the Culture of Reinvention*, Hastings writes that the company strategy was based on "a culture that valued people over process, emphasized innovation over efficiency and had very few controls." Few companies have survived and prospered as Netflix has, especially with an operating philosophy that is very different from most other large companies.

It is important for communications people to look at corporate cultures and mission statements and interpret them into communications and the brand promise of the organization. Some executives suggest that they are guided by the Black Swan Principle. Nassim Nicholas Taleb, a professor at the University of Massachusetts, identified the principle as "a highly improbable event with three principal characteristics: it is unpredictable; it carries a massive impact; and, after the fact, we concoct an explanation that makes it appear less random and more predictable than it was."

PR professionals must be aware of the tendency to normalize unusual situations and explain them as routine or expected. That kind of thinking can seriously damage an organization's reputation and brand.

To be effective and valuable, you must understand how the organization works.

First: how does it want to be viewed by its various audiences?

Second: is it reaching that goal, based on feedback and research with key audiences and stakeholders – defined as people who have an interest in the organization and who range from employees and customers and shareholders for public companies to constituents and donors for nonprofits?

Third: does it operate as it says it does, or is there a disconnect between words and actions?

Sample Lists of Stakeholders

Business Enterprise	Nonprofit Organization
Employees	Employees
Customers	Constituents/recipients
Shareholders	Donors/supporters
Vendors/suppliers	Vendors/suppliers
Government regulators	Government agencies
Associations	Communities
Communities	National associations

Thinking strategically is part of all that. It's recognizing major trends – seeing, for example, some of the impact that the transition to digital information can have on everything.

How to see the actions of an organization can be difficult until you learn to think about being the boss. Then you have to balance competing demands for time, resources and people. You have to learn how to manage warring factions like sales versus manufacturing. And you have to understand how to sell or convince others that your ideas will work and are the best.

PR professionals need to understand all of those vectors of ideas, demands, public pressures and social trends and explain them, both inside the organization and outside. In short, PR people need to empathize with stakeholders – and to explain positions that may be very attractive or may be very unappealing.

The Page Society report, based on interviews with 24 chief executive officers in late 2016, demonstrates how the role of communications has evolved and become more critical than ever, at least in the eyes of those chief executives. Here are the key priorities for chief communications officers and their functions, according to these CEOs, all of which ran multi-billion-dollar enterprises:

- Be always on; be always monitoring.
- Social value must be baked into the business plan.
- The CCO must oversee corporate character across the whole enterprise.
- The line between internal and external communications is now blurred.
- Communications is officially a central part of the corporate strategy.

- Get everyone on the same page.
- Determine the ideal key performance indicators (KPIs) for the organization.
- Help build the CEO's personal brand externally.

That's quite a job description. And while this came from commercial enterprises, the responsibilities will be similar at nonprofits and nongovernmental organizations, also known as NGOs.

Harold Burson, who was hailed by the industry publication PRWeek in 1999 as the most influential PR person of the 20th century, was to have said, according to his 2020 obituary in the *New York Times*, that he

> was less interested in hiring reporters with contacts than in finding good writers who could capture the essence of a client. As business and financial news reporting improved in the 1970s and '80s, he sought writers adept at detailed analysis, not the old puffery about chief executives and companies.

This book will go into these areas in later chapters.

Writing strategically is a key skill that comes from adopting the strategic mindset. But it is not easy. You have to be able to understand the big, big picture and its implications while reducing decisions and imperatives to headlines and concepts easily grasped by a wide range of people – those stakeholders, who include customers, donors, shareholders, employees, government regulators and a potentially wide range of others.

Chapter Summary

- Thinking, acting and communicating strategically has become an integral part of the role of communications professionals.
- Strategic thinking and acting involve a deep understanding of the goals, processes and mission of the organization being supported, whether a client or an employer.
- Strategy is looking at the horizon or even beyond it. It is planning and thinking how things can be.

Exercises

1. Look at the list of Fortune 500 companies or a large nonprofit like the United Way or the American Cancer Society or a nongovernmental organization like the United Nations to find its mission statement and the title of its chief communications officer. Compare a recent press release to the mission statement and note how well they are aligned. In other words, do they use some of the same vocabulary? Does the release reflect the tone and direction of the mission statement? What is the title of the chief communications officer? Does he or she work directly for the chief executive?

2. Review the mission statements of three organizations of your choosing. For best comparisons, they should be in the same industry or have similar orientations.

In other words, choose car companies or banks or nonprofits or similar NGOs. Compare and contrast the mission statements. Do they use similar language? Are they similar in length? Very unemotional and businesslike or more personal and emotional?

3. Pick a company that you deal with regularly, whether the make of your phone or the cellular service you use or the car you drive or your favorite brand of clothes. Look up the company and think about what that company has for stakeholders. Be sure to think about people who might not be readily visible – for example, neighbors near company headquarters or near a distribution location. You may also use your college and think about its stakeholders beyond students and parents.

4. Think of an experience you have had with an organization and write a short essay regarding your experience and what it told you about the way the organization operates. In other words, if you were treated rudely, do you think that was part of the way the organization wanted to be known or was that a reflection of the attitude of one or a couple of employees? How do you think corporate culture develops? In other words, how do employees learn to act within an organization? Use your own experience if you have some in jobs or as a volunteer.

Glossary

Stakeholders – groups or individuals who have more than a passing interest in an organization. The interest may be financial, social or environmental. The needs and expectations of shareholders are part of the calculation that goes into any communications activity.

References

Arthur Page Society. (2017). *CEO View: Communications at the Center of the Enterprise*. https://knowledge.page.org/report/the-ceo-view-communications-at-the-center-of-the-enterprise/

Bossidy, L., & Charan, R. (2009). *Execution: The Discipline of Getting Things Done* (Rev. ed.). Crown Business.

Center for Management and Organization Effectiveness. (n.d.). *The Need for Strategic Perspective*. https://cmoe.com/blog/the-need-for-strategic-perspective/

Cision, Inc. (2021). *2021 Global Comms Report*. www.cision.com/resources/white-papers/2021-global-comms-report/

Dilenschneider, R. L., & American Management Association. (2010). *The AMA Handbook of Public Relations*. AMACOM.

Hastings, R., & Meyer, E. (2020). *No Rules: Netflix and the Culture of Reinvention*. Penguin Press.

McFadden, R. (2020). Harold Burson, a Giant in Public Relations, Dies at 98. *The New York Times*, January 10, 2020. www.nytimes.com/2020/01/10/business/media/harold-burson-dead.html

Taleb, N. N. (2007). *The Black Swan: The Impact of the Highly Improbable*. Random House.

Welch, J., & Byrne, J. A. (2001). *Jack: Straight from the Gut*. Warner Business Books.

2 CREATING NEWS

The question "What is news?" sounds simple and straightforward. A journalist might just reply something snarky like "news is whatever my editor tells me it is." Or "I know it when I see it." But it is a question of vital importance both to the media and to the strategic practice of public relations writing.

Academics and media scholars spend a lot of time trying to define the essential elements of what constitutes news. A study by Tony Harcup and Deirdre O'Neill in 2017 says, "We have found that potential news stories must generally satisfy one and preferably more of the following requirements to be selected" by journalists for publication:

- Exclusivity: Stories generated by, or available first to, the news organization as a result of interviews, letters, investigations, surveys, polls, and so on.
- Bad news: Stories with particularly negative overtones such as death, injury, defeat and loss (a plane crash or oil spill, for example).
- Conflict: Stories concerning conflict such as controversies, arguments, splits, strikes, fights, insurrections and warfare.
- Surprise: Stories that have an element of surprise, contrast and/or the unusual about them.
- Audio-visuals: Stories that have arresting photographs, video, audio and/or which can be illustrated with infographics.

DOI: 10.4324/9781003248330-2

- Shareability: Stories that are thought likely to generate sharing and comments via Facebook, Twitter and other forms of social media.
- Entertainment: Soft stories concerning sex, show business, sport, lighter human interest, animals, or offering opportunities for humorous treatment, witty headlines or lists.
- Drama: Stories concerning an unfolding drama such as escapes, accidents, searches, sieges, rescues, battles or court cases.
- Follow-up: Stories about subjects already in the news.
- The power elite: Stories concerning powerful individuals, organizations, institutions or corporations.
- Relevance: Stories about groups or nations perceived to be influential with, or culturally or historically familiar to, the audience.
- Magnitude: Stories perceived as sufficiently significant in the large numbers of people involved or in potential impact or involving a degree of extreme behavior or extreme occurrence.
- Celebrity: Stories concerning people who are already famous.
- Good news: Stories with particularly positive overtones such as recoveries, breakthroughs, cures, wins and celebrations.
- News organization's agenda: Stories that set or fit the news organization's own agenda, whether ideological, commercial or as part of a specific campaign.

For you as a public relations writer, understanding "What is news?" is a question that can determine success or failure. After all, one of the most important strategic tasks of PR professionals is making news for their organization or client. There are many ways to make news. It can range from a pharmaceutical company announcing the availability of a lifesaving drug to a cookbook author issuing tips on how to properly cook a turkey.

And another important role is deciding what specific news outlet is appropriate for the news you are pitching. The term "media" has come to encompass print or online newspapers and magazines, broadcast news outlets such as NBC, CNN or FOX News, online news outlets such as the Huffington Post and BuzzFeed, and wire services such as the Associated Press.

The size and demographics of news outlets are vastly different. They are also all in competition with each other. But what they all have in common is that they are in the news business. News is the commodity that they sell. Media outlets succeed or fail by their ability to:

- Be the first to break a news story.
- Provide a different point of view.
- Be the best at explaining a news topic to their target audiences.

So, what does this have to do with strategic public relations writing? The answer: everything! Understanding "What is news?" can determine the success or failure of a public relations campaign. After all, one of the key goals of public relations writing is to convince the media that you have news that is interesting enough for them to print, broadcast or post online. You clearly need to know the central idea that defines news. You basically need to have a **news hook**.

A **news hook** is newsworthy information that will attract the interest of the news media and their audiences.

Successfully pitching a news story is referring as *earned media*. It is an important part of the PESO model. Earned media coverage is not purchased like placing an ad or paying an "influencer" to promote your company or client. It is also uncontrolled media. This means that a journalist may or may not like the story that you are pitching. Details on pitching a news story will be explained and demonstrated in Chapter 7.

To successfully pitch a story to the right news outlet, the PR writer must be able to clearly identify the news or key point of interest to a specific journalist or news outlet. Without a clear understanding of the "news" you are trying to make, the most beautifully written news release or strikingly visual PR tactic will not be successful. Public relations professionals who understand the needs of the media and are able to get positive coverage for their organization or clients have a highly coveted skill.

For example, suppose you are hired by the singer Rihanna (Robyn Rihanna Fenty) as the chief public relations officer for her company Fenty Beauty. A story about her new holiday makeup line would likely not be of much interest to the *Wall Street Journal* or *Bloomberg*. For those news outlets, this is not news. However, if the company was planning to issue an IPO (initial public offering), this would likely be of interest to them. The new makeup line, however, may be of interest to the *Refinery29*, an online publication that focuses on fashion, celebrities, beauty and lifestyle trends. Pitched correctly, her story as a successful entrepreneur of color may be of specific interest to magazines such as *Black Enterprise*, *Essence* or *BET Nightly News*.

Positive media coverage provides valuable credibility to products, services and issues. It is publicity that can't be purchased. It must be earned. That is one of the reasons that publicity or public relations coverage is referred to as "earned" media. The other reason is that when journalists write, post or broadcast a positive story about your company or client, they are providing a third-party or independent endorsement. Journalists strive to be objective and some may have sophisticated knowledge regarding issues, trends or subjects such as technology or finance. This makes earning media coverage more credible than purchasing an advertisement or posting content on the social media channels such as Facebook, Twitter, Instagram or LinkedIn. After all, the news outlet may not have a favorable opinion of your client or organization.

When you buy an advertisement to appear on television, online, in print or even on a large billboard, you are in complete control of what is being communicated, when the message will appear, and how it will look, sound and appear. While advertisements and social media can be creative and memorable, they are far less credible than a rave review in print, broadcast or online news media.

Here is a simple example. A bakery hires you to promote its new brownies. According to your client, they taste great and are healthier than other desserts because they are low in fat and calories but high in fiber and important vitamins.

As the bakery's PR consultant, you can create a website for them, set up social media platforms and present the reasons why their brownies are better than other brownies. This is all great. If the bakery has the financial resources, it can also advertise its brownies online, on television, or in newspapers and magazines. This is all great, too. An effective advertising campaign may result in people trying the brownies. But this information all comes from the maker of the brownie. And most people understand that.

However, what if you came up with an interesting news angle about these brownies and convinced a food writer or "influencer" focused on health and wellness to try the brownies?

And the influencer loved them.

The influencer then states that these brownies taste delicious and that independent analysis shows the brownies to be healthier, too. This has a lot more credibility because an independent third party, a member of the media, has endorsed the new brownie.

Research supports this position that earned media is more credible. In fact, the Institute for Public Relations posted the results of its research in an article titled "Is Earned Media More Credible than Advertising?" on July 15, 2019. The full article can be found here: https://instituteforpr.org/understanding-how-changing-media-sources-in-the-promotional-mix-inform-credibility-and-consumer-action/.

Here are some of the key findings:

- The greatest percentage of participants indicated and explained that they found the **earned media** story the most credible among the sources provided. When examining a message appearing in an earned media story, people seek out and pay attention to cues such as the independence of the journalist writing the story, whether the story is balanced in its coverage, the credentials of the journalist and the prestige of the media outlet where the story appeared.
- Overall, people find blogs written by an **independent blogger** as credible. Participants praised the writing of the blogger (in this case, a man), his credentials, the sense that this person was someone like them, his experience using the product and his independence from the company manufacturing the product, all which impact perceptions of authenticity.
- Not as many participants viewed **advertising** as credible compared with earned media.

This is the power of public relations and the importance of understanding what is news.

How Do News Outlets Decide What to Publish?

What makes a journalist decide to publish or broadcast one story and ignore another? It is not a random decision. When considering a story, a journalist needs to decide if it is newsworthy. And if readers, viewers, listeners or followers are going to be interested in the topic.

The media is a business – a very competitive business! News outlets compete against each other. And journalists within an organization may compete against each other for airtime or space in a publication. Media outlets make money by maintaining and growing their number of readers, viewers or listeners. And by selling advertising. Journalists want to be the first to break or cover a story. This means everything from being the first to report on a disaster to getting a coveted interview with an athlete, author,

newsworthy, but if the speaker is Michelle Obama or Ellen DeGeneres, this would be news.

5. Conflict and Controversy

When people argue about actions, events, ideas or policies, this is of news value. Conflict and controversy attract attention by highlighting problems or differences within society. PR pros can strategically interject their client or corporations into the discussion within the media.

6. Human Interest

The crucial element of a great human-interest story is that it has a strong emotional appeal. These stories aim to evoke responses such as amusement or sadness. Television news programs often place a humorous or quirky story at the end of the show to finish on a feel-good note. Newspapers and television stations often have dedicated areas or segments for offbeat or interesting items. Human-interest stories are a bit of a special case. These stories can be "soft" kid-at-the-petting-zoo snapshots, inspiring comeback accounts or infuriating reports of incompetence on the part of a public figure. They also can be inspirational. For instance, people are fascinated with surfer Bethany Hamilton because she not only lost an arm in a shark attack, but she continued to compete, win and even write a book that was turned into a successful movie called *Soul Surfer*.

6. Newness

If something is truly new, it has news value. This could include a new album from a popular band or a new and innovative app. These have news value because they are new.

7. Weirdness or Novelty

If something is unusual, shocking or bizarre, the strangeness alone could make it newsworthy. For instance, the invention of the cronut – a breakfast treat that is half donut and half croissant – made Pastry chef Dominique Ansel's bakery a viral sensation in 2013 when it was reviewed by a food blogger from Grub Street. It is worth noting that the Associated Press wire service has an entire section on its website focused on "oddities." You may want to view it to get some ideas of the type of stories the media looks for. It can be viewed here: https://apnews.com/hub/oddities?utm_source=apnewsnav&utm_medium=navigation

Creating News

So, what do you do when you don't have any news? An article from Forbes.com answers that question. Titled "How PR Professionals Can Generate News When There Is None," it suggests "key calendar moments":

Another way to spark conversation is to insert companies into key calendar moments throughout the year. Whether it be their own internal calendar, like an earnings report, or the universal calendar, like Mother's Day or Father's Day, using dates is a simple yet impactful strategy to reach the media. It's also important to look at publications' editorial calendars to figure out if your brand could be a fit. Consumer brands need to pay the most attention, since holiday gift guides, back-to-school products and similar seasons are covered heavily by consumer-facing outlets. Be sure to get ahead of pitching because it all starts months earlier than you think.

The full article can be found here: www.forbes.com/sites/forbesbusinesscouncil/2021/09/15/how-pr-professionals-can-generate-news-when-there-is-none/?sh=feff10132854.

There are a number of ways to make news. Here are ten suggestions:

1. **Special Events**

   PR pros will sometimes create a special event with the purpose of creating news. The Celebrity Ice Bucket Challenge for the ALS Association is an excellent example. ALS stands for amyotrophic lateral sclerosis. It is a motor neuron disease also sometimes referred to as Lou Gehrig disease. Gehrig was a Hall of Fame first baseman who played for the New York Yankees in the 1920s and '30s. He retired in 1939 after having been diagnosed with ALS. Gehrig passed away from the disease in 1941.

   The Ice Bucket Challenge encourages nominated participants to be filmed having a bucket of ice water poured on their heads and then nominating others to do the same. The goal of the challenge was to both raise awareness about the disease and money to combat it. When this event was introduced in 2014, it received viral attention and raised over $220 million. The event was an immediate draw for celebrities, including LeBron James and Kermit the Frog.

2. **Polls and Studies**

   The media loves polls and surveys. What the public thinks about issues, celebrities and trends is of news value to the media. The National Endowment for Financial Education (NEFE) conducts an annual survey on New Year's resolutions, for example. This survey has successfully resulted in positive media coverage for the NEFE each year. An organization can create its own polls or surveys or use the findings of another organization to create a news hook. For instance, an auto manufacturer may want to promote the safety features of a new line of cars by using data created by the big federal U.S. agencies such as the Department of Transportation or the National Highway Traffic Safety Administration.

3. **Data**

   News organizations love data because it creates the headlines for them. The *Wall Street Journal* created an article about the speed of recreational marathon runners from around the globe. Using statistics from RunRepeat.com, a website about running shoes, they determined that the United States, the United Kingdom and several Asian nations were among the top ten slowest countries.

4. **Extremes/Superlatives**

Reporters and audiences are interested in stories focused on the largest, the smallest, the best, the worst, the easiest or the hardest. These can be the source of a great human-interest story and are only limited by the imagination. For instance, if you were doing public relations for the ski industry, you would try to determine which mountain gets the most snow, has the most difficult terrain, has the most bars, is the most/least child friendly or has the shortest lift lines.

5. **Top Ten Lists**

A savvy PR pro can create a top ten list on almost any subject. It can be the top ten highest paid athletes or top ten books to read during summer vacation. These don't cost anything to create and can generate substantial media coverage. Magazines frequently create top ten lists to generate publicity for themselves. For instance, *Forbes* magazine yearly issues its lists of the richest people in the world.

6. **Publicity Stunts**

In 1999, the Women's Institute in Yorkshire, England, stripped to create a calendar to raise money for leukemia research. Their efforts created worldwide media attention and inspired a hit movie.

7. **Rallies and Protests**

These have been an effective tactic for years. Approximately 250,000 people participated in the 1963 Civil Rights Movement march in Washington, D.C., where Martin Luther King, Jr. delivered his famous "I Have a Dream" speech.

8. **Awards**

Awards can be great ways to boost brand awareness and get people talking about your client or organization. What better way to get people interested than to create an awards program? Not only will you get industry-wide recognition, but it's a great way to position your brand.

9. **Product Demonstrations**

Showing how to use a product is highly visual and can be used to generated media in broadcast news outlets or online video. Auto manufacturers, for instance, frequently invite journalists to test drive their cars as a way of generating media coverage.

10. Create a Day, Week or Month

A wonderful way to create media attention for an issue is to designate a day, week or month. For instance, the American Heart Association (AHA) created National Wear Red Day on February 7. It is part of the AHA's signature women's initiative, Go Red for Women, a comprehensive platform designed to increase women's heart health awareness and serve as a catalyst for change to improve the lives of women globally.

Case Study: Using Child Abuse Prevention Month as a News Hook

Founded in 1822, JCCA, formerly known as the Jewish Child Care Association, is a major organization that provides child welfare and mental-health services to New York City's neediest and most vulnerable children and families. One of the organization's key concerns is child abuse.

JCCA wanted to bring attention to the problem and make resources available to its three key audiences in New York City:

1. Professionals who work with children and who are legally mandated to report child abuse
2. Friends, neighbors and family members of children at risk
3. The general public

A huge problem in combatting child abuse is the difficult dilemma that some adults face when they suspect a child is being abused. On the one hand, they worry about making an unfair accusation. On the other hand, they worry that if they don't act, a child could be harmed. JCCA, in partnership with the Council of Family and Child Caring Agencies, created a booklet called *Child Abuse Alert*. It is designed to help recognize some of the signs that a child is at risk and to give people the confidence to act.

Here is link to the online version of the booklet: www.jccany.org/get-involved/child-abuse-alert/child-abuse-alert-online/

To promote this information to its target audiences, JCCA's Director of Communications, Leslie Gottlieb, decided to use Child Abuse Prevention Month, which takes place every April, as a news hook. Details about the month can be found at the Child Welfare Information Gateway website (childwelfare.gov).

To reach a broad audience, Gottlieb used the tactic of a television public service announcement (PSA) to educate the public about what can be done about child abuse and to promote the *Child Abuse Alert* booklet.

A PSA is a message in the public interest disseminated by the media without charge to raise public awareness and change behavior. PSAs are aired by television and radio stations and often remain on the air for multiple weeks.

Gottlieb went to a VP at WABC-TV, whom she had known for years, who agreed to do it.

This is a key lesson. Media relations are about building relationships and trust over time. Gottlieb says that she never would have succeeded if this had been a cold pitch.

Another lesson is that Gottlieb knew that the media landscape had changed. Television stations would no longer pay to produce PSAs, so she offered to pay for it with script approval. WABC-TV agreed to run the PSA for the month of April, including spots on network shows and to do a special interview with one of JCCA's experts.

Here is a checklist for understanding what news is:

- Is there a clear news hook?
- Is the timing right for this story?
- What news outlet or part of the news outlet is best for this story?
- Who are the key audiences?
- What are key demographic groups within the audiences?
- What is known or assumed about pertinent knowledge and attitudes within each group?
- What are preferred information sources?
- What words, phrases or concepts resonate strongly with audience members?
- What is the desired opinion or knowledge change?
- What is the desired behavior change?
- Has the outlet/producer/reporter/editor accepted information in the past?
- Has the publication been appreciative of information provided previously?

Summary

Developing a keen understanding of the key elements of what is news is an essential skill for strategic public relations writers. This skill will help you and your client (internal or external) successfully work with the news media. It is also crucial that the PR professional understand how to create news for their client or organization, as this is an essential skill for the strategic public relations writer.

Exercises

1. You are hired to promote the opening of a new restaurant. Using the key elements of news, come up with a few key tactics to promote the restaurant to the news media.
2. Your company has been successfully selling a popular dish detergent. There is nothing new about the product, but your boss would like you to create a media relations campaign. Using what you learned in this chapter about creating news when there is none, how would you generate news coverage?
3. Create a monthly calendar for seasonal news releases. Start with New Year's Day on January 1. List the holidays and then the potential news hooks that could be used. List as many holidays as possible.
4. You have just been retained by a boutique public relations firm known for its cutting-edge media relations services. You have been assigned four very different clients: a model turned food blogger, a midsize accounting firm based in Chicago, a hot new vegan restaurant in New York City and an orthopedic shoe company trying

to expand its reach to younger people. Create a monthly calendar with potential stories for each client. Be as creative as possible.

5. Read the online edition of the *New York Times* for an entire week (or both the print and online editions of your local newspaper). Start on Monday and keep a journal. There are special sections that only appear on certain days. And there are sections that appear every day. Note what they are. What are the major news stories every day? How does the online version differ from the print edition? Make note of the various topics covered throughout the week. For instance, the paper covers everything from wine to national politics.

6. You are hired by the National Restaurant Association. Create a top ten list to generate news.

Glossary

News hook – newsworthy information that will attract the interest of the news media and its audiences.

References

Harcup, T., & O'Neill, D. (2017). What is News? *Journalism Studies*, 18:12, 1470–1488. https://doi.org/10.1080/1461670X.2016.1150193

Heritage Months. https://seramount.com/articles/category/heritage-months/

How Public Relations Professional Can Generate News When There is None. www.forbes.com/sites/forbesbusinesscouncil/2021/09/15/how-pr-professionals-can-generate-news-when-there-is-none/?sh=feff10132854

Is Earned Media More Credible than Advertising? Posted by *Institute for Public Relations*. https://instituteforpr.org/understanding-how-changing-media-sources-in-the-promotional-mix-inform-credibility-and-consumer-action/

Pew Research Center: State of the News Media. www.pewresearch.org/topics/state-of-the-news-media/

3 PERSUASIVE PR WRITING

Learning Goals for This Chapter

After reading this chapter, you should be able to:

- Talk about the three key elements of persuasion according to Aristotle.
- Describe rhetorical devices and convincing approaches for public relations.
- Elaborate on Cialdini's seven principles of persuasion and how to apply them to public relations.
- List some key persuasive tools and approaches to use in crafting convincing messages.

Getting someone to do something takes persuasion. It is the hallmark of great leaders and communicators.

It is a highly valued and desirable skill.

Persuading members of a target audience to accept a new idea, to purchase or think about acquiring a product, or to make a multitude of other changes has always been a goal and test of successful public relations writing and presentations – across multiple media and a vast array of situations.

The definitions of "persuasion" are varied and vast. Whole books and courses are dedicated to the nuances, theories and history of the art of persuasion.

It is not the role of this text to explore that broad panorama of knowledge and practice. But it is the goal of this chapter to highlight the importance of persuasion for PR professionals and describe how persuasive arts are linked to mass communications.

A Long History

The ancient Greeks initiated the formal study of persuasion. Their opinion was that rhetoric and elocution were the ultimate skills for politicians.

DOI: 10.4324/9781003248330-3

"Rhetoric" is often defined as the art of speaking or writing effectively and has two primary branches, according to the American Rhetoric website (americanrhetoric. com/newtop100speeches.htm).

- The study and practice of principles and rules of composition formulated by critics of ancient times.
- The study of writing or speaking as a means of communication or persuasion.

"Elocution" can be defined this way: vocal presentation in a precise and (assumedly) powerful way so that the ideas and suggestions presented come across clearly.

Today, rhetoric has taken on a less valued, even distrusted, meaning, often suggesting communications based on language, not facts or proof. It may even be considered fake news.

Aristotle concluded that persuasion encompasses three appeals: logos, pathos and ethos.

W. Rhys Roberts translated Aristotle from the Greek this way: "Anyone seeking to persuade an audience should craft his/her message with facts (logos), tapping an argument's emotional aspect (pathos), and presenting his/her apparent moral standing (ethos)." These are good elements to use when analyzing persuasive appeals even now, thousands of years later.

Facts are a PR writer's best friends – especially when newly introduced (in other words, news) – and can impact the intended audience or provide new insights that will be viewed as valuable. Facts presented in a compelling way are compelling.

Emotional appeals can be helpful but need to be applied carefully because audiences may interpret such appeals as only working on feelings or impulses and not on reasoned, tested, factual options. Best-case situations mix facts with emotional appeals – as when a new, highly tested and approved medicine can alleviate a dreaded disease – as we saw happen with polio vaccines and recent developments in cancer care.

Moral standing also is difficult to define and portray, but it often is linked with branding appeal and increasingly with good corporate citizenship. Simply put, it is doing the right thing. An organization's reputation can provide a strong platform for messages – effectively paving the way for acceptance.

For example, when the Walt Disney Company pulled out all the stops to try and find a toddler who had been pulled by an alligator into a lake on the grounds of Walt Disney World's Grand Floridian Resort and Spa and communicated forthrightly and often while showing enormous empathy and support for the boy's parents, the company was generally praised for its responsive and caring approach. Company executives acted quickly and responsibly in the face of a tragedy. Some top managers were brought back from China to manage the search and support the parents. Disney was seen as being highly principled and moral.

On the other side of the coin, when the chairman of BP – formerly the British Petroleum Company – told reporters that he wanted the cleanup of the oil spill in the Gulf of Mexico to be finished "so I can have my life back," he was properly and roundly criticized for not empathizing with the people whose lives and livelihoods had been crushed by the explosion on an oil rig. Not to mention showing little compassion for the families of the men who died in the explosion, as well as the terrible environmental impact. He was seen by many people as not acting responsibly or morally.

At times, organizations and management can be discovered to be either consciously or unconsciously behaving in an immoral or illegal way. Such examples, fortunately, are rare, but when they occur, PR professionals may not be able to reverse the powerful winds of public opinion. The best PR campaign can't solve bad behavior. The bad behavior itself must be changed. At that point, the PR writer can strategically communicate what the person or organization is doing to right the wrong.

Historically, PR and corporate communications have played major roles in persuading masses of people to alter their mindsets and behavior. Some change for good and some do not.

For example, convincing great numbers of Americans – and people in other countries – that cigarette smoking is unhealthy and antisocial was a great feat of persuasion, one that is credited with saving untold thousands of lives over decades. No doubt, the communication was accelerated by government communications and regulation, as well as rising social condemnation, but persuasive communications played a defining role.

Anti-smoking campaigns are good examples of the use of all three aspects of persuasion, but in the case of convincing people not to do something, a more precise term is "dissuasion." That's what the anti-smoking campaign was aimed at.

There are all of the medical facts about how smoking causes disease (cancer, heart disease and so on). There is the emotional appeal of the consequences to the smoker and their family. Lastly, there is the ethos of smoking as an example of bad behavior.

Pierce, Gilpin, Emery et al. (1998) detail the effects of a highly focused campaign against smoking in California, showing that "a tobacco control program fronted by a good media campaign can be very effective in changing smoking behavior" (Hornik, page 113). A central component of this program was an anti-smoking media campaign, funded at more than $90 million, between 1989 and 1996. This campaign included paid advertisements that used a variety of communication channels (television, radio, outdoor advertising and print).

It is important to note that the California campaign was based on four key message platforms:

- Attacks on tobacco companies with ads on television and in print showing how the industry was misleading the public and Congress about the harmful effects of cigarette use.
- Messages about protecting nonsmokers from secondhand smoke.
- A series of ads about reducing access to tobacco by teenagers.
- Ads reflecting the tragedy and pain of tobacco-related diseases.

The campaign was correlated to a decline of 1.09% per year in "smoking prevalence" in California between 1989 and 1993, compared with a drop of 0.7% per year in years before the campaign was launched. The numbers might not sound very impressive, but they were compounded year over year and reflected a great number of smokers who quit.

Additionally, the rate of decline in per capita consumption of cigarettes was markedly faster in California than in the rest of the United States during the campaign years – "by a factor of nearly 90%," according to Pierce, Emery and Gilpin.

A similar pattern was seen in the battle against drunk driving. The dangers were demonstrated graphically and repeatedly through mass media. And interest groups such as Mothers Against Drunk Driving – also known as MADD – kept up the drumbeat at the same time that government regulations requiring seat belts in cars and their use accelerated the change in behavior and belief.

MADD's PR tactics are a perfect example of all aspects of persuasion. There were the facts about the high number of deaths due to drunk driving, the emotional appeal of mothers who lost their children to drunk driving and the moral aspect of doing the right thing – not drinking and driving.

In public relations, a critical element of persuasion is finding a sweet spot, or factor that members of the target audience will pay attention to or will react to, even to the point of changing their minds, opinions or behaviors. Smoking and the link to cancer and the perceived anti-social nature of it were sweet spots that set the stage for the California campaign to be successful and result in altered patterns of behavior.

Of course, not all or not even most PR tactics will have such a compelling case. We as PR professionals need to find data or anecdotes or expert opinions that support the changes we are promoting and then present that information in a way that resonates with the intended audiences.

Approaches can be varied and can be mixed and matched depending on target audience, the communications environment where they are appearing, recent events that bring the topic to top of mind, and a variety of other factors, including the history of communications on the topic by the organization and the attitudes of clients. The trick for PR writers is to determine the language, images and communications approach that is likely to be most effective for a given situation. Some approaches include:

- Deadly serious – as when ads and news releases showed crashed cars where people were killed as a way of promoting seat belts.
- Rational – appealing to the notions of intelligence and science as some medical or scientific appeals do.
- Comedic – showing fanciful or clownish situations that make fun of situations but show a product, process or person that can solve the problem that was being parodied.
- Celebrity recommendations – when a popular or famous person supports the use of a product, from cars to sodas to credit cards, whether or not the celebrity has any expertise or experience in the promoted product.
- New or improved products – building on consumer experience with a product, or its competitor, by enticing the audience with the opportunity to have the product do more or be less expensive.
- An opportunity to be first – some people just want to be first, so they stand in line to be among the first to get a new sneaker design or a new smart phone, for example, as a badge of specialness.

Any persuasive pitch should be highly accessible – easily understood and accepted by the intended audience, whether journalists/gatekeepers or ultimate consumers who use traditional media or social media. Concepts and language should be coherent without being simplistic. Esoteric terms, whether financial or scientific or even sports related, need to be explained if there is any hint that the audience may not understand them.

Humor should be used sparingly – very sparingly. People have widely varying understandings of comedic approaches, and language nuances may be misinterpreted. Further, comedy is often time related and may age quickly.

Effective writing for public relations tells an organization's story in an understandable way for the identified audience and simultaneously meets the goals of the organization. It aims to affect the audience in a way that is positive for the organization or person whose message is being projected by the public relations effort.

Persuasive writing is based on a deep understanding of the audience, including knowledge of the topic, interest in the topic and relationship with the organization. The PR writing tools – persuasive language and images, media to be employed, frequency of message distribution, and the spokesperson or persons or influencers – should be defined through observation, experience and examination of effective programs.

The important, even vital, elements of persuasion may not appear to be complicated but putting them into practice can be difficult. It is not always easy to persuade someone to buy something, vote for someone, and so on.

Here are some approaches that can be effective:

Claims and assertions should be based on facts and data. Few parts of a persuasive argument are more convincing than solid information backed up by numbers.

Surveys and financial results show a level of certitude and context that can be convincing and provide the kind of information that is memorable and convincing.

Modern audiences are used to seeing the results of surveys and data collection and using this information as a basis for making decisions, changing opinions and taking action. Ratings of television shows, for example, can help to drive new viewers to a previously unnoticed show or can convince viewers not to try a program if ratings are low. Ratings are key to determining the fate of shows.

By the same token, politicians examining the idea of running for an office often will commission a survey of potential voters to see how much name recognition exists and if there is a pattern of opinion about such a candidacy. Some politicians jump into a race but exit after a while when surveys show that they are not gaining traction or have a negative image among voters.

Large survey and research organizations provide marketers with insights into consumer behavior and desires. From an analysis of consumer research, companies can determine if a new product idea has any traction with consumers or shows little interest. PR writers should make a habit of reviewing public opinion surveys regularly. Many surveys are readily available from major research firms such as the Pew Research Center, NORC at the University of Chicago, Gallup Inc. and Nielsen Corp. Surveys and reports from these organizations can help point to changes in public opinion, new topics that can provide direction for PR outreach, or projects or suggestions for media contacts.

The internet has made gathering information much faster and easier. Insights from the reaction to an announcement can be gathered overnight and adjustments made to make the announcement or product image more palatable and attractive to consumers.

PR pros can take advantage of the plethora of data swirling in the communications industry to both help define the parameters of a campaign or announcement and to determine effectiveness.

It is wise to examine any public data to see what has been said about a topic that you intend to promote – from electric cars to computer security to new flavors of ice cream. You may find that there is a dearth of information, which means you have an opportunity to be the first and thus define the parameters of the topic. And, if you are first, you are more likely to get earned media coverage.

Sources of data are critical. There are many self-appointed "experts" who are willing to share their ideas and concepts. There are a few well-renowned experts whose words and ideas have proven valuable and have been confirmed with results. If you are working for a client, the client representatives can be helpful in identifying trusted, reputable sources of industry information.

PR pros should know how to review a study to see if it is well founded and professionally done.

Some warning signs:

- How recently was the work done? The world moves so fast that even a lag of a month or two can render a study questionable.
- How many responses were there? There are serious statistical tools that can help you understand if a sample is large enough to be valid – if the right people were surveyed. However, a study based on responses from students in two classes at a university should be looked at every carefully. It might provide valid insights into the thinking of those students but very likely cannot be generalized across a wide geographic area or broad range of ages.
- Was there a clear point of view evidenced by the survey team or the sponsor? Asking questions in a certain way can lead to expected or desired answers.
- Was the methodology statistically valid? If the methodology is not explained in some detail, you should be cautious. Reputable, professional researchers do tell you how they collected data, how it was statistically calculated or manipulated, and what the possible deficiencies were.

Being first is a powerful position. It can be a foundation for a persuasive presentation, argument or information release.

You can create the terms of the debate, define the market in your own way and often make competitors look like followers. In addition, being first is a powerful persuasive advantage. It can make a company or person appear to be innovative and inventive.

Claiming to be first or the best can be a two-edged sword. Being first means more than just claiming the number one position; it takes some proof points. Otherwise, a competitor or opponent can point out flaws in the argument and self-promotion to make the claim look false, which can be very harmful to branding and public image.

Cialdini's Principles of Persuasion

Simply stated, the goal of effective public relations is to persuade audience members to do something they may not have contemplated doing or have not decided to do yet. Persuasion, according to Dr. Robert Cialdini (2021), is "a study of compliance." He has developed seven principles that "cause one person to say yes to another person."

His seven principles demonstrate and illuminate the breadth of persuasion and suggest some approaches that can be effective. They are:

- Reciprocity. People often feel obligated to give back by way of an act, a gift or a service as a response to something that they have received. In a PR transaction, the initial presentation may be an idea, a story suggestion or background information on a new or complex topic. The reciprocity does not have to be immediate. The concept can work for both journalists/gatekeepers and for target audiences.
- Scarcity. This principle plays to a basic human instinct. Most of us want things or more of things that are not readily available or which we value. Simply put, people want more of those things that they can have less of. Think of the lines of people waiting to buy a newly available smartphone or pair of celebrity-endorsed sneakers. For PR professionals, it is important to acknowledge that much of the information we deal with is scarce or previously unavailable – which makes it attractive and persuasive on its face.
- Authority. This principle says that people are likely to believe and follow the lead of credible, knowledgeable experts. A 2021 survey of journalists by Muck Rack, a multifaceted PR management platform, showed that 86% of journalists rate academic subject matter experts as their most trusted sources. Next, at 74%, were chief executive officers. Third, at 55%, were company PR people. This knowledge can be leveraged by making subject matter experts or CEOs available to the press or bloggers.
- Consistency. Information recipients, whether journalists or members of a target audience, appreciate reinforcement of information or actions that they know. This principle points to the value of a strong, consistent, clearly explained

brand for organizations. Such an approach builds confidence and results in repeated interactions with the brand and a trust that can result in giving an organization or person the benefit of the doubt in unusual situations.

- Liking. People in general like to deal with individuals whom they like or have had positive interactions with. PR pros find that it is easier to deal with some people than others. The reverse is also true. Journalists, consumers and other stakeholders are more likely to act positively and agree with a company or person who is comfortable and approachable.

- Social proof. This principle was put in place before the explosion of social media use but has been proven even more powerful and valuable with social media interactions. People in general, when faced with uncertainty or a new situation, look to the experiences of others for guidance and reinforcement. PR people can apply this principle by using reviews of products or services or having endorsements from popular celebrities.

- Unity. The shared identity that an influencer shares with the person who is the object of influence is valuable. Influencers have become important purveyors of opinion and persuasion in the digital world and in marketing in general.

Cialdini adds, much to the appreciation of PR and marketing professionals, that his principles "can be commissioned by a compliance professional to deftly incorporate them into requests for purchases, donations, concessions, votes, assent, etc."

For example, when a communications technology firm brings out a new device with newly developed features, the consumer audience is likely not concerned about the development process but about the advantages over similar, previous products. In other words, "What are the benefits for me?"

On the other hand, journalists, bloggers, influencers and even hobbyists who are interested in such technological advances want to know how the new thing was made, the scientific principles underlying the new use or capabilities, and every other detail. A PR writer must meet the needs of all key audiences.

One important, but sometimes overlooked, use of persuasion is convincing a media or news reporter or producer of the value of a function or new feature of your organization. Here's an example.

Case Study: A New Medical Treatment Approach That Was Highlighted on National Television News

Johanna Younghans, who was on the media relations staff at Brigham and Women's Hospital in Boston, provided this case to highlight the value of providing exclusive access to a story that fits with a journalist's coverage area and demonstrated a new, innovative process with the added attraction of saving money. The pitch to a national TV producer was persuasive because it provided exclusive information and it fit the needs of the producer for brand-new concepts.

At Brigham and Women's Hospital, Harvard Medical School's teaching hospital, the public relations team was brought in to help promote an innovative program called "Home Hospital," which was just getting piloted.

The newly established program allowed patients with certain medical conditions to be treated and monitored closely, from the comfort of their own homes through cutting-edge technology, like a skin patch that monitored vital signs remotely.

The program not only resulted in significant benefits to patient outcomes, but also documented massive savings when compared with treating those same types of patients in a hospital setting.

The data from the program had been submitted to a medical journal, which had first publication rights by agreement with the doctor who was the lead author of the paper at the hospital. While I awaited the publication in the embargoed academic journal, I pitched the concept of the remote treatment and its savings to a national health producer at CBS Evening News as an exclusive television pitch.

After continuing to pitch and follow up for over six months, I finally secured filming, which consisted of two full days of one-on-one interviews with the doctor and well-known medical journalist Jonathan LaPook, as well as one with a patient at home who was enrolled in the program.

When we received word of the official publication date, I alerted the station and together we planned to release the story as breaking news when the embargo lifted that day.

The institution was thrilled with the placement because the story demonstrated how Brigham was a prominent leader in the space, trying to reduce health care-related costs while improving patient care.

The PESO model, which was introduced earlier, is valuable for planning persuasive campaigns because it views four media types as complementary and helps PR people decide which ones – or all of them – to use for a particular situation.

Checklist for persuasive messages:

- Who are the key audiences?
- What are key demographic groups within the audiences?
- What is known or assumed about pertinent knowledge and attitudes within each group?
- What are preferred information sources?
- What words or phrases or concepts resonate strongly with audience members?
- What is the desired opinion or knowledge change?
- What is the desired behavior change?

Summary

Persuasive PR is a goal and highly valued measure of success. It can be achieved in multiple ways. Most often, however, it is the result of strategic thinking, creative writing, and a highly refined and sophisticated understanding of the communications equation:

what is being described and is it being presented in a way that is attractive and valuable to the intended or target audience?

Multiple options are available in the 21st-century world of communications, from simple tweets to highly refined and polished multimedia productions. But it is imperative to remember that messages must be clear, succinct, interesting and compelling.

That can be a tall order. But leaders and innovators in public relations agencies and departments do it day in and day out. You can learn to do it as well.

Exercises

1. Review the case about Brigham and Women's Hospital and remote medicine. Are there other persuasive principles that might have influenced the national reporter to accept the story and then work on it to play on the news? Try to put yourself in the place of the reporter and think about what elements would attract you to the story. Write an essay about your thinking and how pitching a story to media follows principles of persuasion.

2. Think about your personal experiences and preferences for a product or organization. What makes you feel positive? Personal good service, perhaps? Or the public perception that you have? Because your family or acquaintances have recommended it? Or possibly because of social media reviews and recommendations? Have you been disappointed by online recommendations or by some from people you know? Write about your experiences, trying hard to define specifics that persuaded you to try, buy or just look at something new to you. Then describe how you might use that knowledge to develop a news release or set of social media posts about the item or brand.

3. If you were promoting a brand-new product – say, a medical breakthrough that vaccinates people against the flu for ten years – which of the Cialdini principles would you use? Why? Write some sample messages.

References

Cialdini, R. B. (2021). *Influence, New and Expanded: The Psychology of Persuasion*. Harper Business.

DiPietro, B. (2016). Crisis of the Week: Disney Responds to Alligator Killing Boy. *Wall Street Journal*, June 28, 2016.

Hayward's Downfall. (2010). YouTube, July 27, 2010. www.youtube.com/watch?v=O5treUQL-o0

Pierce, J. P., Gilpin, E. A., Emery, S. L., et al. (1998). *Tobacco Control in California: Who's Winning the War? An Evaluation of the Tobacco Control Program, 1989–1996*. University of California, San Diego.

Roberts, W. R. (1952). Rhetoric. In Ross, W. D. (Ed.), *The Works of Aristotle*. Oxford University Press.

4 WORDS MATTER
Editing

Learning Objectives for This Chapter

After reading this chapter, you should be able to:

- Describe the importance of having a process to ensure that writing is grammatically correct.
- Recognize and use writing style guides and other resources for writers.
- Apply and know how to learn correct words and terms for social media postings.
- Explain the power of word choice to communicate in an inclusive and inoffensive manner.
- Recognize the importance of having a system in place to proof PR writing for clarity and strategic focus.

Words matter. Words have power. They can inspire or can be hurtful and destructive. Language is not static. It evolves and reflects societal changes, technical advancements, and business and social trends. In addition to being technically correct and current, your writing should follow basic rules of grammar so that your client or company appears in the best possible light. Poor writing can undermine your hard work as a PR professional.

As an example, the *Associated Press Stylebook* contains on average more than 200 new and modified entries each year. There are also special sections in 2021 related to the Tokyo Olympics, the pandemic economy and holidays. These new entries can also be useful for creating **news hook**s for the product, service or person you are promoting. The importance of news hooks in strategic public relations writing is discussed in Chapter 5 on news releases and in Chapter 7 on pitching a story.

A news hook is newsworthy information presented with the goal of capturing the attention and interest of both the news media and their audiences.

As a PR writer, you must be persuasive and create writing that is clear, concise and contemporary. It is imperative that you monitor new words, terms and phrases that

DOI: 10.4324/9781003248330-4

are added to dictionaries and style guides. By the same token, don't use new terms just because they are new. Otherwise, your writing may sound like you are trying too hard and it may not connect with some audiences that don't understand newly minted terms. Instead, only use new terms when they make strategic sense. Your writing must also be respectful. This means being sensitive to the use of personal pronouns as well multicultural references.

In many organizations, the public relations department is also viewed as the authority on good writing. Executives from many parts of your organization may ask you to review their work. If you work for a PR firm, your clients will also rely on your writing and editing skills. There will be the expectation that you know what is appropriate in terms of inclusive language.

Master Established Grammar

The most brilliant proposal, article or blog post will not be taken seriously if it contains even a few spelling errors, grammatical mistakes or misused words. You can't simply depend on spell check. A word may be spelled correctly but it may be the wrong choice for the strategic purpose of your writing. You may even have software that checks grammar. It may alert you to a mistake, but it is up to you as a PR writer to determine if a sentence is grammatically correct or not. You need to master the basics of good grammar and get into the habit of looking up the meaning of words and phrases.

There may also be times when you may want to "break" a grammar rule on purpose – for the shock effect or to get noticed. The California Milk Board famously used "Got milk?" to great effect. And Apple seemed to err grammatically with "Think different." Grammarians said the correct word would be "differently" – but Apple countered that it was using "different" as a noun, not an adverb.

While this textbook is not focused specifically on learning proper grammar, it does focus on helping you assess your understanding of the rules of grammar. If you feel you need to brush up on these skills, now is the perfect time to work on it. Take advantage of the services that most colleges and universities offer to their students. For instance, most schools offer a variety of writing labs and seminars. If you are already a good writer, consider these services to enhance your skills. Great writers, like musicians, artists and athletes, constantly work on their craft.

Build a Writer's Tool Kit

Most effective writers use reference books on grammar and style as well as a dictionary and online sources. You can build a personal library of print books, download them, or use the reference materials at your school or local library in addition to all the online resources available. The format does not matter. You simply need to get into the habit of using these references as you write, edit and proof your work.

Following are three types of reference books for PR writers.

One: Grammar Guides

There are many excellent books on grammar and usage. Here is a list of some of the most popular publications, in alphabetical order:

- *Eats, Shoots & Leaves: The Zero Tolerance Approach to Punctuation* by Lynne Truss. Truss creates an amusing (in the opinion of this book's authors) approach to understanding the rules of grammar.
- *Elements of Style* by William Strunk. A classic grammar guide that is required reading in many high schools and colleges. It is has gone through several editions since it was first published in 1919. A popular version of the book was co-written by E. B. White in 1959. A Kindle edition, edited by James McGill, was published in 2020, which includes guidance on emails and texting.
- *Grammar Girl's Quick and Dirty Tips for Better Writing* by Mignon Fogarty. Fogarty's website, www.quickanddirtytips.com/grammar-girl, is also a good reference and offers free podcasts and videos on grammar and usage.
- *On Writing Well, 30th Anniversary Edition: An Informal Guide to Writing Non-fiction* by William Zinsser, a writer, editor and teacher.
- *Rules for Writers* by Diana Hacker and Nancy Sommer. The 10th edition was scheduled for release in 2022 as this book was written. The book states that it provides "explanations of writing and grammar topics, step-by-step advice for writing and doing research."
- *Write Right!: A Desktop Digest of Punctuation, Grammar, and Style* by Jan Venolia. The most recent edition was published in 2021. The section "The Craft of Writing" is particularly useful for public relations writing, in the opinion of this book's authors, because it focuses on how to write in a clear and simple manner.
- *Woe Is I: The Grammarphobe's Guide to Better English in Plain English* by Patricia T. O'Conner. The latest version was published in 2019. This book addresses both standard grammar and the evolution of language.

There are also a variety of online resources. One is Grammar Underground by June Casagrande, who also writes a grammar/humor column, "A Word, Please." Grammar Underground can be accessed at www.grammarunderground.com. Another online resource is Grammarly.com. It is a "writing assistant" to help proofread and edit documents. It is a fee-based service. However, it also offers free resources such a blog focused on grammar and usage. For instance, there is a blog titled *30 Grammar Mistakes Writers Should Avoid*. It can be accessed at www.grammarly.com/blog/30-grammar-mistakes-writers-should-avoid. Here are some of the top mistakes, according to Grammarly.com:

1. Overuse of adverbs. In excess, they're an indicator of weak verb choices. For example: "The boy ran really fast to catch the runaway ball." In this example, the adverb "really fast" modifies the verb "ran." Consider using a verb like "sprinted" instead. So, instead: "The boy sprinted to catch the runaway ball."

2. Run-on sentences. This occurs when two complete sentences are squashed together without using a coordinating conjunction or proper punctuation, such

as a period or a semicolon. Run-on sentences can be short or long. A long sentence isn't necessarily a run-on sentence.

3. Wordiness (inflated sentences). Keep your writing simple and direct. An average of 20 to 24 words is a good measure. Some sentences can be only three or four words. Wordy sentences frustrate readers, so get to the point. Streamline your sentences by using strong verbs and nouns. Don't overuse words such as "that," "just" and "now."

CNBC.com also posted a great article on the most common grammatical errors in an article: "The 11 Extremely Common Grammar Mistakes That Make People Cringe – and Make You Look Less Smart." Published on March 24, 2021, the full link can be found here: www.cnbc.com/2021/03/24/common-grammar-mistakes-that-make-people-cringe-and-make-you-look-less-smart-word-experts.html.

Here is an excerpt:

1. Apostrophes

- Wrong: *We need to get our sale's numbers up.*
- Right: *We need to get our sales numbers up.*

You use an apostrophe in a contraction (e.g., "there is" to "there's") or to show possession (e.g., "the manager's pet peeve"). You don't use one if the "s" is there simply to make a word plural.

2. Everyday/every day

- Wrong: *He starts work everyday at 8 a.m.*
- Right: *He starts work every day at 8 a.m.*

"Everyday" is an adjective describing something that's very common, like an everyday occurrence. "Every day" (with the space) is an adverbial phrase that means "each day."

3. I/me

- Wrong: *The marketing manager told Riley and I to talk with her.*
- Right: *The marketing manager told Riley and me to talk with her.*

The general rule: Use "I" when it's the subject of a verb (e.g., "I walked to the store"). Use "me" when the pronoun is the object of the verb or when the verb is doing something to someone or something (e.g., "the dog followed me to the store").

4. Its/it's

- Wrong: *The company just celebrated it's eighth year since it went public.*
- Right: *The company just celebrated its eighth year since it went public.*

We've seen a lot of people write "it's" when they want to show possession. But that's the incorrect usage! Only do so when you're writing a contraction of "it is."

5.   Less/fewer

- Wrong: *Less than 50 people showed up for the presentation.*
- Right: *Fewer than 50 people showed up for the presentation.*

Use "fewer" for numbered, countable things (e.g., "100 fewer purchases"). Use "less" for things that can't be counted (e.g., "there's less sand at this beach").

6.   Lie/lay

- Wrong: *I could just lay down and go to sleep.*
- Right: *I could just lie down and go to sleep.*

To "lie" is intransitive, which means it doesn't have an object and doesn't do anything to anyone or anything else (e.g., "I lie down"). To "lay" is transitive, which means it does have an object, as in something or someone the verb is doing something to (e.g., "I lay down my head").

7.   Lose/loose

- Wrong: *If we stay on this track, we can't loose.*
- Right: *If we stay on this track, we can't lose.*

Just remember that "loose" is almost always used as an adjective meaning "not tight" and "lose" is a verb meaning "to suffer a loss."

8.   That/who

- Wrong: *The people that reach their sales target will get a reward.*
- Right: *The people who reach their sales target will get a reward.*

Use "that" when you're talking about things or animals and "who" when you're talking about people.

9.   Then/than

- Wrong: *That presentation was better then the first one.*
- Right: *That presentation was better than the first one.*

This is such an easy mistake to make (and one that autocorrect might not catch). So, remember this: Use "then" when you're talking about time (e.g., "I'm going to go to the meeting, then to lunch") and use "than" when you're comparing things (e.g., "I'm older than he is").

10. There/their/they're

- Wrong: *There going to they're office over their.*
- Right: *They're going to their office over there.*

"There" is a location, as in "not here." Sometimes, it's also used as an exclamation (e.g., "So there!"). "They're" is a contraction of "they are." And "their" is a possessive, showing ownership by more than one person.

11. Your/you're

- Wrong: *Your my favorite supervisor.*
- Right: *You're my favorite supervisor.*

Here's another one that autocorrect often doesn't catch because it's spelled right even if it's grammatically wrong. But be careful! "You're" is a contraction only used to mean "you are." "Your" is a possessive of "you" and is used when you want to show possession. Remember this: You're going to be just fine if you watch your grammar.

Listen to Learn Grammar

If you enjoy listening to podcasts, consider *You're Saying It Wrong* on National Public Radio (NPR). Hosted by KMUW's Fletcher Powell, each episode features a conversation with sister and brother Kathy Petras and Ross Petras. It can be accessed at www.npr.org/podcasts/642595029/you-re-saying-it-wrong.

Two: Writing Style Guides

While proper grammar follows very specific rules, styles in citation, the spelling of new words, and how numbers or technical information is communicated can vary. **Writing style guides** can also help you navigate the changes in English language so that your writing is modern and respectful.

A writing style guide is a set of standardized writing practices required for a project, brand, industry or field of study. Style guides establish rules for writers and editors so they can produce content with consistent capitalization, spelling, punctuation, formatting and grammar conventions.

Most organizations will pick one writing style guide for everyone within the organization to use so there is consistency. A large organization may even create its own style guide for use by everyone within the company to address company- or industry-specific terms or formatting. It may also be used for corporate branding and identity purposes so that written materials have a specific look.

Writing style guides can also be useful for quickly checking grammar or spelling. They are particularly helpful in looking up how to spell new words. Most of the major style guides are available in both print and online versions with a variety of services to update users on a regular basis.

Here, in alphabetical order, are some of the most important style guides to consider:

- *APA Publication Manual.* Produced by the American Psychological Association (APA), this is a useful guide for scholarly writing and strategic public relations writers who work in the fields of psychology, nursing, business, engineering and related fields. It specifically addresses the preparation of draft manuscripts being submitted for publication in a journal. It includes guidance on choosing the headings, tables, figures, language and tone for writing for these fields. The latest version includes a section titled "Bias-Free Language Guidelines" for writing about people "with respect and inclusivity in areas including age, disability, gender, participation in research, race and ethnicity, sexual orientation, socioeconomic status, and intersectionality." The APA manual also has a free blog, which can be accessed through its website: https://apastyle.apa.org/products/publication-manual-7th-edition

- *Associated Press Stylebook.* Created for journalists who write for Associated Press news outlets, this is a useful guide for organizations writing news-centric content. The stylebook's alphabetized organization makes it easy to navigate and it is updated frequently. The 55th edition, published in 2021, includes chapters covering data journalism, business, religion and sports terms, as well as media law, news values, punctuation, social media, and polls and surveys. The classic, spiral-bound edition is published every other year. There is also an online version, grammar quizzes and a free to its Twitter feed for continuing updates.

- *Chicago Manual of Style.* First published in 1891 by the University of Chicago Press, it's now in its 17th edition. It is a popular style guide for authors, editors, proofreaders, indexers, copywriters, designers, and publishers. It also has a free blog called *Shop Talk.* More information can be found at www.chicagomanualofstyle.org/home.htm.

- *The MLA Handbook.* Published by the Modern Language Association, the ninth edition was issued in 2021. While it offers some style and usage recommendations, its primary concern is documentation and citation. The latest version includes new chapters on capitalization, spelling, numbers, italics, abbreviations and principles of inclusive language. There is also a new appendix with "works-cited-list entries by publication format, including websites, YouTube videos, interviews, and more." More information can be found at www.mla.org/MLA-Style.

AP Common Style Recommendations

In AP style, italics (*italics*) are exceedingly rare – virtually never used. In the following examples, they are used only to show examples. The examples would be used without italics in normal writing. Here are 12 of the most common mistakes according to AP style:

1. Use a person's full name and title the first time you mention him or her in an article. For example, write *Don Swanson, professor of communication*, not *Prof. Swanson*. Once people have been fully identified, refer to them by last name only. There are exceptions, so always check the AP stylebook.

2. Spell out abbreviations or acronyms on first reference, unless defined in the stylebook (like *FBI, CIA* and *AIDS*). For example, use *Passaic County Community College* the first time you refer to the college in a story. You may use *PCCC* on any references made after that. Another example would be to use *DAR* only after you have spelled out *Daughters of the American Revolution* on first reference. Do not put acronyms or abbreviations in parentheses after the noun.

3. Abbreviate months when used with days, and use numerals (1, 2, 3, etc.), not ordinal numbers (1st, 2nd, etc.). Exceptions are March, April, May, June and July – write them out; don't abbreviate. For example, write *Sept. 2, 2021*, not *September 2nd, 2021*. But, when using only the month and year, spell out the month.

4. Generally, spell out the numbers zero through ten and use numerals for higher numbers. Note, however, that numbers used at the beginning of a sentence are spelled out. Example: *Five hundred twenty-four students attended.* It is better, however, to rewrite the sentence so that it doesn't begin with a number. Example: *Attending the event were 524 students from local colleges.* Years are one of the exceptions. For example: *2008 was a bad year for investors.*

5. But use numerals even for ages younger than ten. This is another exception to the aforementioned number rule. When used like an adjective, say *X-year-old*, including the hyphens. Otherwise, don't use the hyphens. For example: *The 5-year-old girl kicked her brother, who is 8 years old.*

6. Use the percent sign when paired with a numeral – no space between them. Examples: *Participation increased 5%. Nearly 28% of all students don't like algebra.*

7. To indicate time, use figures and lowercase letters (e.g., *9 a.m.*, *6 p.m.*). Put a space between the figure and the letters. Exceptions are noon and midnight. Do not say *12 noon* or *12 midnight* – it's redundant.

8. Capitalize formal titles used before a name. For example, write *Secretary of State Hillary Clinton*. Very long titles may be shortened or summarized unless they are essential to the story, but the shortened form should not be capitalized (for example, you may use *spokesperson* instead of *Vice President for Public Affairs and Communications*). Use lowercase when formal titles follow a name (e.g., *Hillary Clinton, secretary of state*). General titles, such as *astronaut Neil Armstrong* and *actor Matt Damon*, are lowercase.

9. Capitalize names of people, places or things to set them apart from a general group. These include proper nouns such as *Mike, Canada, Hudson River* and *St. John's Church*. But use lowercase for common nouns (i.e., nouns not coupled with a proper name), such as *the river* or *the church*. Also, put a word in lowercase when you have more than one proper noun sharing the word. Example: *Ocean and Monmouth counties.* Capitalize the first word in a

sentence. Refer to a dictionary or the *AP Stylebook* if needed. When in doubt, use lowercase.

10. Do not use courtesy titles such as *Mr.*, *Miss*, *Mrs.* or *Ms.* except in direct quotes or where needed to distinguish between people of the same name. Using courtesy titles may be polite, and the *New York Times* uses them in its articles, but it is not AP style.

11. Do not abbreviate names of states, even in text. Never use postal abbreviations (e.g., *GA, SC, NY*).

12. For what the AP calls "compositions," here are general rules and examples from the 2017 edition:

- Never underline or use italics for titles of books, magazines, video games, TV shows and so on. Capitalize the principal words, including prepositions and conjunctions of four or more letters. Capitalize an article – the, a, an – or words of fewer than four letters if it is the first or last word in a title.
- The following are used as is: names of newspapers, magazines, reference works (e.g., *Webster's Collegiate Dictionary*), websites, apps, catalogs, almanacs, directories, dictionaries, encyclopedias, gazetteers, handbooks and similar publications. Do not use quotation marks around software titles such as Windows or Adobe Acrobat.
- The following take quote marks: books, operas, video games, software, movie titles, song titles and musical composition titles. Here are some examples: "The Star-Spangled Banner," "The Rise and Fall of the Third Reich," "Gone With the Wind," "Of Mice and Men," "For Whom the Bell Tolls," "Time After Time," the NBC-TV "Today" program, the "CBS Evening News," "Pretty Little Liars."

Three: Dictionaries

The other reference book that you should have access to is a good dictionary. Here are three respected ones:

1. Merriam-Webster: www.merriam-webster.com
2. Webster's New World College Dictionary (used in the *AP Stylebook* and available to its subscribers): www.yourdictionary.com/about/websters-new-world-college-dictionary.html
3. Oxford English Dictionary: www.oed.com

Pick a dictionary that fits your budget and that is easy for you to use. It does not matter if it is in book form or online.

Language Is Not Static

The language we use evolves and changes. As a PR writer, it is very important to be sensitive to the words and phrases people are currently using. Once a new word or expression becomes widely used, it is then added to standard dictionaries. Here are a few of the words and phrases that Merriam-Webster introduced in 2021:

- **Cancel culture:** The practice or tendency of engaging in mass canceling as a way of expressing disapproval and exerting social pressure.
- **Long-hauler:** A person who experiences one or more long-term effects following initial improvement or recovery from a serious illness (such as COVID-19).
- **Crowdfunding:** The practice of obtaining needed funding (as for a new business) by soliciting contributions from a large number of people, especially from the online community.
- **Gig worker:** A person who works temporary jobs, typically in the service sector as an independent contractor or freelancer.
- **Hygge:** A cozy quality that makes a person feel content and comfortable.
- **Second Gentleman:** The husband or male partner of a vice president or second in command of a country or jurisdiction.

Occasionally, there is a word that is not new but it becomes a new word for the general public. For instance, before 2020, the word "coronavirus" was known mostly by those who work in the medical profession. It was considered **jargon**.

Jargon is a technical word that is used or understood by a specific industry.

According to Merriam-Webster's website

the word was largely ignored as the 2020 year began, but that changed on January 20th, with the announcement of the first U.S. case of COVID-19. The largest spike in lookups came on March 19th; overall, "coronavirus" was looked up a staggering 162,551% more in 2020 than in 2019.

Knowing when to use a word that is considered jargon is an important skill. Jargon is appropriate if your target audience is within your industry. A trade association, which represents a specific industry, frequently will use jargon when communicating internally within its industry. Jargon may also be useful and strategic in a B2B (business-to-business) campaign. In fact, using jargon in these situations can be an effective way of communicating. It shows that you speak the language of the profession.

Tech Talk

Technology – or "tech" – uses many industry-specific words and phrases. People who work in tech love jargon. They use words and phrases that are understandable to others in the profession. But technology, digital communications in particular, effects almost every aspect of our lives. Using tech-specific language correctly is crucial. It is also important to match the words you use to your target audience. In the *AP Stylebook*, new terms are listed as individual entries throughout the book, reflecting the prominence of these terms in everyday life.

The 2020–2022 *AP Stylebook* states that the word "technology" is "shorthand for information technology such as computing, robotics, communications as well as artificial intelligence." Since tech evolves so quickly, the book recommends that you refer to its online source, as it is updated in real time rather than every two years.

The *AP Stylebook* also recommends this:

> Consider your audience carefully when describing technology. Younger generations have grown up with technology and require less explanation of terms and services they find familiar, while the same language may bewilder some older readers. It is safe to say that services in widespread use – such as Facebook and Google – for instance will be recognized by all demographics. Other terms, such as "zero-day vulnerability," are not familiar to many and should be explained for general audiences. When in doubt, explain potentially unfamiliar terms and avoid online or technical jargon.

There are also a number of tech-specific style guides that may be useful in your writing, such as the following:

- **Apple's Style Guide:** https://books.apple.com/us/book/apple-style-guide/id1161855204
- **DigitalOcean's Technical Writing Guidelines:** www.digitalocean.com/community/tutorials/digitalocean-s-technical-writing-guidelines
- **Microsoft Style Guide:** https://docs.microsoft.com/en-us/style-guide/welcome/
- **The IBM Style Guide: Conventions for Writers and Editors (IBM Press):** available from Amazon and other booksellers

Trending Words

Using the correct words for your target audience is essential to strategic public relations writing. This not only applies to the jargon used by a specific industry, but to new words and phrases. It is also important to know when it is appropriate to use a trending word. You may want to avoid using a word that you hear a lot. For instance, the word "unprecedented" was used in nearly every media report describing the coronavirus pandemic in 2020. If you do a Google search on usage of the word, you will find article after article talking about the overuse of the word and many articles begging the media to stop using it. So, at that time, you would need to use that word with caution, as it was a word the public was tired of hearing.

One way to figure out if a word is trending is to research which words are looked up the most in dictionaries. Here are three of the most looked-up words in the Merriam-Webster dictionary in 2020 (in alphabetical order):

- **Defund:** In response to the killing of Black people by police officers, the word "defund" rose in lookups beginning in June. The word was used in reference to the best way to address police violence. Overall, "defund" was looked up 6,059% more in 2020 than in 2019.

- **Kraken:** On July 23, 2020, Seattle's brand-new National Hockey League franchise chose "Kraken" as its team name. Searches for the word increased 128,000% that day. A kraken is a mythical Scandinavian sea monster. Krakens have been featured in Marvel comics. For instance, in the 2010 remake of *Clash of the Titans*, Zeus commands his underlings to "release the kraken."
- **Mamba:** When Kobe Bryant, along with nine other people, including one of Bryant's daughters, died in a helicopter crash, people searched for a word strongly associated with the player and settled on "mamba." It was a nickname the player had chosen for himself more than a decade before. A mamba is "any of several chiefly arboreal venomous green or black elapid snakes of sub-Saharan Africa." The word "mamba" spiked in lookups on the day of Bryant's death, with users looking up the word 42,750% more than is typical; the next day, that number increased by 66,366%. Overall, "mamba" was looked up 934% more frequently in 2020 than it had been in 2019.

Keeping up with changes in the English language can seem like a full-time job for a PR writer. That is why working with a variety of reference guides is so important. It is also helpful to sign up for email alerts and blogs to stay up to date on new terminology. It is also why it is important to double-check the meaning of a word or phrase and use the appropriate spelling.

Be Respectful and Inclusive

When you are writing, you need to follow general principles to ensure that your language is free of bias. According to the Linguistic Society of America's website, "inclusive language acknowledges diversity, conveys respect to all people, is sensitive to differences and promotes equal opportunities."

For the PR writer, it is crucial that your writing is respectful, which is demonstrated by using the correct words and phrases. It is important to remember that the words you select are a reflection on your client or organization. This is particularly important if your writing discusses age, gender, disabilities or race.

As the collective consciousness of society evolves, our language has evolved to reflect these changes. The challenge is to make sure your writing reflects what is considered appropriate today. The University of Idaho provides resources to writers on inclusive language. It recommends that "when writing content, always consider whether a person's or group's identity is relevant to the content. Do not identify someone's race, gender, orientation, ethnicity, disability status, etc. . . . unless it adds value and context."

When your writing uses terms or addresses topics that may be sensitive, take a moment to determine if you are using the correct words. Look it up in a writing style guide or dictionary. You can also refer to specialized style guides such as *The Diversity Style Guide*. You can access it here: www.diversitystyleguide.com/about/. It includes terms and phrases related to race/ethnicity, religion, sexual orientation, gender identity, age and generation, drugs and alcohol, and physical, mental, and cognitive disabilities. *The Diversity Style Guide* was originally a project of the Center for Integration and Improvement of Journalism at San Francisco State University.

You can also check with an association that represents the group you are writing about for clarification. The important thing is that you take the time to make sure your language is inclusive and does not offend – even by accident. It is also important to ask the person being mentioned what her/his/their preference is.

Here are some specific guidelines (in alphabetical order) when writing about the following topics:

Abilities/Disabilities

When writing about a person with a disability, be careful to not use terms such as "disabled person" or "handicapped." An individual is not their disability. It is important to not use words that connote pity. Avoid wording such as "afflicted," "battling" and "suffering from." When writing about a person with a disability, if possible, ask them how they would like to be referenced. The Center for Disability Rights offers specific tips for writing about disabilities. It can be found here: https://cdrnys.org/.

Gender and Sexual Identity

Over the past two decades, Americans have experienced a significant evolution in their understanding and cultural acceptance of the lesbian, gay, bisexual, transgender and queer (LGBTQ) community.

GLAAD, the Gay and Lesbian Alliance Against Defamation, created a media resource. It is geared toward journalists, but it is a useful reference guide for public relations writers who are not sure about terminology. It can be downloaded here: www.glaad.org/reference. It provides details on what is and is not acceptable terminology. According to GLAAD:

> The Associated Press, Reuters and the *New York Times* all restrict usage of the term "homosexual" – a word whose clinical history and pejorative connotations are routinely exploited by anti-LGBTQ extremists to suggest that people attracted to the same sex are somehow diseased or psychologically and emotionally disordered.

Using the style guides of these three news organizations, GLAAD came up with the following guidelines:

- **Gay:** The word "gay" is used to describe men and women attracted to the same sex, though "lesbian" is the more common term for women. It is preferred over "homosexual" except in clinical contexts or references to sexual activity. Include sexual orientation only when it is pertinent to a story and avoid references to "sexual preference" or to a gay or alternative "lifestyle."
- **Husband, wife:** Regardless of sexual orientation, "husband" or "wife" is acceptable in all references to individuals in any legally recognized marriage.
- **Gender:** People generally have a clear sense of their own gender, sometimes called gender identity, which may conflict with their sex at birth. When in

doubt, ask people what gender pronouns they prefer. Respect their wishes if they ask not to be identified as either male or female. If it's not possible to ask their preference, use pronouns that are most consistent with the way they present themselves. Do not use quotation marks around names or pronouns used for transgender or gender-nonconforming people.

- **Transgender:** This adjective is an overall term for people whose current identity differs from their sex at birth, whether or not they have changed their biological characteristics. Cite a person's transgender status only when it is pertinent and its pertinence is clear to the reader. Unless a former name is newsworthy or pertinent, use the name and pronouns ("he," "his," "she," "her," "hers") preferred by the transgender person. If no preference is known, use the pronouns consistent with the way the subject lives publicly. "Transgender" is generally preferable to the older "transsexual." Do not use the offensive slang "tranny."
- **Sexual orientation:** Never use the term "sexual preference," which carries the disputed implication that sexuality is a matter of choice.

Another way that language has evolved is the use of non-gender nouns. If not, your writing can sound dated and sexist. Use terms for jobs and roles that can apply to any gender. Here are some examples:

Gender-neutral	Inappropriate
Spokesperson	Spokesman
Firefighter	Fireman
Chair	Chairman
Council member	Councilman
Workers' compensation	Workman's compensation

In your writing, it is also important to make sure you use the preferred personal pronouns for people you are writing about.

Pronouns are the way that we refer to people in place of their name or in third person (referring to that person while talking to someone else). Often, pronouns have an implied gender, such as "he" to refer to a man or boy or "she" to refer to a woman or girl. Don't make assumptions about the gender of a person based on their appearance or their name. When you use someone's correct pronouns, it serves to create an inclusive environment where you demonstrate that you care about and respect them. If you are not sure, ask the person you are writing about how he, she or they would like to be referenced.

Older People

Generally, the terms "senior citizen," "seniors" and "elderly" are no longer considered appropriate to use in your writing. Instead, the preferred terms, according to the *AP Stylebook*, are "older adult," "older person" and "older people."

The AARP, formerly known as the American Association for Retired People, suggests that the following terms are also appropriate:

- **Ageless:** The Isabella Rossellini of appellations. The ageless person perpetually exists in a liminal state where time is irrelevant.
- **Vintage:** It becomes more valuable as it gets older and is revered and passionately pursued by those of all ages who are truly in the know.
- **Distinguished:** It conveys dignity, authority and a healthy investment portfolio.

The AARP suggests that you avoid "of a certain age" and "spry." It is important to be specific in your writing. For instance, if you are creating a strategic communication campaign for a new treatment for people over 70 with high blood pressure, write that. Don't write, "There is a new treatment for senior citizens" or, worse, "a new drug for old people."

Racial and Ethnic Identity

Terms used to refer to racial and ethnic groups continue to change. Words can become dated and may hold negative connotations. What was acceptable in the past may be offensive today. The APA manual offers specific guidelines for bias-free language. You can access it here: https://apastyle.apa.org/style-grammar-guidelines/bias-free-language/racial-ethnic-minorities.

The APA recommends that racial and ethnic groups be referenced by proper nouns and be capitalized. Therefore, use "Black" and "White" instead of "black" and "white."

To refer to non-White racial and ethnic groups collectively, use terms such as "people of color" or "underrepresented groups" rather than "minorities." The word "minority" may be viewed pejoratively because it is usually equated with being less than, oppressed or deficient in comparison with the majority (i.e., White people).

Here is a checklist for clarity and inclusivity:

- Is the writing grammatically correct?
- Are any of the terms or phrases used potentially offensive?
- Is the writing level appropriate for the target audience?
- Are the words and terms used appropriate for the specific social media site?
- Does the writing style adhere to the organization's agreed upon style guide?
- Is the writing clear?
- Is the content appropriate for the target audience?
- Is the tone appropriate for the target audience?
- Does the writing accomplish what it was intending to do?
- Are there any words or phrases that may be offensive?

Editing and Proofing Your Work

Writing means rewriting. And rewriting means editing. You will likely rewrite your work several times before you are pleased with it. Effectively editing your work is the hallmark of great writing.

The last step in the writing process is proofing your work. As you write a draft of your tactic, here is a useful checklist. Ask yourself if the writing is all of the following:

- Clear and concise
- Appropriate for the target audience
- Free of bias
- Grammatically correct
- Free of spelling errors

Before you submit your work to your boss or client, it must be carefully proofed. If possible, show your work to a trusted co-worker before submitting it to a person in authority. It sometimes helps to ask someone who does not work within your specific area to review your work to make sure your writing is clear and your key messages are communicated.

Most PR departments have a process in place for proofing work. If you work alone, you will need to create your own mechanism to proof your work. This may include taking a break from reviewing your work, printing it out or even moving to another location to proof your final copy.

Here are some other tips from the Writing Center at the University of North Carolina at Chapel Hill:

- **Be careful with grammar checkers**. These programs work with a limited number of rules, so they can't identify every error and often make mistakes. They also fail to give thorough explanations to help you understand why a sentence should be revised.
- **Read slowly and read every word**. Try reading out loud, which forces you to say each word and also lets you hear how the words sound together. When you read silently or too quickly, you may skip over errors or make unconscious corrections.
- **Separate the text into individual sentences**. This is another technique to help you read every sentence carefully. Simply press the enter key after every period so that every line begins a new sentence. Then read each sentence separately, looking for grammar, punctuation and spelling errors. If you're working with a printed copy, try using an opaque object like a ruler or a piece of paper to isolate the line you're working on.
- **Circle every punctuation mark**. This forces you to look at each one. As you circle, ask yourself if the punctuation is correct.
- **Read the paper backwards**. This technique is helpful for checking spelling. Start with the last word on the last page and work your way back to the beginning, reading each word separately. Because content, punctuation and grammar won't make any sense, your focus will be entirely on the spelling of each word. You can also read backwards sentence by sentence to check grammar; this will help you avoid becoming distracted by content issues.

You can access the website of the Writing Center at the University of North Carolina at Chapel Hill here: https://writingcenter.unc.edu/tips-and-tools/editing-and-proofreading/.

When drafting a communications plan, include time to edit and proof your written tactics. This can make writing tactics on schedule much easier.

There are, however, many types of PR where you must respond quickly with a written response. This is particularly true if you work in crisis communications or need to jump into the news cycle so that your company or client is the first to respond. In these situations, speed is more important than perfection. When you need to get work out quickly, edit for what is most important. If your goal is to communicate a number or statistic, make sure it is correct. And look for mistakes that would be very embarrassing. For instance, if you are quoting a CEO, get their name spelling correctly. This may sound like simplistic advice, but when you are quickly working, it is sometimes the simplest things that are easy to overlook and can have damaging repercussions.

Keep in mind, however, that time-sensitive public relations should also have a planned strategy. If you know that you may need to respond quickly in writing, draft a few tactics that can be easily updated. That way, you are not starting from scratch. You may also want to create internal fact sheets so that you can easily find relevant facts. And plan ahead for a quick process to write, review and distribute the tactic. It will make drafting a quick written response much easier.

Chapter Summary

Strategic public relations writers should create a tool kit that includes a grammar guide, a writing style guide and a dictionary. Good writers use proper grammar and spelling, and they also monitor language to make sure the words and phrases they use are relevant and respectful. Lastly, an important component of writing is rewriting and editing. You need a mechanism to edit and proof your work.

Exercises

1. Review the list of grammar guides. Pick one that you think would be of value to you both as a student and a PR professional. Why did you pick this book? What interests you about it?
2. Review the major style guides and describe them. Who is the key audience for each book?
3. Look up some trending words. Would you use them in your writing?
4. Pick an industry that has a lot of technical jargon. See if there are any industry-specific writing style guides. Identify some new words.
5. Pick an area of diversity or inclusion that interests you. Are there any trade associations that represent the target audience you are trying reach? Draft a short report of dos and don'ts.
6. Create a mechanism for editing and proofing your work.

Glossary Terms

Writing style guide – a set of standardized writing practices required for a project, brand, industry or field of study.

News hook – newsworthy information presented with the goal of capturing the attention and interest of both the news media and their audiences.

Jargon – a technical word that is used or understood by a specific industry.

References

The 11 Extremely Common Grammar Mistakes that Make People Cringe – And Make You Look Less Smart, March 24, 2021. www.cnbc.com/2021/03/24/common-grammar-mistakes-that-make-people-cringe-and-make-you-look-less-smart-word-experts.html

American Association for Retired People (AARP). www.aarp.org/disrupt-aging/stories/ideas/info-2018/ageist-language-glossary.html

APA Publication Manual. https://apastyle.apa.org/products/publication-manual-7th-edition

APA Style Guide on Bias Free Language. https://apastyle.apa.org/style-grammar-uidelines/bias-free-language/racial-ethnic-minorities

Apple's Style Guide. https://books.apple.com/us/book/apple-style-guide/id1161855204

The Center for Disability Rights. https://cdrnys.org/

Chicago Manuel of Style. www.chicagomanualofstyle.org/home.htm

Diversity Style Guide. www.diversitystyleguide.com/about/

Gay and Lesbian Alliance Against Defamation (GLAAD). www.glaad.org/reference

Grammar Girl's Quick and Dirty Tips for Better Writing by Mignon Fogarty. www.quickanddirtytips.com/grammar-girl

Linguistic Society. www.linguisticsociety.org/resource/guidelines-inclusive-language

Merriam Webster Dictionary. www.merriam-webster.com/words-at-play/word-of-the-year/pandemic

MLA Style. www.mla.org/MLA-Style

Oxford English Dictionary. www.oed.com

Writing Center at the University of North Carolina at Chapel Hill. https://writingcenter.unc.edu/tips-and-tools/editing-and-proofreading/

For Further Reading

Apple's Style Guide. https://books.apple.com/us/book/apple-style-guide/id1161855204

Asian American Journalists. Association www.aaja.org/

Digital Ocean's Technical Writing Guidelines. www.digitalocean.com/community/tutorials/digitalocean-s-technical-writing-guidelines

Guinness, H. (2020). How to Edit your Own Work. *The New York Times*, April 7, 2020. www.nytimes.com/2020/04/07/smarter-living/how-to-edit-your-own-writing.html

Media Takes: On Aging. www.ilc-alliance.org/images/uploads/publication-pdfs/Media_Takes_On_Aging.pdf

Microsoft Style Guide. https://docs.microsoft.com/en-us/style-guide/welcome/

National Association of Black Journalists. https://nabjonline.org/ NABJ Style Guide; www.nabj.org/page/styleguide

National Association of Hispanic Journalists. https://nahj.org

National Center on Disability and Journalism and Its Disability Style Guide. https://ncdj.org/style-guide/

NLGJA Stylebook Supplement on Lesbian, Gay, Bisexual, & Transgender Terminology. www.nlgja.org/stylebook/

Northern Arizona University Writing Style Guide. https://nau.edu/writing-style-guide/inclusive-writing/

Racial Equity Tools Glossary. www.racialequitytools.org/glossary

Religion News Association (RNA). www.rna.org/default.aspx

Religion News Association Style Book. http://religionstylebook.com/

University of Idaho Inclusive Writing Guide. www.uidaho.edu/brand-resource-center/print-digital-content/inclusive-writing-guide

5 NEWS RELEASES

Learning Goals for This Chapter

After reading this chapter, you should be able to:

- Explain the importance of having a goal for your news release.
- Demonstrate how to write a news release that grabs the journalist's attention with a snappy title and a compelling first paragraph.
- Write a news release in the inverted pyramid style.
- Create a multimedia news release.
- Understand the key aspects of a news release.

Knowing how to write an effective news release is one of the most important tactics that a PR professional can master. It is the central piece of writing in strategic public relations.

According to award-winning communications consultant Sherry Goldman, president of Goldman Communications Group and an adjunct professor in PR at the City College of New York:

> A news release is the official announcement or statement of corporate or organizational news which PR pros send to print, broadcast and online media to alert them of the news. News releases should be timely and be written similar in structure to a newspaper article. In some instances, a newspaper or online site will run the press release verbatim in their print or digital editions if it is written properly and effectively tells the news.

Sometimes referred to as a "press release," the term "news release" is increasingly preferred by many organizations. The authors of this textbook also prefer the term "news release" because the press or the media is not the only audience for the document. Two of the other audiences for a news release are:

1. The readers, viewers and listeners of the content produced by the journalist.
2. Individuals who want to read the news release itself rather than believing the media's interpretation of the news in the release.

DOI: 10.4324/9781003248330-5

However, in a professional setting, use the preferred term of your client or the organization where you work. For consistency's sake, this textbook will use "news release." In the end, it does not matter what you call it; what matters is that it is written properly and executed correctly.

Ivy Lee is credited with creating the first news release following a train wreck on October 28, 1906, in Atlantic City, New Jersey. The train was owned by the Pennsylvania Railroad, one of Lee's clients. In response to the disaster, he convinced the railroad to issue a statement about what had transpired. The accident caused the death of 50 people and is known as the Atlantic City train wreck. At the time, the news release was written specifically for newspapers since that newspapers were the dominant media. Allegedly, his news release was printed verbatim.

For many years, the target media for news releases were print newspapers. For that reason, the basic format for the news release is that of a news article in a newspaper. In the beginning, news releases would be written, printed and distributed by mail or messenger to newspapers. Later, the news release was faxed to newsrooms at the major print and broadcast outlets. It was considered an effective way to get broad coverage. As the media evolved, so has the news release.

An effective news release today is written for the needs of a specific target audience and type of media. It is also a multimedia document designed to be read and saved online.

Today's news release includes links to video, audio, web articles, social media and more. In fact, according to Business Wire's 2020 Media Survey, the three most important elements of a news release are:

- Multimedia assets such as video, pictures, logos and infographics (57%)
- Contact information (51%)
- Company background (38%)

More details can be found at https://blog.businesswire.com/what-to-include-with-your-news-releases-to-get-a-journalists-attention-insights-from-business-wires-2020-media-survey.

Why Write a News Release?

With the proliferation of social media, you may question how relevant this tactic is today. After all, a well-known influencer can create significant attention for products and issues. And big news is now announced on Twitter. In fact, "Is the News Release Dead?" is a popular title for seminars at public relations and communications conferences. It is a provocative name for a presentation, and it attracts attendees. But the reality is that a well-executed news release is still one of the best and most efficient ways of controlling the narrative for your client or company.

News releases are also very cost-effective. Other than the cost of your time (or that of members of your team), you don't have to pay to create and distribute a new release as you would if you were paying for advertising. A well-written news release can successfully promote the opening of a small business such as a shop or restaurant, as well as get attention for important issues.

Reporters often find story ideas from news releases. A key finding from the Cision white paper on the 2021 Global State of the News Media found that "the vast majority of journalists (78%) want news announcements and press releases (which is also the source of content journalists said they find most useful)." You can view the full report here: www.cision.com/resources/research-reports/2021-state-of-the-media/.

When thoughtfully written, a news release is a powerful tool. It is also a highly strategic document. You don't write news releases just to write them.

Before writing a news release, you need to be able to answer these three questions:

1. What do you hope to accomplish?
2. Who are you writing the news release for?
3. How will I know the release was successful?

Unfortunately, many clients or executives feel the need to simply issue a news release. It may be because this is the way an organization has always done things. At times, management or clients may hold a dated or uninformed opinion of what a news release should be and can do. It is your job as public relations professional to explain when it makes sense to issue a release and when it does not. If there is no real news, you may need to spend some time creating news and developing a news hook. This topic was discussed in detail in Chapter 2.

There are many reasons to draft a news release. They include:

- Encouraging reporters to interview a subject matter expert at your organization.
- Promoting a special event such as a pop-up shop or a charity fundraiser.
- Announcing a new product or service.
- Providing archival data for an important event or issue.
- Offering key facts and data to feed the 24-hour news cycle.
- Providing consumer tips that focus on events or holidays.
- Announcing annual reports and communicating financial data.
- Boosting the SEO of your website.
- Telling your side of the story when there is a contentious issue.

Identifying the Audiences for the News Release

The PR writer also must be able to identify the various audiences for the news release. This is more complicated than it sounds. Yes, news releases are written for journalists. However, journalists are simply a conduit to your target audience – their readers, listeners or viewers. So, you need to use words and phrases that will make sense to the journalist's audience.

For instance, imagine that you are hired to promote a residential real estate broker. The target audience is people who are looking to buy or rent a new home. Logically, you could try to get coverage for the company by writing a news release for journalists who cover real estate. People who routinely read the real estate section of a newspaper are knowledgeable about the topic. The readers may include consumers who are interested in buying or renting a new home, as well as professional investors and others who follow the economics of real estate. The writing and the focus of the news release should be geared to these readers.

As a strategic public relations writer, you may want to consider other types of media to reach your target audience of people seeking to buy or rent a new home. The most successful PR professionals draft different releases for different types of news outlets. After conducting some research, you decide that personal finance reporters may also be a great way to reach your target audience. In addition to print newspapers, personal finance reporters also produce content for magazines, blogs and other online media as well as television and radio. These outlets provide opportunities to reach members of your target audience who may not read newspapers.

Your strategy is to draft news releases with tips and important "news you can use" geared toward the readers of personal finance media. Your writing needs to be understandable to someone with little or no background in real estate. And the focus of your news release should be similar to the types of topics that personal finance reporters cover. For instance, titles that may be of interest might be "How to Decide if You Should Buy or Rent" or "Hidden Costs of Homeownership."

The releases would need to be written in a very consumer-oriented manner. Your tips should be short and snappy. When writing the release, imagine how your tips would sound if they were spoken on air or how they would read in a short blog. They must be clear and easy to understand. That way, the reporter can simply provide the tips with your client as the source.

Drafting a news release that is used by a reporter is an example of earned media. You "earn" the coverage by convincing a journalist to cover your proposed story. This means that your release needs to be compelling enough for the journalist and/or their editors/producers to use in their news outlet. In some academic books on public relations, you may hear these journalists referred to as **media gatekeepers**.

Since you have to get past the media gatekeeper, and the journalist will ultimately use your information as they see fit, you don't have complete control over what will appear in the media. A journalist will create the content for their outlet. That is why a positive story in the media is so powerful. The information and the key message you are trying to communicate are presented by the media, who is a trusted third party to many people.

As the writer of the news release, you want to make it as easy as possible for the journalist to cover your story by providing as many resources as possible for them. With the size of newsrooms shrinking, journalists find themselves with more and more tasks to complete every day. For instance, according to the Pew Research Center's State of the New Media posted in July 2021:

> In 2008, there were about 114,000 total newsroom employees – reporters, editors, photographers and videographers – in five industries that produce news: newspaper, audio, broadcast television, cable and "other information services" (the best match for digital news publishers). By 2020, that number had declined to about 85,000, a loss of about 30,000 jobs.

Many reporters also need to create social media content to accompany their article, broadcast segment or podcast. One way to build positive relationships with journalists and get your news releases read is by building a reputation for providing useful and credible information that makes their job easier.

Lastly, keep in mind that people other than journalists read news releases on an organization's website. For instance, if you write a news release promoting a new cholesterol-lowering drug, you should expect that doctors, health insurance representatives, and individuals with high cholesterol, as well as health, science and consumer reporters, will be reading the release.

Potential investors also frequently read a company's news releases, as well as its annual reports and other publicly available information. They may not want to only rely on what the financial media has to say about the company.

Marry Your Key Message to the Needs of the Media

In addition to having a goal for your news release, you need a key message. You need to know exactly what you want to say. But it also has to be something that is of interest to the media.

The business news website www.Inc.com posted a great article on this topic called "How to Write a Press Release that Will Pique Reporters Interest."

It stated that "the primary question a journalist would have is "Why would I care?"

The "news" in your news release has to be obvious. You can read the full article at www.inc.com/guides/2010/09/how-to-write-a-press-release.html.

Catching and Keeping a Journalist's Attention

For a news release to be of any use, it must be read by the media. That means your release needs an attention-grabbing headline. Most journalists will only read the first few words in your news release before deciding to hit "delete" or continue reading.

You may have heard the expression "Don't bury the lead." For the PR writer, this is vitally important. Writing a great headline can take time. It is not easy. For ideas and inspiration, read newspaper or blog headlines. Identify some strong words or phrases you can use in your own writing. Great writers are good readers.

After you have grabbed the attention of the journalist with your headline, you need to make the journalist continue to read your release. You need an opening paragraph with a few snappy sentences summarizing the key facts and messages.

Basically, to get your news release read, you need to:

1. Grab the attention of the journalist with a compelling headline.
2. Keep them reading with an interesting opening paragraph.

Analyze News Releases

This is a type of writing that requires practice. It also helps to study and analyze news releases that successful organizations distribute to the media. Here are a few suggestions for analyzing successful news releases:

- Read the news releases of companies or organizations that you admire.
- Also, review the many releases posted on news release distribution websites such as Cision or Business Wire. They can be viewed at www.cision.com/ and www.businesswire.com/portal/site/home/.
- When there is a trending news story that is getting significant media attention, go to the organization's website and try to find the news release that created the media attention.

Write in the Inverted Pyramid Style

News releases should be written in the inverted pyramid style. This means that the most important information should be on the top of the release, followed by additional details. The inverted pyramid writing style is designed to grab the reader's attention as quickly as possible, presenting the most important details in the lead paragraph and then providing additional information.

Writer Malcolm Gladwell, author of the books *Blink* and *The Tipping Point*, notes in a MasterClass article how to use the inverted pyramid style for news releases and article writing:

- "Start with the lead. In your story's lead, you should be answering five important questions:

    - Who did the thing of interest?
    - What did they do?
    - Where did they do it?
    - When did they do it?
    - Why did they do it?

    Your lead should offer these key points as quickly as possible, getting to the essence of your story in approximately 30 words or one to two short paragraphs. The lead may also include a hook to your story, such as an enticing quote or provocative detail, which encourages people to keep reading.
- **Continue with the body**. The body is where you offer supporting details, quotes from sources, and additional supplementary information. The information in the body should be organized in terms of importance, with the most essential info appearing earlier in the story.
- **Finish with pertinent background information**. Appearing last in inverted pyramid story structure is a section of additional related information. While this info is still helpful to fully understand the context of the story, it is less important than the information contained in the lead and the body."
    You can read the full article here: www.masterclass.com/classes/malcolm-gladwell-teaches-writing.

Key Elements of a News Release

If you read a number of news releases, you will notice that they may look slightly different. Some may use artistic fonts or very corporate graphic designs. Some organizations will also create their own news release template to reflect organizational or personal identity. News releases may also be formatted to the specifications of a release distribution service. There are, however, key elements that should be included in all standard news releases. In general, news releases should also be short – not more than two pages.

Here are the key elements to include in your release:

- **Company logo**

  This should be prominently displayed in the release. Traditionally, it is on the top, but this may differ depending on the design of an organization's news release template.

- **Media contacts**

  Clearly state who the media should contact for interviews and follow-up questions. Provide the name, title and/or area of expertise, phone, email or other contact information such as a Twitter handle. Some organizations may also list the names of subject matter experts who are deputized to speak to the media. It is okay to have the contact information on both the top and bottom of your release.

- **Release status**

  The words "FOR IMMEDIATE RELEASE" should be in all caps in the top left-hand corner of your news release. This information lets the media know that the information can be used. There may be times when you want to send the release out prior to formally releasing the information. In that case, put the words "EMBARGOED FOR RELEASE" in the top left-hand corner and then add the date and time the release can be used by the media. If you use this approach, only send the release to reporters you trust.

- **Headline**

  A headline appears at the top and center of your news release but below the logo and release information. The goal of the headline is to get the attention of the journalist. It should be short and to the point. Traditionally, a headline is 14-point size, bold and centered. However, some organizations use another format. The language, however, should be clear and easy to understand. This is one of the most important parts of the news release.

- **Subheadline**

  This is optional, but it can be very useful for providing additional information to entice the journalist to cover your story. It can be up to 120 characters in length and should appear directly below the headline. This helps you reinforce your story angle with more information and encourages further reading. Traditionally, it is italicized in 12-point Times New Roman font, but other styles are being used today.

- **Location and date**

  Put this information immediately in front of the lead or first sentence in your release. You need to provide the location where the news is being made as well as the date the news release is being issued to the media. Traditionally, you should provide both the city and state, as well as the full date, including month, day and year.

- **Lead**

  The first paragraph should answer these fundamentals:

  - Who
  - What
  - When
  - Where
  - Why
  - How

  Stick to basic facts and avoid exaggeration. Text should be single-spaced in regular (not bold or italicized) 12-point Arial or Times New Roman font. Include hyperlinks to your company's website and links to the bios of those quoted in the release. You should also link to relevant information such as white papers, infographics, photos and video, as well as articles. This is an excellent way to drive traffic to your website. It allows you to provide a lot of information and still keep the release itself short.

- **Body**

  The next few paragraphs should complete the story you introduced in the headline and first paragraph. Use short paragraphs – about two to four sentences. Try to include only one idea per paragraph.

- **Quotes**

  Adding quotes to your release allows you to communicate your key messages. They may be used verbatim by the reporter, or they may prompt questions by reporters. They are also a strategic way of controlling the narrative and telling your story. They can also provide a human face to an issue.

- **Boilerplate**

  The final paragraph of your press release is called a boilerplate. It's your company's "About" section that appears at the very bottom of your news release. This is where you write about your company's background, awards, amount of time in business or anything else that might be of interest to the media about your company. If more than one company is mentioned in the release, include boilerplate information for each of them.

- **End notation**

  At the end of your release, you need to add "###" or a similar notation, which tells the journalist that there is no more information. Some organizations will put their company initials or a small logo. If your release is more than one page, put "more" centered on the bottom of each page.

News Releases Should Be Multimedia and Sharable

The more relevant multimedia you can add, the better. This means adding links to sections of your website, as well as to video, audio, infographics and photos. Creating links to additional information allows you to write a short news release while providing a lot of information. It can also help to increase SEO for your website. You also want to make it easy to share the release by email or social media. It is standard practice to include hashtags and links to social media sties.

Consider How Your Release Will Be Viewed

Your news release needs to be easily read on both a phone as well as a computer. Take this into account when formatting it. There should also be an option to print the release. Make sure that when it is printed, it looks professional and reflects your brand.

Where Does the News Release Fit in the PESO Model?

In the PESO model, the news release is an example of earned media. It is a primary tactic to get a journalist to cover your story. It is also a tactic that is shared media on social media. News releases are sometimes distributed to the media through social media, too. And they are content for the owned media of an organization's website. If you pay for placement of the news release, it would fall into the category of paid media. Paying for placement is different from paying for distribution, as the media who receive the news release in this manner may or may not use the release.

News Release Template to Use as a Guide

Following is a sample news release from Cision.com. It is a useful guide to drafting a news release.

A Brief, Tweet-able Summary of the News that Mentions Your Organization

This is one or two subheadlines that explain your organization's news and who it impacts.

Include additional information here that helps add context and will intrigue readers, but keep it brief.

CITY, STATE – Date – Start your release with a clear, concise statement of the news. Restate your organization's name and provide the necessary details for the story, linking to a web page that is directly related. Your readers should know the who, what and when within the first paragraph. Include key statistics and the names of key players in this paragraph, but keep it brief; audiences will often read just the first few lines of your release, so you need to pack these sentences with all of the key information. End the first paragraph (or add a standalone line) with your call to action – it should be direct and easy to understand.

The second paragraph is where you can tell your readers why the information in the first paragraph is important. You've gotten the crucial details out; now it's time to give them more context. How does the information in the first paragraph impact them? How does it impact your company? Include more here to back up what you're saying, and remember to show, not tell. If you're including hard numbers, incorporate one hyperlink here to show where you got them, or use a chart to visually showcase your story. By this point, your readers should be able to tell you why this story is important enough for them to keep reading.

When applicable (don't force it), include a list to:

- Highlight important takeaways for readers
- Lay out future effects of your story
- Recognize customers, employees or organizations
- Summarize key figures related to your news
- Boost your SEO results
- Make your release more visually appealing and easier to scan

Says Emily Engle, customer marketing specialist at Cision:

Focusing on the facts doesn't have to take the personality out of your release, but personality shouldn't get in the way of the facts. Including quotes from key people at your organization lends credibility to your release and humanizes your organization to your audience. I've worked with our customers on press releases for years, and good quotations really take a release to the next level. Reporters can also use the quotes in your release to write their own story about your announcement.

If your readers are hitting your fourth paragraph, congratulations – you've really caught their interest! Now is the time to fill in more of the details about the news and your company. If you're announcing a new product line, for instance, this is where you explain more of the specifics around where it's available and even where it will be available in the future. Regardless of what you're writing about, make sure you tell them what they can expect to happen as a result.

Any other relevant information should go after your fourth paragraph, along with any other quotes (unless you have two equally important people who both need to be quoted early on). Take the opportunity to direct your readers to supporting resources with one more hyperlink. If your news is very technical or industry specific, feel free to take more time here to explain what it is and how it works at this point. Be careful not to ramble; think like a journalist. Restate your call to action at the end of your release.

Information About Your Organization

This is your boilerplate – it gives journalists and readers a brief overview of your organization. Tell them who you are, what you do, where you're located, and who you serve. Include one sentence on your organization's values, notable achievements, certifications or anything else that your audience and the media benefits from knowing. Tell them where they can go to find more information about your organization and include a link to your home page here as well. If you'd like, include your social media handles here, too.

Your Name (or the Name of the Person You Want the Media to Contact)

Include, after the name, title, phone number and email address.

Case Study: Earth's Hottest Month on Record (and Surrounding Circumstances)

This case study demonstrates how to use regularly provided data as a news hook for a highly successful news release when events provide an opportunity. The National Oceanic and Atmospheric Administration (NOAA), part of the U.S. federal government, has a mission to understand and predict our changing environment and to manage and conserve America's coastal and marine resources.

Among NOAA's numerous services, every month, it releases climate data and statistics for the United States and the globe from the preceding month.

The information is available to the public and the media. But in terms of newsworthiness, not all months are equal. Some months, the data and statistics are more newsworthy than others.

In August 2021, NOAA announced that the preceding month, July 2021, was the hottest July on record for the planet. And a combination of related high-profile events helped amplify the news. With records dating back to 1880, the planet's record hottest month was especially noteworthy. Adding to the news value of the announcement were ongoing events at the time such as record heat, historic drought and raging wildfires in the western United States. Additionally, just a few days prior to the routine release of NOAA's climate information, a major international report from the United Nations' Intergovernmental Panel on Climate Change released a comprehensive assessment of our changing climate.

In a NOAA press release, dated August 13, 2021, the agency broke the news ("It's official: July was Earth's hottest month on record") and then provided the raw data and statistics that set the month apart from any other in the previous 142 years.

The press release:

- Included a fresh quote from the NOAA administrator, who spoke to the context of the news
- Provided the climate statistics in concise chunks

- Used graphics, bullets, subheads and bold font to enhance readability
- Referenced the recent IPCC report and provided an opportunity to reiterate an excerpt from the NOAA administrator's statement about the IPCC's findings

Collectively, this resulted in widespread local, national and international media interest in the announcement that cited NOAA's data, quoted the NOAA administrator and provided another bounce to the news of the IPCC report.

News Release Referenced in the Case Study "It's Official: July Was Earth's Hottest Month on Record"

August 13, 2021

A collage of typical climate and weather-related events: floods, heatwaves, drought, hurricanes, wildfires and loss of glacial ice. (NOAA)

July 2021 has earned the unenviable distinction as the world's hottest month ever recorded, according to new global data released today by NOAA's National Centers for Environmental Information.

"In this case, first place is the worst place to be," said NOAA Administrator Rick Spinrad, Ph.D. "July is typically the world's warmest month of the year, but July 2021 outdid itself as the hottest July and month ever recorded. This new record adds to the disturbing and disruptive path that climate change has set for the globe."

July 2021 by the Numbers

- **Around the globe**: the combined land and ocean-surface temperature was 1.67 degrees F (0.93 of a degree C) above the 20th-century average of 60.4 degrees F (15.8 degrees C), making it the hottest July since records began 142 years ago. It was 0.02 of a degree F (0.01 of a degree C) higher than the previous record set in July 2016, which was then tied in 2019 and 2020.
- **The Northern Hemisphere**: the land-surface only temperature was the highest ever recorded for July, at an unprecedented 2.77 degrees F (1.54 degrees C) above average, surpassing the previous record set in 2012.
- **Regional records**: Asia had its hottest July on record, besting the previous record set in 2010; Europe had its second-hottest July on record – tying with July 2010 and trailing behind July 2018; and North America, South America, Africa and Oceania all had a top-ten warmest July.

Extreme Heat and Global Climate Change

With last month's data, it remains very likely that 2021 will rank among the world's ten-warmest years on record, according to NCEI's Global Annual Temperature Rankings Outlook.

Extreme heat detailed in NOAA's monthly NCEI reports is also a reflection of the long-term changes outlined in a major report released this week by the Intergovernmental Panel on Climate Change offsite link.

"Scientists from across the globe delivered the most up-to-date assessment of the ways in which the climate is changing," Spinrad said in a statement. "It is a sobering IPCC report that finds that human influence is, unequivocally, causing climate change, and it confirms the impacts are widespread and rapidly intensifying."

Here is a link to the full release: www.noaa.gov/news/its-official-july-2021-was-earths-hottest-month-on-record. It should be noted that this release, when viewed on the NOAA website, is also a great example of a well-executed multimedia news release that includes links, images and an educational infographic.

This case study was provided by Chris Vaccaro, senior media relations specialist at NOAA, who is also former assistant editor at the newspaper *USA Today*.

As a media relations expert and former print journalist, Vaccaro also offers the following perspectives on working with the news media:

- News releases are not outdated tools. There is always value to crafting a communications strategy that includes a well-written and internally vetted document solely focused on a matter related to your organization and its audiences.
- Speak to your audience. Assume nothing, explain everything and don't use jargon unless you're also including a clear explanation. Use plain language.
- Praise the BLUF (Bottom Line Up Front). Clearly explain the "So what? Why should I care?" part of your announcement first – do not delay in communicating to your audience how or why the announcement is important.
- Mind the flow. Formatting techniques can help the writer and the reader. Embrace the use of bullets and bold font to break up text. Paragraphs should be brief with no more than two or three sentences. Make every word count.
- Say something useful. Quotes from internal sources need to say something substantial and newsy – worthy of publication. Quotes should not be filled with branding, which is covered elsewhere in the release, nor should they over-communicate cliché personal feelings such being "excited" or "proud."

Chapter Summary

A news release is a highly strategic and goal-oriented tactic as part of a public relations program or campaign. You need to have clear goal for the release. In addition, you need a key message that will be of interest to your target media. Lastly, a news release has very specific elements that must be included in it. It is a type of writing that takes practice.

Here is a checklist for writing an effective news release:

- What is the primary goal of the news release?
- Who is the key audience or audiences?
- Are keywords included to boost SEO of the company's website?
- Is the title descriptive and enticing enough to grab the attention of the media professional?

Exercises

1. What is the inverted pyramid? What does it have to do with news release writing?
2. Pick a news story that has received significant media attention. Try to find the news release that announced the news. What did you learn from this?
3. Imagine that you were just hired by Google. Pick any job you think you would like to have. Draft a news release announcing that you accepted this position. Link to your bio or LinkedIn profile if you have one.
4. Read the Pew Research Center's State of the News Media for 2021. What are some trending topics that may be useful news hooks for a news release?
5. Read Cision's white paper on the 2021 State of the Media. How can you apply its findings to drafting your next news release?
6. Your client wants to rewrite the same news release it distributed last year. It is about a product that makes a lot of money for the company but there isn't anything newsy about it. The executives at the company like seeing their name in the release, but it did not generate any media coverage last year and is likely to not generate any attention again. How would you advise your client to take another approach?
7. Read the news releases of a company you admire. What do you think about its news releases? Are they strategic? Do they follow the general guideline for a news release?
8. Identify a nonprofit or charity that you support. Write a news release announcing that Amazon is donating $10 million to support its good works. There are no strings attached to the donation. Make sure to include the boilerplate information from both organizations. Create hyperlinks from resources from their respective websites. Draft a quote from a real executive at both of the organizations.

Glossary

News release – an official written statement provided to newspapers, magazines, television news programs, online media and radio stations.

Media gatekeepers – the people who decide what information is used or not used in their news outlets.

References

BusinessWire. https://blog.businesswire.com/what-to-include-with-your-news-releases-to-get-a-journalists-attention-insights-from-business-wires-2020-media-survey

Cision's 2021 State of the Media. www.cision.com/resources/research-reports/2021-state-of-the-media/

How to Write a Press Release and that Will Pique Reporters Interest. www.inc.com/guides/2010/09/how-to-write-a-press-release.html

Malcom Gladwell on the Inverted Pyramid. www.masterclass.com/classes/malcolm-gladwell-teaches-writing

NOAA News Release. www.noaa.gov/news/its-official-july-2021-was-earths-hottest-month-on-record.

Pew Research Center. www.pewresearch.org/fact-tank/2021/07/13/u-s-newsroom-employment-has-fallen-26-since-2008/

For Further Reading

The Ad Council's Five Tips for Writing a Winning Press Release. www.adcouncil.org/5-tips-
for-writing-a-winning-press-release?gclid=EAIaIQobChMIkZe5m_HU8gIVKNSzCh2fdw-
xEAAYAyAAEgK_P_D_BwE

How-to Guide: Instructions on Writing a Reporter-Friendly News Release Featuring Best Practices from Ann Wylie, Wylie Communications. https://services.businesswire.com/resources-
education/writing-a-reporter-friendly-news-release

Sample New Release by BusinessWire. https://services.businesswire.com/resources-education/
sample-press-release

6 MEDIA KITS
Advisories, Q&As, Bios, Fact Sheets and Corporate Profiles

Learning Objectives for This Chapter

After reading this chapter, you should be able to:

- Understand the key elements of a strategic media kit.
- Know how to create an online media kit to accommodate the 24/7 news cycle.
- Develop the key contents of a media kit to advance organizational goals and objectives.
- Identify the goals and objectives of creating the media kit and its contents.

A media kit, sometimes referred to as a press kit, is a collection of PR tactics focused on a specific topic or event.

Both terms are used in the public relations business. However, the authors of this book prefer the term "media kit" because the kits provide information that is of interest to both traditional press and broadcasting, as well as other media.

This chapter focuses on describing what should be in a media kit, why it should be created and how to create some of the tactics that may be included in it. This includes a detailed description of how to strategically write media advisories, Q&As, bios, fact sheets and corporate profiles.

Regardless of the term used, media kits are intended to provide content to the news media, as well as to bloggers, podcasters, influencers and other target audiences and gatekeepers. They can be created for a press event or product launch or as a repository of information for easy 24/7 access by reporters. They also contain a selection of visual and auditory elements, including photos, infographics or charts for use by reporters.

Media kits bundle together important tactics for a PR campaign. They can also be used to package relevant tactics focused on specific issue. A media kit may also be

DOI: 10.4324/9781003248330-6

created to provide all of the essential background about an organization or even a person, such as a celebrity, author or athlete.

The goal of a media kit is to make it easier for the media and other key audiences to find and use important resources by curating the tactics that are most relevant. Virtually all of the tactics discussed in this book can be incorporated into a media kit, from the news releases described in Chapter 5 to the speeches and video scripts of Chapter 11.

The 24-Hour News Cycle

Today's news cycle is fast. It is 24 hours a day, seven days a week. It's always moving, always changing. The immediacy of news through digital and social media has completely altered the way news gets reported and disseminated. The media and the public want to get information when they want it. If you as the PR professional do not offer your key audiences the content they need, they will go somewhere else. This may not work to your advantage. It's always better to tell your story by providing your own content and information.

A well-executed media kit can provide one-stop shopping for journalists looking for information during the middle of the night or on weekends. This is particularly important if you work with international media who may not work on the same schedule as your PR team.

Format of a Media Kit

In the past, a media kit was just that – a kit. It was a physical binder or folder containing copies of news releases and other tactics, ranging from technical specifications to photographs to company logos. The contents were carefully designed with company or campaign-specific branding and were distributed at press events or handed out at meetings with journalists.

While physical media kits are still handed out at special events or press conferences, they are now designed to be saved on a website and distributed by social media or email. The Centers for Disease Control and Prevention has an example of a digital press kit: www.cdc.gov/eis/conference/digital-press-kit.html.

A website may also be created for a specific media kit. For seasonal topics or scheduled events, some organizations will build the kit but keep it dark or unavailable to the public. That way, they can work on all of the key elements and quickly update the content and make it available to the media when needed. Increasingly, the contents of a media kit are also saved on a thumb drive or made available by a QR code for easy access by journalists at an event. This makes it faster and easier for a reporter to cover your event or story.

Each tactic in the kit should be on branded letterhead and designed to stand alone. Each should also be formatted to look good if printed out. Web content, in general, should be designed this way to provide the most extensive use of the content. That way, if a physical media kit is needed, it can be created quickly. The media kit as well as the individual tactics should also be designed to be shared by email or text or on social media.

The tactics in the kit should also be written to support the other tactics. If appropriate, consider embedding individual tactics into other tactics. For instance, you may want to link the fact sheet or bios into the news release.

Media kits can be proactive tactics to be used before, during and after a specific event. Or they can be powerful reactive PR tactics designed to be used when someone is looking for information. The goal is to make it as easy as possible for your target media to use the tactics and cover your event, issue or client.

A strategic media kit is increasingly a multimedia tactic and may include digital sound bites for use on podcasts or radio, as well as videos and B-roll, which can be used in broadcast and online media, as well as photos and infographics.

The Key Elements of a Media Kit

Deciding what to include in a media kit is an important strategic decision. It should be based on your goals and objectives. In fact, before you decide to create a media kit, you need to have a specific goal for it.

In other words, what do you hope your media kit will accomplish?

You also need to decide if you plan to update the tactics in the kit or if it is a static document for use during a specific period of time.

There are some key basic elements to include:

- Bios of key executives or subject matter experts.

  Photos of these individuals should be included, as well as links to their relevant social media sites.

- Boilerplate information about the organization.

  This is information about the company. It is also sometimes referred to as a corporate profile. On many websites, it is also the "About" section.

- Images.

  Make sure you include images in your media kit that journalists can use for their stories. Most journalists require high-resolution images. This can include photos, logos, graphs, infographics or other visuals. These tactics are detailed in Chapter 13.

- Media contacts.

  Include the name or names of people who are deputized to speak to the media. If your organization is international, also add the physical location of the media contact. That way, users of your media kit also have a sense of when a person is likely to be available by phone or email.

- Media advisories and news releases.

  Your news release should include quotes from the person who is available for interview. Details on drafting a news release can be found in Chapter 5.

Other tactics to consider include:

- Audio clips.

  With the popularity of podcasts and other auditory tactics, it is important to provide audio tactics. If you have the budget, you can create tactics that can be used in a podcast or on radio or even used by television producers to narrate their stories. If you don't have the budget, consider taping a few sound bites to advance your key messages. This is a helpful tactic for journalists, as it draws them to the key points of your story or issue. Details can be found in Chapter 10.

- Annual reports or other financial information.

  If your media kit is focused on the financials of a publicly traded company, you may want to include a link to the company's annual report or other financial information required by the Securities and Exchange Commission. While this textbook is not focused on the communications requirements of publicly traded companies, it is worth noting that a strategic media kit should consider including this information if appropriate.

  Nonprofits or other noncommercial organizations should consider reports of ratings by nonprofit oversight groups as well as annual reports. While nonprofit organizations are not required by law to publish annual reports, it may make sense to have one, as it is a means of showing that the nonprofit is transparent about its finances and governance. For instance, the nonprofit Girls Who Code publishes a comprehensive annual report. You can access its 2020 annual report, "Bravery in a Crisis," here: https://girlswhocode.com/2020report/.

- B-roll and video

  Visual tactics are increasingly important in all aspects of public relations. This can also include PSAs and recordings of broadcast interviews. Details on these tactics are presented in Chapter 10.

- Fact sheets

  These are short documents that quickly and efficiently communicate the most relevant information about a particular topic, ranging from countries served to number of employees to years in business.

- Relevant media coverage

  You may want to include media coverage on your topic or issue if you believe it will help generate more coverage. This may be useful if you are introducing a new brand – media coverage may provide credibility.

- Testimonials

  These are quotes from pleased customers. It could also include examples of positive reviews of your product or service. For instance, if you are creating a media kit to promote a new play or movie, you may want to include positive reviews. Testimonials can be written quotes, videos or social media posts.

- Q&As and FAQs

    As the name applies, you may want to include questions and answers in your media kit. This can be a very strategic tactic, as it focuses a journalist's attention to the most important facts. They can also form the basis for interview questions by journalists. Frequently, this information is also shared on social media.

Types of Media Kits

A media kit can be created for many reasons. Nonprofit organizations, NGOs and governmental agencies can have educational goals. They may create media kits and other tactics with the goal of educating their target audiences about important issues They generally want to give information away. For instance, the nonprofit National Fire Protection Associations (www.nfpa.org) has the goal of preventing fires, but its key audiences include diverse audiences such as scientists, firefighters, children and even pet owners.

For-profit organizations generally create media kits to promote products, explain organizational objectives or communicate financial information. The company Seventh Generation, for example, has a media kit on its website that includes comprehensive information about the company. You can view it here: www.seventhgeneration. com/press. It includes information on the history of the company, its values, the CEO, its mission and awards. A media kit may also be created for the investor relations section of a publicly traded company to bundle important tactics together to make it easy for business media to find important information.

Drafting Key Elements of a Media Kit

The five key elements that should be considered for inclusion in a media kit that were not discussed in other chapters (or are outside the purview of this book, such as annual reports) are bios of key executives or subject matter experts, corporate profiles, fact sheets, media advisories and Q&As.

Following are details on how to draft each of these important tactics.

1. Bios of Key Executives or Subject Matter Experts

An effective bio should be between one and two pages in length. It should be written in third person. This means you don't use the word "I." Instead, you would write "he," "she" or "they." If you are writing a bio for someone and don't know their preferred pronoun, ask them. You will also want to vary your writing by referring to the executive or spokesperson by their name. You can use a formal title such as Dr. Smith or Ms. Smith. You can also choose to refer to them by their first or last name. The decision should reflect the image of the organization. For instance, an organization that wants to appear informal or friendly may decide to only use first names.

The bio is not a full resume. It is a narrative that should be filled with facts and information that explains why the person is qualified to speak to the media about the main focus of your media kit.

Bios should include:

- Name
- Title
- Relevant work experience and/or expertise
- Education if appropriate
- Personal information if relevant

Lastly, you should include a photo and/or video, which are increasingly included with bios. They are particularly useful if you have a video of your executive talking about the topic that is the focus of the media kit. Broadcast and multimedia journalists like to see how someone speaks on camera and are more likely to interview someone who has a good on-camera presence.

You can find some examples of bios provided by Apple at www.apple.com/leadership and by Delta Airlines at https://news.delta.com/leader-bios-a-b.

2. Corporate Profiles

A corporate profile is a professional summary of your organization or business and its activities. It is a sort of bio or resume for your organization. This is the same type of information that can be found in the "About" section of your website and in the boilerplate information that is included in a news release.

Some organizations will use the same content for their boilerplate "About" section and corporate profile. Other companies will have a concise description in the news release's boilerplate and provide expanded information in the "About" section and/or the corporate profile. The corporate profile created for the media kit may even include long and short versions. The long versions are useful to journalists who may be working on complex stories and the shorter versions are useful for social media posts and for introducing your spokesperson when interviewing them on radio, television or a podcast.

All of these approaches work. What is important is that the information about your organization can be easily found and that it is consistent. You need to make sure that all of the factual information is correct and up to date and that the writing reflects the organization's brand. A good corporate profile details how/when the company began and its plans for the future. It tells the story of your organization.

A strategically written corporate profile is a powerful document that can be used both externally with the media as well as internally with employees. It can be used to shape how employees talk about your organization by providing a cohesive and consistent vision. Tiffany & Co. is an interesting example of using this type of information in a strategic manner.

The company has a very smart boilerplate description on its news releases and media advisories. It can be viewed here.

About Tiffany & Co.

In 1837, Charles Lewis Tiffany founded his company in New York City where his store was soon acclaimed as the palace of jewels for its exceptional gemstones. Since then, TIFFANY & CO. has become synonymous with elegance, innovative design, fine craftsmanship and creative excellence. During the 20th century its fame thrived worldwide with store network expansion and continuous cultural relevance, as exemplified by Truman Capote's *Breakfast at Tiffany's* and the film starring Audrey Hepburn.

Today, with a workforce of more than 14,000 employees, TIFFANY & CO. and its subsidiaries design, manufacture and market jewelry, watches and luxury accessories – including nearly 5,000 skilled artisans who cut diamonds and craft jewelry in the Company's workshops, realizing its commitment to superlative quality. TIFFANY & CO. has a long-standing commitment to conducting its business responsibly, sustaining the natural environment, prioritizing diversity and inclusion, and positively impacting the communities in which we operate.

The Company operates more than 300 TIFFANY & CO. retail stores worldwide as part of its omni-channel approach. To learn more about TIFFANY & CO. as well as its commitment to sustainability, please visit tiffany.com.

This corporate profile does an excellent job of not only telling the organization's story but also sending the message that the brand is elegant and timeless and that its products are produced by expert craftsman.

The following are elements that can be included in a corporate profile:

- Company name as the full legal name
- Description of the business, as well as its vision or mission
- Description of products and services
- Physical location or locations
- Safety, health and environmental policies
- Top management team
- Client portfolio – with permission of the clients
- Awards
- Certifications
- Special programs and projects
- Key events in company history (e.g., the first drug created or the major computer system developed)

Starbucks also has a great corporate profile. It is both descriptive and inspiring. You can read it here.

Our Heritage

Our story begins in 1971 along the cobblestone streets of Seattle's historic Pike Place Market. It was here where Starbucks opened its first store, offering fresh-roasted coffee beans, tea and spices from around the world for our customers to take home. Our name was inspired by the classic tale, "Moby-Dick," evoking the seafaring tradition of the early coffee traders.

Ten years later, a young New Yorker named Howard Schultz would walk through these doors and become captivated with Starbucks coffee from his first sip. After joining the company in 1982, a different cobblestone road would lead him to another discovery. It was on a trip to Milan in 1983 that Howard first experienced Italy's coffeehouses, and he returned to Seattle inspired to bring the warmth and artistry of its coffee culture to Starbucks. By 1987, we swapped our brown aprons for green ones and embarked on our next chapter as a coffeehouse.

Starbucks would soon expand to Chicago and Vancouver, Canada and then on to California, Washington, D.C. and New York. By 1996, we would cross the Pacific to open our first store in Japan, followed by Europe in 1998 and China in 1999. Over the next two decades, we would grow to welcome millions of customers each week and become a part of the fabric of tens of thousands of neighborhoods all around the world. In everything we do, we are always dedicated to Our Mission: to inspire and nurture the human spirit – one person, one cup, and one neighborhood at a time.

Here is the link to Starbucks' full corporate story and website: www.starbucks.com/about-us/.

Other great corporate profiles are Warby Parker at www.warbyparker.com/history and REI at www.rei.com/about-rei.

3. Fact Sheets

A fact sheet informs the media about your business, organization, product, service, campaign, event or issue. It should center around one issue and have a clean, easy-to-read layout. Since it will be included in your media kit, it should be formatted to look like the other tactics in it. This means it should have a branded heading and logo. Try to make your fact sheet visually appealing and use tables, charts, graphs and bullet points.

The information you include in a fact sheet will differ depending on its subject and its intended audience. However, most fact sheets should contain the following content:

- Headline
- Summary of most important information in paragraph form
- Bullet point list of supporting facts
- Call to action
- Sources or attributions
- Where to go for more information

The headline, like all good headlines, should catch the attention of the reader. It should entice the reader to then read the summary. The call to action is what you want the reader to do.

A call to action is a statement designed to get an immediate response from the person reading or hearing it.

The goal of the fact sheet is to provide major facts of your story at a glance. It is a way of presenting facts and figures that support your key message. It is also an opportunity to provide more information that can be included in the news release or media advisory. You can find samples of fact sheets (20 Free Fact Sheet Templates) at https://business.tutsplus.com/articles/free-fact-sheet-microsoft-word-templates--cms-37526

4. Media Advisories or Alerts

A media advisory, or media alert, is essentially an invitation to the media to attend an event such as press conference, an SMT (Satellite Media Tour), special event or opening of a new store.

It may also be used in a crisis situation to alert media to who is deputized to speak during an evolving situation. For instance, the Insurance Information Institute (I.I.I.) frequently issues a media advisory during hurricanes and other disasters to alert media to I.I.I. experts and resources. For instance, to alert reporters to I.I.I. resources in the aftermath of 2021's Hurricane Ida, the I.I.I. issued a media advisory, titled "Media Advisory: Triple-I Available to Discuss Ida's Insurance Implications." The full media advisory is available here: www.iii.org/press-release/media-advisory-triple-i-available-to-discuss-idas-insurance-implications-083021.

If the event or crisis has passed, a media alert isn't appropriate and you should consider sending a news release instead.

Media alerts should be distributed a few weeks before the event. In particular, they should be sent to planning editors at the news outlets. They should then be sent again closer to the event and then immediately before the event.

Media alerts are brief and should simply provide:

- Who
- What
- Where
- When
- Why
- How

The headline is generally an announcement of the event itself. The first paragraph is very short and covers details of the event – location, time and so on. It might also include information on where to enter the building, where to park and whether refreshments or a meal will be served.

Here are seven elements to include in the media advisory:

1. "MEDIA ALERT" written at the top of the page
2. Your contact information written in a place that is clearly visible
3. The date of the event

4. Enticing headline (and sub headline if needed)
5. Introductory sentence with date, as well as the city and state in which the advisory is being issued
6. Boilerplate information
7. The word "end" or the symbols "###" at the bottom of the page, which indicates the end of the media alert

Here is a template that you can use:

Logo

Month, Day, Year

For more information, contact:

Full name, office phone number, cell phone number, email address

THE HEADLINE GOES HERE AND CAN BE UP TO FOUR LINES LONG, BOLD AND ALL CAPS. IT SHOULD CAPTURE THE READER'S ATTENTION.

A subtitle may be used for additional context.

CITY, STATE – Great opening paragraph

What: Name of event

Who: Name, role and organization of speakers or important attendees

When: Date and time

Where: Location and address

###

Add boilerplate information

The American College of Midwives and Nurses distributed a sample media advisory to its members and encouraged them to send it to their local news outlets regarding National Midwifery Event Week. It is a nice example of a media advisory and it provides a demonstration on how to use national events as a news hook. You can view it here: www.midwife.org/Sample-NMW-Media-Advisory.

The National Science Foundation has an entire page on its website of its media advisories: https://search.nsf.gov/search?query=media+advisories&affiliate=nsf&search=.

Here is another example of a media advisory from the National Association for the Education of Young Children: www.naeyc.org/our-work/public-policy-advocacy/media-advisory-template.

5. Q&As and FAQs

Q&As are a very smart tactic to include in a media kit.

A similar document is a list of FAQs.

Both tactics are similar in that each is simply a document with questions related to your topic with written answers. These tactics can provide a great way to provide more detailed answers to the topics in your media kit. They can sometimes provide direction to reporters on what is important and what is not. If they are well thought out, they can also form the basis of potential media interviews. They are also frequently picked up by social media. The Metropolitan Museum of Art uses this format with the news media: www.metmuseum.org/press/press-faqs.

Media Kits for Influencers

If your client is an influencer, a media kit is essential. It would include the same key tactics in a well-executed media kit, as well as the following:

- Number of followers – This gives brands a quick idea of the kind of reach an influencer has on social media. A well-executed influencer media kit should include all of their social media accounts with the number of followers on each platform.
- Audience demographics – Brands collaborate with influencers who have followers that are similar to their target audience. Provide details about the target audience of the influencer and their demographics. Mention their age group, gender and country of origin.
- Website statistics – Include website statistics in your influencer media kit. Include metrics like the number of unique visitors, page views, total subscribers and duration of visits. You can use Google Analytics to retrieve this data easily.

Case Study: Pets Need Dental Care, Too!

The campaign was created by Lea-Ann Germinder, APR, Fellow PRSA.

The "Pets Need Dental Care, Too!" campaign was launched in 1995 to focus on the importance of oral care for pets. Research showed that 80% of dogs and 70% of cats exhibited some signs of oral disease by the age of three. Preventative care (similar to humans) was the answer, but veterinary dentistry was a specialty in its infancy.

To educate both veterinarians and pet owners about the need for pet oral care, the American Veterinary Dental Society (AVDS) proclaimed February as National Pet Dental Health Month. Unfortunately, it did not have the resources to fund an educational campaign.

The American Veterinary Medical Association (AVMA) had also identified educating veterinarians to include oral care in their practices as a key initiative but also did not have a funding sponsor. Hill's Pet Nutrition had developed an oral care product for dogs and also wanted to address veterinarians and pet owners. To address this problem,

Germinder and her team at the time created "Dogs Need Dental Care, Too!" and after the first year, "Pets Need Dental Care, Too!" The educational campaign was a strategic partnership between the AVDS, the AVMA and Hill's Pet Nutrition. Hill's underwrote the cost of the campaign.

The primary goal was to highlight the importance of pet dental care through an earned media campaign and in-clinic materials.

In the first year, the campaign resulted in over 500 million media impressions within a 45-day period and rapid engagement from the veterinary profession to educate pet owners about caring for pets' teeth. Elements of the campaign included:

- A press conference and press kit for the veterinary trade announcement
- In-clinic promotional materials and press materials including a consumer "Healthy Smile" pet contest and a "Practice Builder" contest
- A national media tour
- Free dental checks through local veterinary medical associations
- Presentations at veterinary schools and veterinary dental conferences
- PetDental.com – one of the first veterinary websites
- A post-campaign survey of veterinary clinic participation

A strategic media kit was created and included the following tactics:

- Cover pitch letter
- Announcement release
- Home-care tips for preventing dental disease among pets
- Fact sheet about gum disease in pets
- Backgrounders
- Announcement and description of National Pet Dental Health Month
- Background on the AVDS, AVMA and Hill's Pet Nutrition
- Potential media questions with suggested answers
- Research cartoon graphic
- Spokesperson bios and photos

Over several years, the campaign has won multiple awards, including the American Animal Hospital Association Gold Key Award of Excellence and the Public Relations Society of America Silver Anvil Award of Excellence. The campaign was recognized in the Colgate (Hill's parent company) annual report with building the oral care category for pets. Dental care is still celebrated during National Pet Dental Health Month, but pet dental care has become a core category in both the veterinary clinic and consumer pet products. More details of the campaign can be found here: https://goodnewsforpets.com/the-pets-need-dental-care-too-campaign/.

Here is a checklist to use in defining the contents of a media kit:

- Why is the media kit being created?
- What type of media will use the media kit?

- Is the media kit being created for a specific event or is it designed to be used for a longer period of time?
- What tactics should be created for the media kit?
- Is there consistent branding for all of the key tactics in the kit?
- Do the contents of the kit look good printed out?

Summary

In summary, a media kit can be a very strategic tactic. It bundles important tactics to promote an event or topic. They provide one-stop shopping for journalists and other members of your key audiences on a specific topic. Media kits are usually saved online so they can be easily shared through email and social media. Most are designed so they can also be easily printed if needed. You can get free templates for media kits at www.adobe.com/express/create/press-kit.

Exercises

1. Pick an organization that you like. Go to its website and look for the corporate profile. Also, read the boilerplate on their website. How does it compare/contrast? What did you learn about the company that you did not know before?
2. Write your own executive bio. It should be based on who you are as a student and as a professional.
3. Pick an influencer that you admire. Make a list of the elements you would include in an influencer media kit.
4. Pick two or three organizations that you admire. Look up the bios of their key executives. Compare and contrast how they are written.
5. You are hired to create a media kit for a new bakery in your town. What questions would you have for the bakery? And what basic tactics would you include in the media kit?
6. Pick a topic that you care about and create a Q&A for it.
7. There will be a midnight run in your town to raise money for St. Jude Children's Research Hospital. Pick a location in your town that would make sense and draft a media advisory. Make yourself the press contact.
8. Pick a government agency or nonprofit. Analyze the content it provides on its website.

Glossary

Call to action – a statement designed to get an immediate response from the person reading or hearing it.

References

CDC Digital Press Kit. www.cdc.gov/eis/conference/digital-press-kit.html
Girls Who Code Annual Report. https://girlswhocode.com/2020report/

Seventh Generation Press Kit. www.seventhgeneration.com/press

For Further Reading

Best Press Kit Examples: What Should a Media Kit Contain in 2021? (prowly.com). https://prowly.com/magazine/company-press-kit-examples/#presskitexamples

The Evolution of the Media Kit. www.pr.co/blog/evolution-of-the-media-kit-and-examples#examples-great-media-kits

How to Build a Rocking Author Media Kit: A 7-Step Template (reedsy.com). https://blog.reedsy.com/author-media-kit-template/

How to Write an Online Bio – With Short, Professional, and Other Bio Examples. www.grammarly.com/blog/how-to-write-bio/

Press Kits: How to Create A Hype Media Kit (2021). www.shopify.com/blog/44447941-how-to-create-a-press-kit-that-gets-publicity-for-your-business

What is in a Press Kit and How to Make One. www.marketing91.com/press-kit/

Why a Good Press Kit Is Essential – And How to Make One. www.forbes.com/sites/forbescommunicationscouncil/2018/02/26/why-a-good-press-kit-is-essential-and-how-to-make-one/?sh=1458ec077822

7   PITCHING A STORY

Learning Goals for This Chapter

After reading this chapter, you should be able to:

- Know how to create and maintain media lists, as well as how to work with outside vendors that distribute news releases to traditional and social media, influencers, blogs and websites.
- Create a strategic "pitching plan" to promote your client or organization to the media.
- Decide what journalists at which specific news outlets should be pitched.
- Draft strategic email pitches and "scripts" for phone or social media conversations.

One of the most essential skills in public relations is knowing how to effectively pitch your story to the news media. It is a skill as old as the profession, and despite the evolution of the media itself and technological advances, it is a skill that must be mastered to succeed in modern strategic public relations.

According to Muck Rack:

> A PR pitch is a short, personalized message that outlines the value of a story and explains why it should be published. It is usually 150 words long but can reach up to 400 words. PR pitches should be short, engaging, and timely for the topic.

You can read the full report, "How to Craft a Winning Media Pitch in 2021: A Guide to Pitching Journalists and Getting Media Attention for Your Company or Client," here: https://info.muckrack.com/guide-to-pr-pitching-2020#mrcs-toc-hs_cos_wrapper_widget_1580699326164.

It is very exciting to see a story that you crafted and pitched appear in a newspaper or to listen to the CEO of your company talking on a podcast – speaking the words you carefully wrote. Heady stuff.

DOI: 10.4324/9781003248330-7

At different phases of your career, you may be either being doing the pitching or supervising it. Either way, you must have a keen understanding of the strategy that accommodates this task.

Writing a perfect news release or creating the most stunning infographic won't help you reach your communications goals if your work is not effectively used by the media.

A key goal of public relations is to get someone to do something. This ranges from getting someone to buy something to watching a new movie to learning a new skill or even changing behavior such as convincing someone to wear a seat belt.

As a public relations professional, you reach these goals by successfully convincing a journalist to cover these topics in order to educate or convince the reader to do these activities.

Here are some examples of pitching goals:

- Encourage reporters to attend a news conference or press event.
- Announce a new product or the opening of a store.
- Convince a reporter to review a book, movie, play or restaurant.
- Have your subject matter expert interviewed on television or in a podcast.
- Place an op-ed in a major newspaper or leading trade press outlet or influential blog.
- Arrange for your CEO or subject matter expert to talk on an important business news outlet.
- Place an infographic in a newspaper or a video or podcast on the website of a news organization.
- Convince an influencer to write a review of your client's book.

However, pitching is not easy. It has become more challenging by the shrinking number of journalists, faster news cycles and fewer traditional news outlets.

Pitching and the PESO Model

When you pitch a journalist and they write an article or create a broadcast segment about what you are pitching, this is considered earned media. That is an essential component of the PESO model. You are not paying for the media mention. Instead, you are earning it by creating information that is of value to the reporter and the news outlet where they work.

It is also uncontrolled media because the reporter may or may not be interested in your pitch or may not use the information as you intended. However, if you successfully pitch a story, you have succeeded in doing something quite powerful. You have earned the media coverage.

When a reporter covers your story or issue, it is communicated by a third party. And in many cases, the journalist is an expert, so what they write has tremendous credibility. That is why a positive media placement is referred to as a third-party endorsement. If you purchase media lists or pay to distribute your news release or other tactic, it still falls into the category of earned media because you have not paid for the coverage, only the distribution of the news release.

Building Relationships With Journalists

It is important to build relationships with journalists. As a PR student, you can begin to build these relationships now by using social media. Twitter and LinkedIn are good choices. Think about the type of industry that interests you or where you may want to work or intern. For instance, you may be interested in doing PR for the sports industry, financial services, high tech, fashion or book publishing.

You want to start searching for the journalists who cover those industries and begin following them. Of course, if there are journalists who you simply like because you enjoy their reporting, you should follow them, too. You can also encourage them to follow you back by letting them know that you are a student who hopes to work in their field. Professionals like to help students, so they may agree to follow you back. Then read their postings. Analyze their reporting. If you like what you read, you can post a compliment or simply "like" the posting. Most journalists are evaluated – even paid or otherwise rewarded – by the number of "likes" they get, so they will be pleased by this type of engagement.

You may also want to look up which public relations firms specialize in the industries that interest you and start to follow them, too. Take the time to see which news outlets and journalists they follow. Analyze how these firms engage on social media with the media. You will gain valuable insight into how these relationships work.

In strategic public relations, everything begins with research, including successful pitching. In most industries, there are a handful of reporters or news outlets that focus on your business or area of specialization like nonprofits or government. There may be two or three reporters who exclusively follow your industry and perhaps a dozen who cover it on a regular basis.

You need to know who they are and follow everything they produce on a regular basis. It is also important that you build a relationship with these journalists. You do this first by following them on social media and then reaching out to them directly. Social media is a terrific way to learn more about the editorial focus of various news outlets, as well as what specific journalists focus on.

In many ways, "pitching" begins before you have something to pitch. It begins with building these relationships. You need to make sure the journalist knows:

- Who you are
- How they can reach you
- What you have to offer them

You want to become a trusted source of information. You do this by:

- Understanding exactly what type of information they need, as well as how they want to receive information
- Knowing their deadlines and who their bosses and editors are so that you can help them do their jobs
- Understanding the types of spokespeople that work best for their article or segment as well as if they need video, audio or still photos

Quite simply, the more helpful you are to the journalist, the more successful you will be in pitching them. Then, when you have a story to pitch the journalist, they will consider it. If you have a good story and have developed a good reputation as an honest and reliable source of information, the journalist may even introduce you to another journalist at their organization who may be interested in your story if it is not right for them.

Creating Media Lists

One of the first steps in pitching is creating media lists. If you work for a PR firm or large PR department at an organization, your employer may have many media lists. You can create a media list in three ways:

1. Pay for media and news release distribution.
2. Buy the media list or access to a media database.
3. Create your own list.

Most companies use a variety of all three methods. If you work for a nonprofit, a start-up or a PR department with a small budget, you may not be able to access a media database or buy lists, and you will have to create the lists yourself. While this may be time consuming, you can still be successful pitching journalists. One of the most exciting aspects of PR is that you can accomplish amazing things with nothing more than a cell phone, a laptop and an internet connection.

In most public relations departments, the media lists will belong to the organization where you work. They are the property of your employer. It is therefore important to build your own list of key contacts. As you build relationships with journalists, start to take notes. If they shared personal cell phone numbers or emails, save them. Also, make note of hobbies, birthdays or interests. This information can strengthen your bonds with the reporter. As a PR professional, your personal relationships with the media are very valuable and will make you a highly coveted public relations professional. Here is an example of what you should consider collecting to build your media list:

- First name
- Last name
- Media outlet/publication/blog name
- Role (journalist, blogger, etc.)
- Beats/topics covered
- Location
- Email or emails
- Cell phone number
- Office or work phone number
- Twitter or other social media accounts
- How they prefer to be contacted
- Deadlines

- Publication schedule. For example, an online or print magazine may work several months ahead of time, so a summer-related story may need to be pitched in the winter.
- Notes. This can be personal information such as the fact that a reporter is a marathon runner or volunteers for charity.

There are many formats for creating and saving your media list. The PR service provider Prowly offers this template: https://prowly.com/magazine/media-list-building.

Broad Media Distribution

In many cases, you will simply use the targeted media lists you have created to distribute your news release or other tactic. You may also want to consider paying for distribution using services such as PR Newswire or BusinessWire. There are many vendors that distribute news releases with a wide variety of services and prices. Some specialize in international news, financial press, social media or highly specialized news outlets that target diverse audiences.

A key part of your distribution plan should be to determine if you need to supplement your in-house lists with external distribution. There may be additional costs that need to be budgeted. In some cases, additional distribution resources can be essential to the success or failure of your pitching plan. In other cases, it may fall into the nice-to-do category.

Broadly distributing PR tactics through internal/external lists is done in coordination with social media distribution as well as individual pitching to journalists.

Pitching the Media and Having a Plan

Pitching the media is a very strategic task. It is conducted on a one-to-one basis. You can pitch by phone, email or social media.

There may be times when it is appropriate to break the news to one or two key journalists. For instance, if you have a big story such as a groundbreaking new drug therapy or you are representing a publicity-adverse celebrity who has decided to be interested in speaking to the press.

You may also consider offering an exclusive to a journalist. This means you will be giving the story to one specific journalist or news outlet before you distribute your story to the rest of the media. In fact, according to Muck Rack's "The State of Journalism 2019: How Journalists Find Their News, Use Social Media, and Work with PR Teams," 76% of journalists are more likely to cover a story if it is offered as an exclusive.

If you have a breaking news story, you may simply want to text or send a tweet to alert journalists about the situation. Either way, you should have a detailed plan regarding who you plan to pitch and when you want to pitch them. For example, if you are hired to promote a new cookbook, you would make a list of the media outlets that would be appropriate and who to contact. It may include the morning talk shows, food bloggers, magazines and radio stations. You will need to decide who to contact

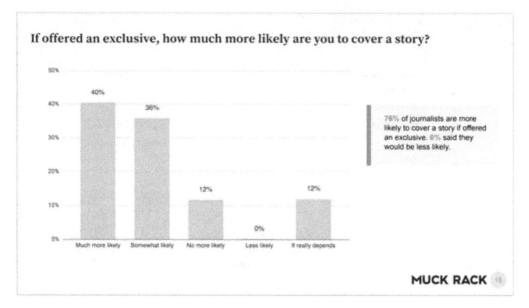

Figure 7.1 Muck Rack
Source: muckrack.com

first, second and third. And your pitch needs to be specific to each journalist and news outlet.

A lot has been written about the pros and cons of pitching by phone or email. By building relationships with journalists, you should know the best way to reach specific journalists with your story. In most cases, however, a carefully drafted email pitch followed by a polite phone call or text is best. Email provides a journalist with the opportunity to read your note when they have the time. A phone call, on the other hand, can be very disruptive to a journalist who is on deadline or focused on an important task. In fact, according to Muck Rack's "The State of Journalism 2021," "66% of journalists wish PR pros would stop calling them to pitch story ideas." The full study can be found here: https://info.muckrack.com/state-of-journalism-2021.

Here are some best practices for writing an email pitch:

- **Create a compelling subject line**.

  - It needs to be eye-catching. Basically, your job is to get the reporter to open the email and read it.

- **Get to your key point immediately**.

  - Journalists are extremely busy people. They receive hundreds of pitches, so it's important to get right into whatever you are trying to pitch.

- **Keep your pitch short**.

  - Most journalists prefer pitches to be fewer than 200 words.

- **Have a unique approach to the story**.

  - You should know why your product or service is different from others. If you don't, you need to refine your pitch.

- **Proof your work**.

  Before hitting send, carefully review your email. Typos, spelling errors and bad grammar can be very off-putting for a journalist and will send the wrong message.

- **Connect your pitch or your story specifically to what the journalist covers**.

  - Don't make them guess why the story is appropriate.

- **Use links**.

  - Don't send attachments in an email pitch unless the journalist asked for them. Most journalists delete emails with attachments as a standard precaution against viruses, and the servers of some publications will even send your email directly to spam.

- **Let them know how they can reach you and when and how you plan to follow up**.

  - There's nothing worse than writing a great pitch and then not including follow-up information. Sure, the journalist can reply to the same email address you sent the pitch from, but also including a phone number gives them the choice of calling you directly in the case of an urgent question.

- **Thank the journalist for their time and end with something personal**.

  - If appropriate, end by complimenting some of their recent work or asking how their vacation was or how their daughter's soccer season is coming along. But use your judgment regarding the addition of personal comments or questions.

Cision, a public relations service provider, offers ten tips to get journalists to read your pitch. Here is an excerpt of its recommendations:

1. **Know who and what you're pitching**.

   Before you send a pitch, you should know what topics the journalist does and does not cover. It will take some investigating and digging through past articles, but it can pay off. Pitching a topic that a journalist or publication doesn't cover, or one that she's already written about, will waste your time and cast you in a negative light since clearly you couldn't be bothered to make the effort.

2. **Use email for the first point of contact**.

   Sure, a phone call is direct, and the popularity and reach of social media are impressive, but 92% of journalists agree that email is where they want PR pitches to come from.

3. **Make your subject line sizzle**.
4. **Know the publication's audience**.

The best PR professionals know which journalists to target, but they can also explain why the pitch fits the needs, demographics or interests of their readership. We can't express enough the importance of ensuring that your pitch is relevant.

5. **Find the story in your news**.

When you can take your client's not-so-newsy news and turn it into a compelling story, that's when journalists perk up.

6. **Be accessible**.

Journalists work on tight deadlines, and one of their biggest pet peeves is not being able to reach the PR person who sent them an email when they need additional details. They take note of who replies in five minutes and who takes a day or more (guess which they're more excited to work with). Being available to provide additional details, quotes or photos is imperative if you want the coverage.

7. **Always be helpful**.

Relationships are a two-way street, so if you're looking to build and sustain rapport with journalists, it's important that you're not just contacting them when your company or client wants coverage. Consider how you can add value to a reporter or blogger, even when there's nothing in it for you.

8. **Don't send attachments**.

This should be a no-brainer by now, but there are still PR professionals who send email attachments.

9. **Pay attention to the timing of your pitch**.

A big part of successful pitching is also knowing when not to pitch your story. Doing a little reconnaissance work before emailing a journalist, you might see on Twitter that he's on vacation – or worse, at his grandmother's funeral. He might be at a major conference, or just under a deadline. Clearly, this isn't the ideal time to pitch. You can also use what you discover on social media to your benefit. Ask about that vacation when the journalist is back in the office. You'll show that you're paying attention, which will make the journalist perk up.

10. **Be pushy (but polite)**.

It may sound like counterintuitive advice, but if you've done everything else right, you could stand to be a bit more assertive. Journalists get dozens, if not hundreds, of emails every day, and sometimes they can't open every one. By reminding a journalist of your email, you push your pitch back to the top of the list, where it stands a better chance of being opened and read. If you don't hear back within a week, follow up with a second email. If you don't hear back then, drop it. It's also acceptable to follow up via social media. Sometimes tweeting a journalist to see if he got your email is a great way to remind him to find your email and read it. Other ways you can help include meeting deadlines, providing ample resources for the story and simply being in touch even when you aren't pitching. Journalists say that PR contacts who selflessly work to develop the relationship are the ones whose pitches they always open first.

The full article can be found here: www.cision.ca/resources/tip-sheets/get-journalists-read-cover-pitch/.

Write a Script for a Phone Pitch With a Journalist

When calling a journalist, you should write a script so that you can quickly explain your pitch in a clear, simple manner. You should have details and facts ready in case the journalist has questions. It does not matter if you are pitching for the first time or following up on a previously sent email; write a script. You want to quickly get to your point. The best way to do this is to write out what you plan to say and how you plan to say it. This is particularly useful if you are nervous about calling a reporter on the phone.

You don't want to read your script, but you should have it in front of you and listed as bullet points in order of importance.

If the reporter hangs up or rudely gets off the phone, don't take it personally. They are likely juggling many tasks at once and simply don't have time to talk. Instead, send a short, polite email with your pitch to gauge their interest and ask if there is a better time to talk.

Keep Records

A key part of your pitching plan should be to keep a detailed record of your pitching. You should keep a record of when you emailed someone and when you promised to call them back. If you told a journalist in an email that you would call them back next Monday at 10 a.m., put this on your calendar and call them back. You want to build a reputation of being reliable.

Also, note when you called someone and keep records of the date and time. If you were not able to speak to the reporter, wait a day and call them back. If they tell you to call back in two weeks, call back in two weeks. Unless there is new information, respect their time and call them back when they requested. In PR, it is good to be persistent. It is bad to get the reputation of being a pest.

Tailor Your Pitch by Media Type

As you craft your pitch, it is important to tailor it specifically to the type of media you are pitching. For instance, pitching a print reporter is different than pitching a radio or television station.

Each type of media has its own deadline. However, deadlines may vary dramatically within a specific media outlet. For instance, some magazines plan several months in advance. For the weekly sections at a newspaper or at a radio or television station, writers may have several days to work on a story. You simply need to know their specific deadlines.

Since most news outlets are increasingly becoming multimedia, it is important to let them know if you have video, audio, photos or infographics to add to the story.

Know When to Pitch a Reporter

Based on responses from a Muck Rack survey, the best time to pitch journalists is between 6 a.m. and 11 a.m.

Here is a breakdown of when reporters prefer to receive email pitches.

- 34% of journalists prefer to be pitched between 5 a.m. and 9 a.m.
- 34% of journalists prefer to be pitched between 9 a.m. and 12 p.m.
- 10% of journalists prefer to be pitched between 12 p.m. and 3 p.m.
- 6% of journalists prefer to be pitched between 3 p.m. and 6 p.m.
- 5% of journalists prefer to be pitched between 6 p.m. and 11 p.m.
- 12% of journalists prefer to be pitched between 11 p.m. and 5 a.m.

The study also indicated that Monday is the favorite day to receive pitches (57%), followed by Tuesday (20%). You can access the full study here: https://muckrack.com/blog/2019/07/01/2019-muck-rack-journalist-survey-results.

It is important to note that the preferred time will vary by individual and by media outlet. For instance, a producer at a morning talk show will have a very different schedule than a writer at a weekly newspaper; their preferred times to receive a pitch will vary dramatically.

Social Media and Pitching

Twitter remains the leading social network among journalists according to a survey by Muck Rack. Journalists use it to gather information as well as to promote their work and their news outlets. If you have a relationship with a journalist and they follow you on Twitter, you may consider pitching them directly on this site. However, only do this if you know they would like to receive information in this manner.

Twitter is also a great resource if you need to quickly distribute information. It is great for promoting events or during a crisis. For example, if a fire breaks out in your corporate headquarters or there is a bad accident, your goal may simply be to let reporters know that your press officer or the company CEO is available to answer questions. You can also continue to update reporters via Twitter as more information is available. This can be a very strategic and impactful approach.

If your client, subject matter expert or organization has a large following on social media, make sure you let the journalist know. The experience of the authors of this textbook is that reporters are more likely to interview someone who has a strong social media following or has a popular website. Since the news article or broadcast segment will be saved on the news outlet's website, the reporter and/or news organization could potentially grow its social media presence by linking to the people and organizations referenced in their story.

Best Practices for Pitching From Grant Winter, Veteran Journalist and Producer, Black News Channel

- Find out how a journalist would like to be pitched. Basically, ask them how they would like to be contacted and the best times to reach them.
- If you don't know if they want to receive a phone pitch, text or email them instead.
- Have a very clear pitch. Your whole story should fit in the subject line of an email.
- Make it easy for a journalist to contact you. Put all of your contact information in the pitch as well as in your email signature.
- If a journalist asks for you to call back at another time, believe them. Mark your calendar and get back to them as they requested.
- When you have a complicated story, give them at least two weeks to work on it.
- Be truthful, accurate and factually correct. Provide as much information as possible. Journalists are busy and the easier you make it for them to do their job, the more likely they will want to work with you.
- Believe a journalist if they say no to a story. Don't alienate them by continuing to press a story idea.

Chapter Summary

Pitching is an essential skill for the public relations writer. This chapter explained the importance of building relationships with journalists, as well as how to create media lists and when to pay for outside services. It also detailed how to write a pitch email, create script for a phone pitch and when to use social media for pitching. Lastly, it described how to create a pitching plan.

Here is a checklist for pitching stories:

- Do I have a clear goal for pitching the story and distributing the message?
- Are my in-house media lists current? Are they the right media outlet and journalist for my goals and objectives?
- Should outside vendors be considered to create media lists or distribute the story?
- Is my pitch relevant to the journalist or news outlet? And, have I crafted my most compelling argument?

Exercises

1. Pick an industry that interests you and research the news outlets and journalists who follow this business. Then start to follow them on social media. What do you notice? How do outlets and journalists differ?
2. Develop a media list for ten of the most important journalists who cover an industry such as real estate, beauty or insurance. Review their social media presences as well as professional output, whether stories or video or other media.
3. Write both an email pitch and a phone script for the opening of a new restaurant. Make up the details. Identify a reporter who may be interested.
4. You work for a tech company in California that was evacuated due to a wildfire. You are told that the company's main campus was destroyed by fire. Your CEO wants to get the word out that the company prepared for the disaster and is still fully operational. How would you get the word out?
5. Your boss wants to invest in a media database. Research the top vendors and explain the cost and benefits of each.
6. A key part of your communications strategy is to reach Korean speaking consumers in New York. How would you reach this audience?

References

Building Media Lists Templates. https://prowly.com/magazine/media-list-building

Cision Article on How to Get Journalists to Your Pitch. www.cision.ca/resources/tip-sheets/get-journalists-read-cover-pitch/

How to Craft a Winning Media Pitch in 2021: A Guide to Pitching Journalists and Getting Media Attention for Your Company or Client. https://info.muckrack.com/guide-to-pr-pitching-2020#mrcs-toc-hs_cos_wrapper_widget_1580699326164

https://info.muckrack.com/guide-to-pr-pitching-2020#mrcs-toc-hs_cos_wrapper_widget_1580699326164

Muck Rack State of Journalism Survey. https://info.muckrack.com/state-of-journalism-2021

For Further Reading

Meltwater Resources. www.meltwater.com

Prowly's14+ Tips to Holiday Gift Guide Pitching(w/ Examples). https://prowly.com/magazine/holiday-gift-guide-pitching/

This Month in Bad PR Pitches Posted by Muck Rack. https://muckrack.com/blog/2021/03/24/this-month-in-bad-pr-pitches-40

8 LETTERS TO THE EDITOR, OP-EDS AND EDITORIALS

Learning Goals for This Chapter

After reading this chapter, you should be able to:

- Describe the features and uses of editorials and op-eds for print and broadcast.
- Explain the value of thought leadership for organization reputation and morale.
- Know when and how to write a letter to the editor.
- Create the tactics necessary to support an editorial board meeting.
- Understand the differences between writing a letter to the editor and an op-ed.

Understanding how to work with the opinion sections of newspapers, magazines and other news outlets is an important skill for the public relations writer. This type of writing is focused on issues and innovative ideas rather than selling products, promoting special events or providing consumer tips. It is sophisticated, detailed and highly strategic work.

Writing opinion pieces provides a unique opportunity to establish thought leadership on important issues by an organization or an individual. It is also an opportunity to offer more information on topics in the news or to set the record straight when a news outlet has not covered your organization or industry in a fair and balanced way.

If you are tasked with opinion writing, you will likely work with your company's CEO or key executives. Depending on the issue, you may also be coordinating with departments such as government affairs, corporate social responsibility, legal or investor relations.

This chapter focuses on the differences among letters to the editor, editorials and op-eds. It will also explain how to work with editorial boards as well as how to write and place op-eds and letters to the editor. Lastly, there will be information on how to use social media to self-publish opinion pieces, as well as how to use it to promote published pieces that appear in news outlets.

DOI: 10.4324/9781003248330-8

How Are Editorial Pages Different From News?

The opinion pages are different from the news content that appears in the rest of the news outlet. As the name indicates, opinion pages focus on opinions. Editorials are not news. For example, editorials may criticize or praise the performance of an elected official while the coverage in the rest of the news outlet is supposed to present facts such as their voting record or details about a public appearance.

Editorial pages are under the direction of an editor outside the news division. There is a line between news and opinion that should not be crossed. If it is, the news outlet loses its credibility.

The *Wall Street Journal* website has a section on news literacy that explains the differences between their news reporting and its opinion pages. While the web posting is focused on the practices of the *Wall Street Journal* specifically, it provides an explanation that applies to all major news outlets. It states:

> We draw a clear line between news and opinion. The separation between these two independent departments helps ensure impartiality in our news reporting and freedom of perspective in our opinion pieces.
>
> Our newsroom serves as the definitive source of news and information through the lens of business, finance, economics and money – global forces that shape the world and are key to understanding it. We provide facts, data and information – not assertions or opinions – and strive to be a model for ethical, factual and ambitious news reporting.
>
> *Wall Street Journal* readers want information, but they also want to make their own judgments about what they are learning. Our commentary is intended to inform on the issues of the day, with the added purpose of stirring debate and helping readers decide for themselves what they think.

The full article can be found here: https://newsliteracy.wsj.com/news-opinion/.

The opinion pages are also one of the most frequently read sections of a news outlet. They are read by **thought leaders**, an important target audience. The authors of this textbook define "thought leaders" as the people who have the power and influence to change the opinions of others. Thought leaders may be elected officials, business executives, religious leaders, academics, medical professionals or scientists.

The business publication *Forbes* published an article on thought leaders. It defines a thought leader as

> an individual or firm that prospects, clients, referral sources, intermediaries and even competitors recognize as one of the foremost authorities in selected areas of specialization, resulting in its being the go-to individual or organization for said expertise.

The full *Forbes* article can be accessed at www.forbes.com/sites/russprince/2012/03/16/what-is-a-thought-leader/?sh=6a190c897da0.

As a target audience, thought leaders are valuable for a campaign focused on ideas or issues – in particular, an initiative where an organization is trying to move its target audience to action based on an ethical or philosophical perspective.

In some situations, the goal of appearing in the opinion section of a news outlet is to establish an organization or person as an expert or thought leader, which will position them to effect or influence change. In other words, the author of an opinion piece becomes a thought leader.

There are three key sections to the opinion pages:

1. Editorials written by the editorial board of the news outlet or external guest writers
2. Op-eds submitted from outside experts or commissioned by the editorial board
3. Letters to the editor from readers

Following are details on working with editorial boards, as well as how to write and place op-eds and letters to the editor.

1. Editorial Boards

Printed or online, editorials can be valuable as image-enhancing tactics in public relations. Editorials are recognized as reflecting the opinion of a news outlet.

The editorial board determines what the paper's position will be on an issue and writes editorials expressing that view. The editorial board is comprised of writers and editors of the editorial page. A large paper may have several editorial writers with beats, similar to news reporters, along with an editorial page editor.

To influence what the editorial board writes, your organization or client may want to set up an editorial board meeting. This provides an opportunity get a point of view across to the people that determine what the newspaper's opinion will be about a particular issue.

At a larger news outlet such as a major daily newspaper, if your issue is fairly narrow and falls under the purview of one editorial writer, you might meet just with that writer. That writer could also be joined by one or more interested colleagues. For high priority issues or those that span the interest areas of several writers, you might meet with the entire editorial board.

There are several times when it may be useful to request an editorial board meeting:

• When you are launching a campaign or a new program and wish to ask the newspaper to editorialize in support of your efforts
• If there is a crisis or trending issue that must be addressed
• When you release a report or otherwise have new information that you wish to share with the editorial board
• After a news outlet has opposed your position and you want to share your side of the story with the editorial board

In general, an editorial board meeting gives you the opportunity to discuss your opinions. If you can't change their opinion, you will at least have a better understanding of their perspective. This is valuable insight that can help you develop an ongoing communications strategy about the issue.

The public relations or corporate communications department of an organization is generally responsible for trying to secure an editorial board meeting. Senior members of the public relations team will make recommendations regarding who should attend the meeting. Generally, there will be one to four people from an organization in attendance. In many situations, the head of public relations may attend the editorial board meeting to moderate the discussion.

The role of the strategic public relations writer will be to create the written materials to be distributed before, during and after the editorial board meeting. This will begin with writing to request the meeting. You would write an email that contains the following information:

- Names of executives who will participate in the editorial board meeting
- Suggested meeting times and dates
- An explanation of why the meeting is being requested

Once the meeting has been arranged, you will need to create a background package that will be emailed to the editorial board in advance of the meeting or used as handouts at the meeting itself. You will basically need to create a media kit for the meeting. The contents of the media kit will be determined by the goals and objectives of the meeting and the media outlet itself. However, you will want to include a company profile, bios of the participants, fact sheets, relevant white papers and possibly Q&As.

In preparation for the editorial board meeting, there will likely be a number of meetings to determine what should be said and who should say it. As the strategic public relations writer, you may be asked to write:

- Key messages
- Talking points
- A "script" so that everyone participating in the meeting knows the role they will play at the meeting and what they will be saying

Here is a general description of what occurs at an editorial board meeting:

1. At the meeting, someone should act as the moderator.
2. The moderator will outline the reason for the meeting, introduce himself/herself/themselves and ask other participants to briefly introduce themselves.
3. Each participant will then speak for three to five minutes on their perspective on the issue at hand.
4. The moderator will then ask for questions and direct them to the appropriate member of the team.
5. The meeting will conclude by the moderator asking if there is any more information that you can provide.

6. Finally, the meeting will close by asking the editorial board to do something. This request will depend on the situation. For instance, you may ask the board to editorialize on a specific issue.

After the meeting, it may be necessary to supply additional written materials to reinforce the key messages discussed at the meeting or to supply information that the board requested. This is another task that is generally going to be completed by you as the public relations writer.

While it is rare for organizations or individuals not affiliated with a publication to be asked to write editorials – that space is typically reserved for the staff of the publication – some specialized industry or trade publications will accept contributions or even seek out contributions from executives or experts in fields ranging from aerospace to food.

2. Op-Eds

An op-ed piece derives its name from originally having appeared opposite the editorial page in a newspaper. Today, the term is used to represent a column that represents a strong, informed and focused opinion of the writer on an issue of relevance to a targeted audience. But, as the media has evolved and changed, so has the name "op-ed." Many newspapers still use the term, but other newspapers, magazines and online media outlets use different terms to describe opinion articles submitted by readers. In fact, the *New York Times*, after 50 years of publishing op-eds, retired the term. Articles submitted by outside writers to the *New York Times* are now known as "Guest Essays."

Kathleen Kingsbury, Opinion editor of the *New York Times*, explained why in her April 26, 2021, article titled "Why the *New York Times* Is Retiring the Term 'Op-Ed'":

That important mission remains the same. But it's time to change the name. The reason is simple: In the digital world, in which millions of *Times* readers absorb the paper's journalism online, there is no geographical "Op-Ed," just as there is no geographical "Ed" for Op-Ed to be opposite to. It is a relic of an older age and an older print newspaper design.

Kingsbury's article also stated:

The impulses that made Op-Ed successful from the get-go are still in play. One is the allure of clashing opinions well expressed. As Herbert Bayard Swope, an editor at the New York World newspaper in the 1920s who was a pioneer of the concept of an op-ed page, once said, "Nothing is more interesting than opinion when opinion is interesting." Or in the words of John B. Oakes, a long-ago predecessor of mine who drove the creation of Op-Ed, "Diversity of opinion is the lifeblood of democracy. . . . The minute we begin to insist that everyone think the same way we think, our democratic way of life is in danger."

Kingsbury's full article can be found here: www.nytimes.com/2021/04/26/opinion/nyt-opinion-oped-redesign.html.

Semantics aside, submitting opinion pieces to news outlets for publication is a very strategic and important PR tactic. Op-eds carry the imprimatur of the media outlet and are aimed at thought leaders and influencers. For consistency's sake, this textbook will refer to this type of writing as an "op-ed." The name is not important. What is important is writing a persuasive article for the news outlet that will most effectively reach your target audience.

In addition to name changes, op-eds, because they now appear on websites, are no longer print only. Instead, they have gone multimedia with photos, video and audio.

The nonprofit Op-Ed Project is a great resource for anyone writing an op-ed. They believe that "the best ideas, regardless of where they come from, should have a chance to be heard and to change the world."

The Op-Ed Project offers step-by-step guidelines on writing op-eds, as well as a sample pitch letter. Their website is www.theopedproject.org. It also offers a list of the top online and print publications that accept op-eds with links to the submission details.

Every publication has slightly different requirements. But, in general, op-eds are short. They are typically between 600 and 700 words. You do not write an op-ed for marketing purposes. Instead, it is an opportunity to align yourself, your client or your company with certain topics or causes.

Here are some best practices:

- Forget objectivity. An op-ed is about your opinion and perspective.
- State why you are an authority on the issue.
- Be passionate in arguing your point of view.
- Write as if you are arguing or debating with a friend.
- Use simple language. Avoid using jargon.

When writing an op-ed, a strong voice is critical to a successful column or op-ed piece. It also works well if you provide personal and compelling narratives. For instance, the actress Angelina Jolie wrote an op-ed that was published by the *New York Times* on May 14, 2013, titled "My Medical Choice," where she explained her reasons for choosing to have a "preventive double mastectomy." She wrote:

MY MOTHER fought cancer for almost a decade and died at 56. She held out long enough to meet the first of her grandchildren and to hold them in her arms. But my other children will never have the chance to know her and experience how loving and gracious she was.

We often speak of "Mommy's mommy," and I find myself trying to explain the illness that took her away from us. They have asked if the same could happen to me. I have always told them not to worry, but the truth is I carry a "faulty" gene, BRCA1, which sharply increases my risk of developing breast cancer and ovarian cancer.

My doctors estimated that I had an 87 percent risk of breast cancer and a 50 percent risk of ovarian cancer, although the risk is different in the case of each woman.

You can access the full op-ed here: www.nytimes.com/2013/05/14/opinion/my-medical-choice.html.

While Jolie's fame certainly must have helped to get the attention of the *New York Times*, her op-ed is well written and personal. It was also brave of her to share her personal experience. But, most importantly, the topic is also timely and controversial. The publication of the article sparked conversation and debate, which is one of the things that news outlets look for when deciding to publish an article or not. In fact, a former editorial board editor of a daily newspaper said at a PRSA Meet the Media panel discussion that he looks for "topics that could start a fist fight in a bar."

Op-eds are also a great tactic to promote research studies. For instance, the nonprofit organization LeanIn.org published a new report, "The State of Black Women in Corporate America." Using Black Women's Equal Pay Day as a news hook, Raena Saddler, vice president of people and managing director of the Sheryl Sandberg and Dave Goldberg Family Foundation, and Rachel Thomas, cofounder and CEO of LeanIn.org, published an op-ed to promote the findings. Here is an excerpt:

> Today is Black Women's Equal Pay Day. That means Black women had to work all of 2019 and this far into 2020 to earn what white men earned last year alone – four months longer than white women had to work to accomplish the same goal. Over the course of a Black woman's career, the pay gap accounts for almost $1 million in lost income.
>
> That's a major injustice. It's also part of a much bigger problem.
>
> For five years, LeanIn.Org and McKinsey & Company have run Women in the Workplace, the largest study on the state of women in corporate America. Year after year, the data tell the same story: The workplace is worse for women than for men, worse for women of color than white women, and for Black women in particular, in many ways, it's worst of all.

The full article can be found here:https://fortune.com/2020/08/13/black-womens-equal-pay-day-wage-gap/. It should be noted that Sheryl Sandberg, founder of LeanIn.org and chief operating officer of Facebook, frequently publishes op-eds to advance the objectives of LeanIn.org.

The best op-eds are typically conversational in nature. This tone is driven, in part, by the publication for which you are writing. In many organizations, you, as the PR writer, may be writing the op-ed for your CEO or a subject matter expert. This means that you will need to work closely with them to write in their authentic voice. The person you are writing for may write the first draft or provide key messages for you to turn into an op-ed. Or you may write a first draft for them to review and put in their own words. Either way, a well-written op-ed will take considerable back-and-forth between you as the ghost writer and the person whose name will appear on the opinion piece.

At times, executives and others in organizations may feel the need to assert a point of view or to lash out at critics or gadflies. But a professional communicator will counsel against any unprofessional or emotional displays. Op-eds should demonstrate a demeanor of solid reasoning and the highest possible competence.

Op-eds also can explain little-known or little-recognized features and operations of an organization. For example, Associated Press president and CEO Gary Pruitt in 2021 wrote an editorial that outlined the news cooperative's standards, origins and structure. The op-ed was published by a collection of AP member news organizations, which includes newspapers that contribute to and accept information from the AP. The full link is here: https://blog.ap.org/behind-the-news/what-is-ap-ceo-explains-in-op-ed.

Here is a quote from his op-ed:

> More than half the world sees news from The Associated Press every day, but few know exactly what AP is.
>
> Every hour of every day, AP journalists in all 50 U.S. states and in more than 100 countries gather the news, from statehouses to war zones in the Middle East, and distribute it to thousands of news outlets in the U.S. and across the globe.
>
> That is AP's mission: to inform the world. Fairly, objectively and accurately.
>
> AP is unique, both in our mission and in how we carry it out. No one owns AP. We are truly independent, neither part of a corporation nor funded by any government. We are a not-for-profit cooperative – not a charity but run like a business. Any revenue we generate must be invested right back into AP to help us produce the most comprehensive news report in the world.

Basic Components of an Op-Ed

There are four basics components of an op-ed.

1. **Lead paragraph**. Try to grab the reader with your first sentence. You want to make them read more.
2. **Supporting paragraphs**. Build on your lead with facts, statistics and anecdotes.
3. **A strong concluding paragraph**. If you're trying to move people to action, be sure to answer the question "What can I do?" Make the final sentence as compelling as the first one.
4. **The author's name, title and a one-sentence biography**. This provides information on why the author is qualified to speak about a specific topic or why they would have an interesting perspective on an issue because of who they are or what they do.

The New York Times offers guidance on what its editors look for when deciding to publish an op-ed or a Guest Essay:

> What are we looking for in a Guest Essay? That is always changing, depending on the news and the issues in public conversation at any given moment. But the best opinion essays have a few things in common: They try to challenge and engage audiences who do not necessarily agree with the writer's point of view. They give insight into complicated problems or anticipate big ideas. They start conversations,

influence policymakers and have an impact far beyond the pages of *Times Opinion*. They aspire to delight the reader with great writing and originality, and to open a window into a world we might not otherwise see.

The full article can be found here: https://help.nytimes.com/hc/en-us/articles/1150 14809107-How-to-submit-a-Guest-Essay-for-Opinion.

Pitching Your Op-Ed

The best preparation for pitching an op-ed is to be a regular reader of them. That way, you can get a sense of what the news outlet publishes. Some major newspapers will require you to submit a proposal for your op-ed. If this is your target media, it may make sense to pitch first and write later. That way, if you are invited to write the article, you can gear it specifically to the news outlet and its readers. Newspapers such as the New York Times offer details on "How to submit a Guest Essay for Opinion." There is a form that must be filled out to explain "the professional or personal background that connects you to the argument or idea in your essay."

The Washington Post also requires that you fill out a submission form for an op-ed to be considered. The instructions to submit for The Washington Post include some important information about how it decides who to invite to publish. Here is the full link: www.washingtonpost.com/opinions/submit-an-op-ed/. It includes:

Among the things we look for are timeliness (is it pegged to something in the news?), resonance (is it something that will interest *Post* readers?) and freshness of perspective (is it an argument we haven't heard many times before?). You don't need to have special expertise in a topic. But explaining how your background or experience informs your point of view can make for a more effective op-ed. You also don't need to have an important title – and having an important title doesn't mean we'll publish your op-ed. In fact, because we realize that senators, business leaders, heads of state and the like have access to various platforms where they can express their views, we hold them to a particularly high standard when considering whether to publish them in The Post.

Another newspaper that requires op-ed writers to submit proposals for an op-ed is the Financial Times. Here is what they are looking for:

We particularly relish pieces that highlight unexpected places, explore new ideas and illuminate diverse points of view. We also want our opinion pieces to be punchy, readable articles that make strong arguments; and we have a soft spot for writers who demolish conventional wisdom or dissent from opinions we have already published.

Other newspapers don't accept pitches. Instead, you will need to submit a fully written op-ed. In 2021, this list included USA Today, the Los Angeles Times and the Boston Globe.

Certain newspapers such as the Denver Post not only want to receive the written op-ed but also require a high-resolution photo of the author and a short biographical paragraph. The paper also "gives preference to local and regional writers and issues." You can review their information here: www.denverpost.com/2013/07/09/submission-guidelines-and-contact-information/.

Most major publications will not print an op-ed that has appeared in another publication. So, you will need to create a submission plan by ranking the publications in order of preference and then submitting your proposal or draft op-ed in order of importance. While the major daily newspapers such as the New York Times, the Wall Street Journal, the Chicago Tribune and the Los Angeles Times are coveted news outlets for op-eds, consider pitching regional newspapers and publications such as The Hill (https://thehill.com/opinion), CNN Opinion (www.cnn.com/opinions), Slate (https://slate.com/pitch) or The Conversation (https://theconversation.com/us).

Video Op-eds

With video emerging as one of the most important communications tactics, it should come as no surprise that major news outlets are also accepting opinions in video form. The New York Times, for instance, introduced Op-Docs. This is the New York Times editorial department's "forum for short, opinionated documentaries, produced with wide creative latitude and a range of artistic styles, covering current affairs, contemporary life and historical subjects." Here are their submission guidelines:

> We will consider written pitches that include links to representative footage, as well as completed videos. We cannot consider film trailers, nor can we consider videos that have already been posted online or broadcast on television. In addition to new short works, we can consider pieces that are adapted from longer, topical works-in-progress. Op-Docs are generally 5–10 minutes in length.

3. Letters to the Editor

Writing a letter to the editor (LTE) of a newspaper or other news outlet is another strategy to reach opinion leaders. Even if your letter is not published, your efforts can help educate and persuade editors. The more letters they receive on a topic, the more likely they will cover the issue in the news outlet – both on the opinion pages and in news articles or segments.

LTEs are usually sent to newspapers or news magazines. However, they also appear in trade and technical news outlets, academic journals, as well as radio and television stations. In terms of broadcast news outlets, they may be read on air.

In most cases, you will write an LTE in response to an article or news segment that ran in the news outlet. You would write to provide a proactive statement of support for or opposition against a particular issue that affects the publication's readers. You may also write an LTE to provide additional information. You may also want to write an

LTE to set the record straight if you believe that their reporting of your industry, client or organization has been untruthful or biased.

LTEs are short. Most news organizations require that they be 300 words or less. Here are some basic guideless for writing LTEs:

- Begin by citing the original story by name, date and author.
- State your concern/support of the issue in the article.
- Follow the news outlet's direction.

  - The news outlet will provide information on word count and other requirements.
  - The Op-Ed Project provides links to the top news outlets that publish LTEs. It can be found here: www.theopedproject.org.

- State your qualifications to have an opinion – for instance, if you are doctor with an opinion on health-care legislation or a truck driver responding to a proposed change in highway design.
- Write in a clear authentic manner. The voice of the writer needs to be heard in the LTE.
- Include a call to action. Basically, clearly state what you would like to see happen.
- Provide your name, phone number and email address.

Many advocacy and educational organizations provide detailed information on how to write and place LTEs. The National Association for the Education of Young Children, for example, offers templates for sample LTEs. You can read them here: www.naeyc.org/our-work/public-policy-advocacy/letter-editor-template.

There are also free templates of LTEs available for download. Here is one example: https://templatearchive.com/letter-to-the-editor/.

Since many letters to the editor are written by private citizens, the authors of this textbook chose to not highlight one in this textbook as an example. Quite simply, the author of the LTE intended for their words to appear in a specific news outlet and not in an educational textbook. The best way to find examples of LTEs is to read them in the news outlets of your targeted media.

Most news outlets also provide useful insights into how they decide what to publish. For instance, Thomas Feyer, letters editor at the New York Times, provided answers to some of the most frequently asked questions about LTEs in the following web article: www.nytimes.com/2004/05/23/opinion/editors-note-the-letters-editor-and-the-reader-our-compact-updated.html.

In response to questions about the length of an LTE, Feyer responded:

Your suggested length for letters is about 150 words. Why so short? (Or, as one writer put it after I cited the brevity of the *Gettysburg Address*, "Why does Lincoln get 250 and the rest of us a measly 150?") Ideally, the letters page should be a forum for a variety of voices, and that means letting a lot of readers have a turn. With our limited space, we have room for letters that make their case with a point or two, but not for full-length articles. (For those, try our neighbors at the Op-Ed page.)

In terms of the New York Times policy on editing LTEs, Feyer said, "We reserve the right to edit for space, clarity, civility and accuracy, and we send you the edited version before publication."

News outlets require that you submit the entire LTE. You don't have to submit a request to write one as you are required to do for op-eds for some major news organizations. Some news outlets, such as the Miami Herald, require the writer to fill out an online application and sign their letter. Every news organization has slightly different requirements, so you will need to follow the instructions and tailor your LTE to the news outlet.

Many news outlets also include multimedia elements to their LTEs. For instance, many offer the letter as a podcast that can be downloaded and listened to at any time. One example of this is the Wall Street Journal.

Self-Publish Your Opinion Piece on Social Media

With social media, you have the option of simply posting your opinion to your organization or client's followers on social media. LinkedIn and Twitter are good choices. If the opinion leaders you are trying reach are following your organization or client on these sites, this can be a very strategic option.

Your message won't have the same credibility as one published in an op-ed or LTE in a formal news outlet, but with more and more people going directly to social media for their news and information, your opinions may find a receptive audience.

If your posting is timely and insightful, your opinion article may also go viral. Another option is posting opinion pieces on company websites, intranets or blogs. This could be a useful way of sharing your message with clients, employees or even vendors and suppliers.

Use Published Opinion Pieces for Media Relations Purposes

Succeeding in getting an op-ed or LTE published in a respected news outlet is very prestigious. As a PR person, you can use past success to pitch the author for print and broadcast interviews, as well as with bloggers and podcasters. A link to the op-ed can be embedded in news releases, pitch emails and social media. It would also be smart to include a link in the professional bio of the author as well.

To extend the reach of the published op-ed, consider posting it on social media. Again, LinkedIn and Twitter are good choices.

However, before you post the link, check the guidelines of the media outlet where it appeared. For instance, CNN Opinion requires approval by CNN. Its website (www.cnn.com/opinions) states:

You understand that any other use of the article, if published, would have to be approved by CNN. (You may post the first 150 words of the article on a personal or business website or blog with a required live link back to the article on CNN Digital.)

Other news outlets may have similar requirements. Check the news outlet's website for details or email them for permission if you have any questions or concerns.

Paid Placement of Opinion Pieces – Advertorials

In a controversial event, a Mobil Oil Co. communications executive arranged to buy advertising space on the op-ed page of the New York Times and periodically used the space to present the company's point of view on energy policy and business topics.

The Mobil ads – quickly dubbed "advertorials" – were presented almost as newspaper text, but clearly were sponsored as indicated by the Mobil logo at the bottom.

An advertorial is an article, website page or video programming that is designed to look and read like objective journalistic content but is, in fact, a paid advertisement.

Mobil's PR started the innovative campaign during the oil crisis of the 1970s to provide Mobil's point of view. The sponsored opinion pieces at times commented on current events; sometimes, they talked about broader business and society issues, including mass transit. The company purchased ad space for advertorials in other newspapers as well.

Best Practices

Mike Barry, chief communications officer, Insurance Information Institute, and former editorial writer at the Long Island Weekly (his columns from 2016 and 2017 are archived here: https://longislandweekly.com/author/mike-barry/), offers these three insights for successfully writing opinion pieces:

1. Find an angle to an issue that no one else has used in the publication. Basically, look for a fresh take on an ongoing issue.
2. Look for a historical perspective. Has society seen this issue before? Are there any parallels to other events in the past?
3. Research current events. Find facts or people who can affirm your position.

Opinion Pages and the PESO Model

Op-eds and LTEs are unique types of earned media because the writer controls the message or content. There is no other example of earned media like that. You can also use a published op-ed to pitch other earned media opportunities. You can share your opinion pieces on social media or place them in your owned company website, blog or podcast. Lastly, if you pay to place your op-ed in a targeted news outlet, this would fall into the category of paid media.

America has the world's best highways
And the world's worst mass transit.
We hope this ad moves people...

In recent years the United States has developed a really superb highway system. It's been built with tax revenues earmarked specifically for road building.

But the highway construction boom has been accompanied by a mass transit bust. Train and bus travel in this country, with few exceptions, is decrepit. The air traveler suffers increasing indignities despite bigger, faster planes.

Greater New York is a typical example. You can depend on commuting to and from Manhattan—but only to be undependable and slow. On public transport, the 25 miles to Westfield, N.J. takes 75 minutes at an average speed of 20 miles per hour. The 33 miles to Stamford, Conn. takes 60 minutes at 33 mph. The 26 miles to Hicksville, L.I. takes 55 minutes at 28 mph. When you're on time.

You have to be a stoic with stamina to use public ground transportation for a trip beyond the commuting range. Fly to a nearby city? You can hardly get at our congested air terminals, either by land or air. The ride to or from the airport often takes longer than the flight.

Mass transit seems to work better abroad. Americans are agreeably impressed by the fast, comfortable, and attractive subways in foreign cities. Intercity trains in other countries make ours look pitiful. Japan's high-speed Tokaido line carries more than 200,000 passengers a day. Clean, comfortable French, German, Italian, and British trains regularly attain speeds over 100 mph. European railroads are already planning or building expresses that will do better than 150 mph.

Yet, in the United States, new mass transit systems are for the most part still in the wild blue yonder.

Providing for our future transportation needs will require very large expenditures. We believe there's an urgent need for legislators to reexamine the procedures used to generate and expend transportation revenues. Such a review may yield the conclusion that special earmarked funds are no longer the best approach.

In weighing priorities, no decision-maker can ignore the increasing congestion on those fine highways of ours, especially in and around the great urban centers. But more and better mass transit could stop traffic jams before they start. Just one rail line has triple the people-moving capacity of a three-lane superhighway.

It costs less—in energy consumption and in money—to move people via mass transit than on highways. Thus mass transit means less air pollution.

It also means conservation. Whether the energy comes from gasoline for cars, or fuel oil, natural gas, or coal for electric power plants, it's derived from a diminishing natural resource. So we think all forms of transportation should be brought into a national plan for safe, rapid, economical ways of moving people—consistent with the wisest use of our energy resources.

While Mobil sells fuels and lubricants, we don't believe the gasoline consumed by a car idling in a traffic jam (carrying a single passenger, probably) is the best possible use of America's limited petroleum resources. Our products ought to help more people get where they want to go.

To us, that means a green light for mass transit . . . soon.

Mobil.

Figure 8.1 An example of a Mobil advertorial. From the *New York Times* October 19, 1970
Source: nytimes.com

Summary

In conclusion, writing opinion pieces is an excellent way for an organization or individual to establish themselves on key issues. It is a great strategy to reach opinion leaders. To communicate about issues, you can meet with the editorial board of a major news organization or try to place an op-ed or letter to the editor. You can also self-publish an opinion article on social media or pay for placement in an advertorial. Lastly, it is worth noting that op-eds and LTEs are unique types of earned media because the writer controls the message or content.

Checklist for Editorials and Op-Eds

- What strategic or emerging topics or issues are facing your organization or industry?
- Who are the thoughtful, credible experts in your organization who might be valued sources or who can be approached to create think pieces or offer expert opinions?
- Should you consider self-publishing your opinion on a website or social media?
- What outlets cover the industry or field you are promoting?

  - What are their requirements or needs?
  - What are the schedules for publication or broadcast? What are other technical requirements?
  - Do they accept articles from outsiders, no matter how credible?

Exercises

1. Pick one of the major daily newspapers such as the New York Times, the Wall Street Journal or the Washington Post. Read their opinion pages for one week and keep a diary of what you read. Note what kinds of authors they publish and the topics. Are there any multimedia elements? Also, review the information on how to submit both op-eds and LTEs.
2. Think of an issue that you care about. Write a draft of an op-ed for possible publications. Then make a list of three possible news outlets that you would like to see publish it. Research the submission guidelines and then create a submission plan. Basically, decide which news outlet you will approach first, second and third.
3. Read a regional newspaper for a week. Find an article that you either really like or really dislike. Review the newspaper's LTE submission requirements. Write an LTE. Check with your professor about submitting it.
4. Partner with another student to "ghost write" each other's op-ed. Each student should pick an issue. They should take turns writing each other's opinion piece. Focus on how you would do this to communicate the other student's key messages and voice.
5. Create a pitching plan for an op-ed. Pick ten news outlets of various types. This includes the major daily newspapers, as well as other news outlets. Review their submission requirements and write-up notes. Then decide the order in which you will pitch these news outlets.

Glossary

Thought leaders – the people who have the power and influence to change the opinions of others. Can be an important target audience.

Advertorial – an article, website page or video programming that is designed to look and read like objective journalistic content but is, in fact, a paid advertisement.

References

Associated Press Op-ed. https://blog.ap.org/behind-the-news/what-is-ap-ceo-explains-in-op-ed

CNN Opinion. www.cnn.com/opinions

Editors' Note; The Letters Editor and the Reader: Our Compact, Updated, by Thomas Feyer, May 23, 2004. www.nytimes.com/2004/05/23/opinion/editors-note-the-letters-editor-and-the-reader-our-compact-updated.html

How Can I Submit an Editorial to the Boston Globe? www.bostonglobe.com/2019/12/26/opinion/submit-an-op-ed/

How Can I Submit an Editorial to Fast Company? https://fastcompany.zendesk.com/hc/en-us/articles/360000291906-How-can-I-submit-an-editorial-contribution-

How to Submit a Guest Essay to the New York Times. https://help.nytimes.com/hc/en-us/articles/115014809107-How-to-submit-a-Guest-Essay-for-Opinion

How to Submit and Op-ed to the Denver Post. www.denverpost.com/2013/07/09/submission-guidelines-and-contact-information/

How to Submit an Op-ed to the Los Angeles Times. www.latimes.com/opinion/story/2021-10-20/op-ed-explained\

How to Submit to the Hill.com. https://thehill.com/submitting-op-eds

How to Submit to USA Today. https://static.usatoday.com/submitletter/

Letter to the Editor Templates. https://templatearchive.com/letter-to-the-editor/

Long Island Weekly. https://longislandweekly.com/author/mike-barry/

My Medical Choice. www.nytimes.com/2013/05/14/opinion/my-medical-choice.html

Politico.com: How to Write for Us. www.politico.com/write-for-us

The Redesign of The New York Times Op-Ed. www.nytimes.com/2021/04/26/opinion/nyt-opinion-oped-redesign.html

Wall Street Journal on News Literacy. https://newsliteracy.wsj.com/news-opinion/

What is a Thought Leader? www.forbes.com/sites/russprince/2012/03/16/what-is-a-thought-leader/?sh=6a190c897d

For Further Reading

How to Submit a Letter to the Editor to the New York Times. https://help.nytimes.com/hc/en-us/articles/115014925288-How-to-submit-a-letter-to-the-editor

How to Submit an Op-ed to the Washington Post. www.washingtonpost.com/opinions/submit-an-op-ed/

How to Write an Op-ed. https://pinkston.co/how-to-write-an-op-ed

How to Write an Op-ed. www.thebalancesmb.com/oped-what-is-it-and-how-to-write-it-1360714

How to Write Thought Leadership Pieces that Get Published and Don't Make Editors Want to Die by Shane Snow. It Contains Fast Company's Updated Opinion Submission. www.fastcompany.com/3003516/how-write-thought-leadership-pieces-get-published-and-dont-make-editors-want-die

Influencing Editorial Board Meetings. https://ccf.georgetown.edu/wp-content/uploads/2012/03/influencing-editorials-an-editorial-board-meeting-primer.pdf

Linkedin Learning – Video on How to Become a Thought Leader. www.linkedin.com/learning/paths/become-a-thought-leader

MBooth Web Posting, Five tips for Effective Thought Leadership. www.mbooth.com/blog/5-tips-for-effective-thought-leadership-now/

Muckrack Blog Post on Editorial Board Meetings. https://muckrack.com/blog/2019/12/03/editorial-board-meeting

Rethink Media's Web Posting, Congrats You Have Published an Op-ed. How Do You Make Sure More People See It? https://rethinkmedia.org/blog/congrats-you-have-published-op-ed-how-do-you-make-sure-more-people-see-it

What is an Op-ed and How to Write It. www.thebalancesmb.com/oped-what-is-it-and-how-to-write-it-1360714

www.nydailynews.com/opinion/submit-op-ed-daily-news-article-1.3802506

You Tube Video Featuring Thomas Friedman on How to Write an op-ed. www.youtube.com/watch?v=kD3eHClpnI0

9 SOCIAL MEDIA FOR STRATEGIC PR

Learning Goals for This Chapter

After reading this chapter, you should be able to:

- Create a social media strategy for your organization.
- Define which social media outlets or platforms will meet the strategic PR goals of your organization, project or campaign.
- Analyze target audiences to determine which social media platforms, if any, are most appropriate for reaching them.
- Master social media writing.
- Understand how to use social media for media relations and crisis communications.

Social media has become an integral part of our lives. The *Associated Press Stylebook*, 2020–22 edition, defines "social media" as an "umbrella term for online services that people use to share posts, photos and videos with small or large groups of people."

People use it to get their news, to learn about new products, to educate themselves about candidates for public office and to announce everything from the adoption of a new pet to a death in the family.

It has also become an essential tactic in strategic public relations.

For nonprofit organizations, elected officials and NGOs, as well as businesses large and small, social media has become a central part of how they communicate both internally and externally to key audiences.

It is safe to say that if your business or organization does not have a website and an active social media presence, it will seem as if it does not exist. In fact, it would be virtually impossible to name an organization or important individual that does not have some sort of social media presence.

For the PR writer, it is important to not confuse familiarity with social media as expertise. It is one thing to post vacation pictures on Facebook and another to understand how to use social media to advance business and organizational objectives. Like all communications tactics, social media should be executed in a planned, strategic manner.

DOI: 10.4324/9781003248330-9

The bedrock of an organization's social media presence is its website – the public face of the organization. It must reflect the image, identity and overall "personality" of the organization. Creating and maintaining an effective website is a central tactic for virtually all organizations. To be effective, websites must evolve in tandem with digital technology and must be updated with fresh, engaging content. Website design and maintenance is not the focus of this book; however, creating content and the strategic use of social media will be discussed in detail.

This chapter focuses on strategically harnessing the tremendous power of social media and how to integrate it into the overall communications strategy of the organization as well as individual campaigns and initiatives. Social media is constantly changing. New platforms are launched routinely. And some just gather digital dust. Existing platforms introduce new features and retire others. It is important to monitor these changes. An important strategic role for the PR professional is evaluating if a specific social media platform is right for your client or company, as well as how you plan to use it.

Smart businesses are constantly reevaluating their social media presences and what social media platforms are best for them. For example, LinkedIn may be a great choice for a law firm but TikTok may not make sense. Unless, of course, the law firm finds an innovative use for the site that helps it stand out from its competition. It all comes down to strategy.

Social Media and the PESO Model

In terms of the PESO model, social media can be used in all four types of communications. If your organization pays for advertisements on social media, then it is certainly paid media. In terms of earned media, social media can be used to identify new media outlets, distribute news releases, and pitch individual reporters and build relationships with them. Social media is also an important way of sharing content. Lastly, an organization's or individual's social media account is owned by it because the organization has control of what is posted and when. This makes it owned media.

Social Media Use in 2021

According to the 2021 Pew Research Center Survey on Social Media Use, seven in ten Americans say they use social media, with YouTube and Facebook continuing to be the most popular sites. In fact, 81% of survey respondents use YouTube and 69% are on Facebook. The full report can be accessed at www.pewresearch.org/internet/2021/04/07/social-media-use-in-2021/.

The survey also revealed that the popularity of YouTube, which is owned by Google, is likely to grow. On the other hand, Facebook's growth has leveled off.

When it comes to the other platforms in the survey, 40% of adults say they use Instagram and about three in ten report using Pinterest or LinkedIn. One-quarter say they use Snapchat, with Twitter and WhatsApp close in popularity.

TikTok, an app for sharing short videos, is used by 21% of Americans, while 13% say they use the neighborhood-focused platform Nextdoor. In terms of young adults,

Instagram, Snapchat and TikTok have an especially strong following. In fact, a majority of 18- to 29-year-olds say they use Instagram (71%) or Snapchat (65%), and half use TikTok. It is worth noting that Reddit was the only platform polled (other than YouTube) that experienced statistically significant growth, increasing from 11% in 2019 to 18% today.

Figure 9.1 details the survey results:

Growing share of Americans say they use YouTube; Facebook remains one of the most widely used online platforms among U.S. adults

% of U.S. adults who say they ever use ...

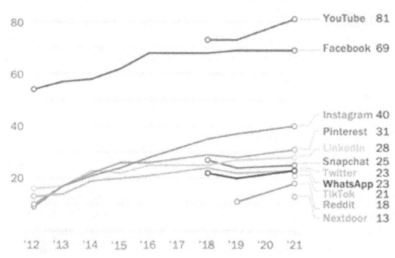

Note: Respondents who did not give an answer are not shown. Pre-2018 telephone poll data is not available for YouTube, Snapchat and WhatsApp; pre-2019 telephone poll data is not available for Reddit. Pre-2021 telephone poll data is not available for TikTok. Trend data is not available for Nextdoor.
Source: Survey of U.S. adults conducted Jan. 25-Feb. 8, 2021.
"Social Media Use in 2021"

PEW RESEARCH CENTER

Figure 9.1 Pew Research Center on use of YouTube and Facebook
Source: Pew.org

Demographics of Different Social Networks

When deciding which social media platforms to use, it is important to have a detailed understanding of not only the number of participants, but who is using the site. That way, you can select the site that will reach your target audience. The Pew Research Center's survey reveals the following information:

Instagram

- About half of Hispanic (52%) and Black Americans (49%) say they use the platform, compared with smaller shares of white Americans (35%).

WhatsApp

- Hispanic Americans (46%) are far more likely to say they use WhatsApp than Black (23%) or white Americans (16%).

LinkedIn

- Those with higher levels of education are more likely than those with lower levels of educational attainment to report being LinkedIn users.

- Half of adults who have a bachelor's or advanced degree (51%) say they use LinkedIn, compared with smaller shares of those with some college experience (28%) and those with a high school diploma or less (10%).

Pinterest

- Women continue to be far more likely than men to say they use Pinterest when compared with male counterparts, by a difference of 30 points (46% versus 16%).

Nextdoor

- Adults living in urban (17%) or suburban (14%) areas are more likely to say they use Nextdoor. Only 2% of rural Americans report using the site.

Relationship Between PR and Social Media Engagement

When social media was in its infancy, it was generally viewed as its own form of communications. It was separate and apart from the advertising, marketing and public relations functions. Today, these functions are integrated to maximize their potential. That is one reason the PESO model is so important.

PR and social media work best when they are in sync with each other. PR and social media are based on communication, but social media, with its real-time messaging, amplifies your message, allowing PR tactics to be stronger and more impactful. Social media has also made PR more "friendly" to all stakeholders, resulting in a new area of marketing called "relationship marketing." This helps companies to be warmer, more inviting and more approachable.

Creating a Social Media Strategy

When using social media as part of your communications plan, it is crucial that you develop a social media strategy. This is a document that outlines:

- Your social media goals
- The tactics you will use to achieve them

Hootsuite.com, a social media service provider, offers tips to create a social media strategy. Here is a summary of their suggestions:

- Choose social media goals that align to your business objectives.

  Use the SMART approach to choosing goals. "SMART" stands for specific, measurable, attainable, relevant and time-bound.

  You may want to track different goals for different platforms, or even different uses. For example, if you use LinkedIn to drive traffic to your website, measure click-throughs. A click-through is the action or facility of following a hypertext link to a particular website.

- Learn everything you can about your audience. Knowing who your audience is and what they want to see on social media is key. That way, you can create content that they will like, comment on and share.
- Know your competition. Your competitors are using social media, and you can learn from what they're doing. Conduct a competitive analysis. This allows you to understand what they're doing well (and not so well). It may also help spot opportunities. If one of your competitors is dominant on Facebook, for example, but has put little effort into Twitter or Instagram, this may provide an idea for an interesting opportunity for your client or company.
- Do a social media audit. Take stock of your efforts so far. Determine what is meeting your goals and what is not. And plan to improve what you are currently doing.
- Set up accounts and improve profiles.

  After your audit, you may decide to include new social media sites or retire old ones. As you decide which social networks to use, you will also need to define your strategy for each platform. Remember to use consistent branding (logos, images, etc.).

- Find inspiration.

  While it's important that your brand be unique, you can draw inspiration from other businesses that are great on social media. Case studies can offer valuable insights that you can apply to your own social media plan. You could also check out the winners of the Facebook Awards (www.facebook.com/business/news/facebook-awards-winners-announcement) or the Shorty Awards (https://shortyawards.com/).

- Create a social media content calendar.

  Sharing great content is essential. You need to schedule when you'll share content. Your social media content calendar will contain dates and times when you will publish different types of content on each site. The social media service provider Meltwater offers this free template to build a social media calendar: www.meltwater.com/en/resources/content-calendar-template.

- Evaluate and adjust your strategy.

  As you implement your plan and track results, you may find that some strategies don't work as well as you'd anticipated, while others are working even better than expected.

  A template to create a social media strategy can be downloaded from Hootsuite.com at https://blog.hootsuite.com/how-to-create-a-social-media-marketing-. Another template is available from Ring Central, a cloud communications company, at www.ringcentral.com/us/en/blog/social-media-campaign-planning/.

Create Hashtags

Using the right hashtags can show that you're in tune with current trends, allowing you to take part in the conversations that matter to your organization or client. Hashtags also work well for monitoring your brand. They're a great way to increase the visibility of your content beyond your own followers. Many brands latch onto trending topics to contribute to the conversation or sell their products. You can also create your own hashtags to draw attention to your brand or events you are holding.

Only use hashtags that are relevant to your content. For example, if you tweet about starting a business, you might use the hashtag "#entrepreneurship." You should also limit how many hashtags you use. The more you use, the less likely people are to interact with your content because they'll find your posts spam-like. Every social media site uses hashtags slightly differently, so it's important to know what the conventions are on each platform.

How to Use the Top Social Media Sites

Social media is constantly changing. As a communications professional, it is your job to stay on top of these changes. Your clients and senior management will rely on your judgment regarding using a new platform or not. For instance, the CEO of your organization may become interested in a social media platform because his or her grandchildren are obsessed with it. Or your client may have just returned from a social media conference and is now questioning the social media strategy that you and your team just spent the last month working on. Look at these suggestions as opportunities to evaluate what you are doing in social media. There may be the germ of a good idea. You just don't want to start working with a new social media site simply because it is trendy or abandon what you are currently doing because you have been on the site for a while. It is all about working with the social media platforms that will advance your goals, will reach your target audience and can be maintained within allotted resources.

Over time, the list of the top social media sites will likely change, and, as it does, you will need to reevaluate your social media strategy. Following are the top social media outlets in 2021 with descriptions of what they are and how to use them.

YouTube

YouTube is an online video sharing and social media platform. It is also the second most popular search engine after Google. In fact, Google, after a failed attempt to launch its own video sharing site, purchased YouTube for $1.65 billion in stock in November 2006.

Content on YouTube covers a huge range of topics and can be an excellent platform for your organization or client to share their unique expertise with a captive audience. Many consumers land on YouTube after searching for "how-to" content. Developing this type of content can be an effective way to drive viewers to your YouTube channel and capture their interest.

As you plan your video topics, think of the common questions your organization receives from its key audiences. For instance, if your company develops health-care software, you might select a common pain point that your software solves and develop a how-to video showcasing your software as one of the potential solutions to the problem.

When planning your YouTube strategy, be sure to include plenty of content that displays your organization's expertise and positions its leadership as thought leaders. The site itself offers some great best practices to working with it. It can be found here: www.youtube.com/intl/en_us/ads/resources/best-practices/.

Facebook

According to Sproutsocial.com, about 75% of women use Facebook, while about 63% of men use it. Representation across age groups is fairly equal but highest among adults 18 to 64 years old. Facebook is a social media networking site that allows users to connect with friends, family, co-workers and others, including groups of people who share a similar interest.

People tend to go to Facebook for news, entertainment, staying connected with others and shopping. Users share pictures, videos, articles and opinions with their friends. You can also learn a lot about how to use the site by going directly to the site and accessing the "About" section at: https://about.facebook.com/company-info/. They also offer best practices for businesses working with Facebook, as well as Instagram, which Facebook also owns. Here is the link: www.facebook.com/formedia/blog/best-practices-for-facebook-and-instagram.

The online publication *Business News Daily* suggests that Facebook can benefit a business in a number of ways, including:

- Building an online brand. As the largest and first social media network to achieve mainstream success, it also offers the most integration tools compared with other platforms, such as follow buttons, account logins and photo sharing. These can lead customers back to your website and other online content you want to highlight.
- Forming professional bonds between competitors. This can help your client or organization become a leader within their business.
- Offering life advice. Facebook users can share knowledge in areas from parenting advice to practical business solutions.

Here is the link to the full article: www.businessnewsdaily.com/2534-facebook-benefits. html.

An example of how a government agency uses Facebook can found at the Centers for Disease Control and Prevention (CDC), which publishes a social media guide for this platform. It can be accessed at www.cdc.gov/socialmedia/tools/guidelines/ facebook-guidelines.html.

Instagram

Since its inception, Instagram has proven to be a powerful marketing tool for a business looking to expand its presence and the visibility of its products. It is hugely popular with millennials and Gen Zers. Like Facebook, Instagram is slightly more popular with women than with men.

It is a highly visual social network – which means it's best for brands with really cool or interesting-looking products. Users of this social media platform expect high quality from businesses. If your client or organization is not naturally visual, you will need to create interesting visuals. Make sure to create a cohesive look that reflects your graphic standards as well as branding and organization values. Here are some best practices:

- Create well-written captions. They are as important as visuals because they help engage viewers. Use clear, concise writing and urge viewers to comment.
- Include hashtags. They group together photos that have commonalities or share a meaning.
- Use the Instagram Stories and Instagram Live Function. Instagram Stories are short segments of media (photo and/or video) that play in a sequence and disappear after 24 hours. Keep your content in Stories both educational and informative to engage the audience. Instagram Live Videos can last up to an hour and disappear afterwards.
- Make use of locations. Make sure your company has a set location to tag, if applicable. When consumers take photos at a particular place, they often like to tag their locations.
- Choose an appropriate handle and fill in your company bio. Instagram users are known by their handles, so choose your name wisely. Ideally, you'll choose your company/brand name, but if that is unavailable, pick one close to it. Don't choose a handle that is completely off-brand because users will have a hard time finding and remembering it. The PR service provider Cision offers tips for businesses to work with Instagram. It can be found here: www.cision.com/ resources/white-papers/what-your-business-needs-to-know-about-instagram/.

Pinterest

Content on Pinterest is driven by visuals. In fact, you can't share something on Pinterest unless an image is involved. Pinterest has its own lingo. When you share something on Pinterest, each bookmark is called a pin. When you share someone else's pin on Pinterest, it's called a "repin." Like Twitter, Pinterest is driven by reposts (only they call them "repins").

Pinterest can be a great public relations tool. For example, you can pin infographics from your company website. If your company is attending trade shows or conferences, be sure to document it by taking pictures/videos and pinning them during and after the event. Or, if you manufacture and sell a consumer product, capture pictures of your product so your Pinterest images tell a story about the value of your product in people's lives.

It is also a great platform to hold contests in order to spread the word about the products and services of your business. Think about some innovative contest ideas, ask customers for "repins," participate on specific boards or ask customers to create boards on their own. Their creativity might help you with ideas for future contests.

LinkedIn

LinkedIn is the largest professional network on the internet. In fact, it has been described as Facebook for business. It can help showcase your organization or client's unique professional story. It provides an opportunity to establish your client or someone at your organization as a subject matter expert and a thought leader. It is also an appropriate platform to communicate financial success or promote a corporate social responsibility initiative.

You can also use LinkedIn to organize events, join groups, write articles, post photos and videos, and upload PowerPoint or SlideShare presentations. According to LinkedIn, posts with images receive 98% more comments than those without. LinkedIn also finds that custom collages that include three or four images in one post perform well. Videos see five times more engagement on LinkedIn than any other content type. An advantage of LinkedIn video is that it auto-plays when someone scrolls by it. As a result, it does a better job at catching someone's attention. LinkedIn can also help you identify relevant media and build relationships with journalists. It is a powerful business-to-business tool.

Most organizations have a Linkedin page for the organization itself as well as for chief executives and subject matter experts. It may be your responsibility to manage these accounts for your organization or client. You would need to create a calendar for posting content as well as identify the topics that would best meet communications and organizational objectives.

Twitter

Media personalities, politicians and the public turn to Twitter for real-time information and reactions to the day's events. It is the site where news organizations post their latest information and where individual journalists showcase their individual work as well as look for sources and story ideas. This is one of the reasons that Twitter is such a powerful tool for media relations. If you want to work effectively with the media, you need to be where they are, and the media is on Twitter.

The top Twitter accounts are an eclectic group. They include people such as billionaire business leader Elon Musk; singers Justin Bieber, Taylor Swift, Lady Gaga,

Ariana Grande and Rihanna; soccer star Cristiano Ronaldo; and politicians such as Barak Obama.

Twitter profiles have six parts: your Twitter handle, username, profile picture, bio, header image and a pinned tweet. All of these elements should work cohesively to be an accurate representation of your organization or client. A tweet itself can be up to 280 characters. Hashtags are a great tool for Twitter. You just need to make sure it's relevant to your brand and that you use the trending phrase. Here are some best practices for using Twitter:

- Direct message (DM) someone who follows you.

  This tool is great for working directly with journalists and is also useful for handling problems. It's smart to handle individual customer complaints and issues through DMs. This takes the problem offline. Also, there is no character limit on DMs, which gives you the freedom to help customers properly.

- Include photos, GIFs and polls.

  Twitter allows you to add up to four photos per post. You can also create graphics to add to your tweets. Twitter has a built-in GIF keyboard; you simply search for a keyword and choose the clip that best suits your tweet. One way to involve your followers is to create a poll. You can list up to four answer options in your poll; each option can be up to 25 characters. The poll stays live for 24 hours by default, but you can shorten that time frame if you prefer.

- Live tweet.

  Live tweeting is another potential way to get a topic trending on Twitter. If you organize an event and want your attendees to live tweet about it, it's a good idea to create your own hashtag for the event and share it with your attendees so they can spread and follow it. When you're live tweeting or using multiple tweets for the same topic, make them responses to the original tweet. This makes it easier for users to follow the entire conversation.

- Chat on Twitter.

  A Twitter chat is when several Twitter users discuss a specific topic simultaneously using a shared hashtag. Usually, one Twitter user hosts a chat at a specific time, with prepared questions and discussion points. Twitter chats usually last about an hour.

Twitter itself offers the best description of how to use the site. It can be found at https://help.twitter.com/en/using-twitter/how-to-tweet.

Snapchat

Snapchat is a social media app that allows users to send short, temporary photos, videos and chats that disappear after a few seconds. Snapchat also offers interactive features like Snap Maps, where you can view the locations of people or places. It also offers Stories, which live on a profile for 24 hours, as well as a Discovery tab for finding new content. It is popular with millennials, so if they are your target audience, this can be an effective social media tool for you to consider.

Unlike other types of social media, Snapchat obligates people to pay immediate attention. The time limit on Snapchat content creates a sense of urgency. This provides a powerful strategic opportunity. For example, if you offer an exclusive deal containing a coupon that is only visible for ten seconds, this can be a great call to action. It may also be a useful tool for those trying to get attention for a special event, meeting or press conference.

The New Orleans Saints is an example of an organization that successfully uses the app. Through Snapchat, the Saints have been able to show their fans what goes on away from the home stadium. They post intimate footage of the team during training. It has proven to be immensely popular with their fans and followers.

WhatsApp

While WhatsApp is a messaging app, many professionals and organizations define it as a social media platform because of its ability to enable users to interact and share media. The app supports voice and video calls and group chats, Users can also share various media types such as videos, GIFs, PDFs and geo locations. The calls can also be made internationally as long as the user has data or a Wi-Fi connection.

Social media platforms such as Facebook and Twitter enhance businesses' public profiles, whereas WhatsApp's focus is on its private connections. This advantage could strengthen the connection between a business and its customers. It is also a great tool for those who have an international target audience, as it can save the cost of costly long distance conversations.

TikTok

The platform consists of 15- and 60-second user-recorded videos. It includes in-app editing and integration with other social media sites. Most TikTok users are between the ages of 16 and 24. It allows brands to engage with users through video, only in shorter, bite-sized clips.

Elf Cosmetics, for example, has been active on social media. They commissioned a song specifically for a TikTok campaign. The song, which takes inspiration from Kash Doll's 2018 hit "Ice Me Out" and is called "Eyes Lips Face" after the brand name's acronym, is believed to be the first original song commissioned for a TikTok campaign. They created the #eyeslipsface challenge to activate a key brand pillar: "e.l.f. is for every eye, lip and face." The challenge was an instant success, becoming the fastest-growing TikTok campaign of all time. TikTokers contributed nearly five million videos, reaching seven billion views. More details on the campaign can be found at https://moversshakers.co/elf-tiktok-challenge.

In 2021, Mattel's Barbie also launched a campaign creating videos for the site. They also posted these videos on their YouTube channel. It is also worth noting that this site is where a lot of young people go to get news. So, it may be a strategic choice for an educational campaign on a serious issue. You just need to present the information in an entertaining manner.

Reddit

Reddit is an online platform that resembles a giant forum. The platform consists of subreddits – subdivisions on any topic, from fitness and needlework to marketing and startups. The pages of these communities resemble news feeds with individual publications. The more involvement the post gets, the higher it rises in the newsgroup. The most popular posts with viral content appear on Reddit's home page.

Each user earns karma – that is, the rating consisting of two indicators: the karma of publications and the karma of comments. Voices "for" add pluses to karma; votes "against" take away points.

For a promotion to be successful at Reddit, you must become part of the community and gain the audience's credibility. Do not try to promote your company or client with an empty account and zero karma. Reddit is first of all a community. It is not a platform for direct sales. Contribute to the community: entertain, share your experience, ask questions, and take part in discussions. Only by establishing a relationship of trust and understanding with the Reddit audience will you be able to use the full potential of the platform to promote your organization or client.

Nextdoor

The Nextdoor app is a social media platform for neighborhoods. The idea behind the app is to help neighbors communicate with each other, organize local events and share information about what's happening in their community. Nextdoor also has a business page that lets you promote your company locally by interacting with members of their neighborhood and surrounding areas.

Nextdoor describes itself as "The neighborhood hub for trusted connections and the exchange of helpful information, goods and services." Nextdoor requires new users to prove where they live before signing up. This can be done by phone or postcard. You can use this site to:

- Ask questions or post a poll
- Sell products
- Organize events
- Get recommendations
- Post alerts

This platform can be a useful tool for promoting a business or event within a community. The site itself offers tips to how to use it. It can be found at https://about.nextdoor.com/.

There are also other social media sites that have smaller followers that may provide unique opportunity for your strategic needs. For instance, Yelp and Quora are not as large as the social media sites discussed in detail previously. Yelp is emerging as the leading consumer review site for many types of businesses and it currently receives high priority from the Google search engine results. And Quora, as a question-and-answer platform, may help establish an organization as subject matter expert. It all gets down to being smart and strategic.

Best Practices for Posting Online

While each social media platform is different, there are some best practices that apply to all of them. The online publication *Social Media Today* offers seven tips for social media posting.

1. Do Your Research

If you want your audience to notice and engage with your social posts, you need to make them highly relevant to that target audience. The more relevant your posts are, the more success you will have – but relevance, in general, is not enough. You need to take the time to understand your audience. Pick a need or challenge that research or experience has shown might be a high priority for the audience and develop content and social media posts that provide a solution.

2. Speak Their Language

Use language when writing your posts that resonates with your audience. This will help show that you truly understand them and their challenges. For example, a post you write on LinkedIn for senior-level executives will read very differently than a post you write on Facebook for new moms. Not only do these two groups of people have different challenges and points of view, but their language – the exact phrasing they use to speak about their needs and challenges – differs significantly.

3. Develop Your Voice

Although you should write social media posts in the language of your target audience, the overall message should be written in your own voice (or the voice of your organization, client or brand). This voice is influenced by your personality or your company's personality – your "why" story and the language used by your ideal customers. This voice needs to be consistent throughout the content you create and the posts you share on social platforms, as well as the engagement you have on those networks. This consistency will help your audience connect with you emotionally, as well as build trust.

4. Be Positive

This doesn't mean every post needs to be happy. You want your audience to be excited and inspired by your posts, and that doesn't always mean happy posts. In some of your posts, you may choose to share your opinion or take a stand on something important to you and your brand. But there's a difference between taking a stand and attacking or criticizing others. Whatever you do, avoid criticizing anyone (or any business) publicly. Criticizing others is not only unprofessional but also dangerous – it can draw more negative people to your page and can hurt any trust or credibility you've built with your existing followers.

5. Keep It Short and Simple

Make your content and posts easy to read by writing at an eighth-grade reading level. Most newspapers also write at this level. This means that you need to write simply and clearly. Use headings, bullets and lists where possible to make your content or posts easier to scan. Keep paragraphs short and try to keep to one idea per paragraph.

6. Use Images and Videos

Visual content is more engaging and can tell the story more quickly than words alone. People respond well to video; it can humanize your company or client.

7. Add a Call to Action

At the end of your content or social posts, consider prompting your audience with the action you'd like them to take next by including a call to action (CTA). Here are some suggestions:

- Ask them to rate or like or share your social media posts.
- Ask a question they can answer in the comments.
- Suggest that they access another piece of content.
- Direct them to your website.
- Get them to subscribe to your newsletter.
- Ask them to connect with you on other social media channels.

The full article can be viewed here: www.socialmediatoday.com/news/7-social-media-content-writing-tips/555805/.

Media Relations

Social media is a powerful tool for working with the news media. It can be used to:

- Distribute or share media kits, news releases and media advisories
- Pitch journalists
- Research what topics are of interest to specific news outlets
- Build relationships with specific journalists
- Showcase the social media presence of company executives and subject matter experts

A very effective way to broadly distribute news releases, media advisories and press kits is through social media. Twitter and LinkedIn, for instance, are good choices for mass distribution of earned media tactics. It is also standard practice today for news releases themselves to have links to social media so that they can also be shared online. This is a simple and cost-effective way of expanding the reach of your news releases and media advisories.

Social media is also an effective pitching tool to use for contacting journalists you already know. For instance, a direct message on Twitter about an issue or upcoming event will get their attention a lot quicker than an email, and it is less intrusive than a phone call. LinkedIn can also be used to directly pitch a journalist. You can also strengthen your relationship with journalists that you are working with by reading or viewing their work. If you like something, post a positive comment or share their work with others. Many journalists are evaluated by their news organizations based on their social engagement, so they will appreciate your support.

The goal is to establish a long-term relationship. If you only interact with a journalist for a short period of time on social media right before you pitch them, this can be a dead giveaway that you aren't genuinely interested in establishing a long-term relationship. That's why it's important to keep engaging, even when you don't have anything to pitch. This type of organic and thoughtful interaction allows you to build trust over time, so reporters know that you are a valuable resource and not just someone who only wants to promote your own interests.

Some social media sites may be better for building rapport with journalists than for pitching. For instance, if you have a shared hobby on Pinterest, keep your communications on this platform to your mutual interest. The same goes for platforms such as Facebook or Instagram. If your interactions are about vacations, pet photos or sports activities, keep it that way. It may be seen as an invasion of privacy to pitch a story idea. Of course, it is okay to reference your shared interest in an email pitch or phone conversation.

Social media is also an excellent way to identify news outlets and journalists who may be a good strategic fit for your organization or client. You can see how they cover issues or products. If you don't have access to a database of journalists or are just starting to create media lists, social media can be an excellent place to begin.

Social Media and Crisis Communications

Social media can be a useful tool during a crisis because it allows you to respond quickly in real time. For instance, if a business needs to be evacuated because of a wildfire, sending messages out on social media regarding how to reach the media team, as well as providing real-time updates on people who may be at the business is very important. For other types of crises, using social media to tell your story and get out your key messages can help control the narrative of your company or client. If you don't tell your story, someone else will and you may not like their version.

But sometimes, a crisis itself starts in social media. It could be as simple as a reporter who posts a message looking for negative stories. For instance, a journalist posts that they are hearing that flood claims are not being paid after a storm and want to know if this is happening to others. Or they want to know if people are experiencing rude salespeople at a particular store or chain. The journalist is looking for victims who can make for compelling news. If you ignore such situations, they can turn into a crisis of negative reporting.

You may want to reach out to a journalist directly. If you can't stop such postings, you will need to develop a plan. If the accusations are true, the problem needs to be fixed. You can follow up with positive messages about how your client or organization has positively responded. If the accusations are false, you need to quickly set the record straight, and social media is an effective tool for doing this.

There are also other types of crises that can occur in social media. The social media monitoring company Mediatoolkit states that there are four types of social media crises:

1. **Multichannel crisis**. This is extremely dangerous because it has the potential to go viral and generate a great deal of negative publicity very quickly.
2. **Emerging crisis**. If it is not anticipated and dealt with as soon as possible, it can quickly escalate into a bigger scandal.
3. **Industry crisis**. This occurs when a vendor or competitor is experiencing a social media crisis – for example, when many fashion brands are suddenly all attacked for nontransparent actions.
4. **Fake news**. In the age of social media, a post can go viral in just one click. The ability to detect rumors about your brand quickly is essential.

All of these crises demand immediate responses. For instance, if a customer is unhappy, your social media team needs to reach out directly to the customer and help them offline. This needs to be done immediately. Generally, if this is handled properly, there will be no social media crisis. If there is no response – or worse, there is a computer-generated response that is not helpful – this could snowball into a much larger crisis. For complicated social media crises, your organization or client's crisis communications department will need to step in and handle the strategic response. You as the PR writer may be tasked with developing content for various parts of the crisis response.

Mediatoolkit, on its website, offers this well-known case study of a social media crisis that could have been avoided. Here is a link to Mediatoolkit with the full case study: Mediatoolkitwww.mediatoolkit.com/blog/social-media-crisis-examples.

This is an example of how to turn a PR social media crisis into a total disaster. One day in 2017, United Airlines Flight 3411 was overbooked. The airline decided to draw four random passengers who would not be able to fly and asked them to vacate their seats to make room for four airline employees. When the crew requested a pulmonologist to surrender his seat, he refused, saying that he needed to see a patient the following day (which was understandable, as he had paid for that seat).

After that, security appeared on the plane and forcibly dragged the man off the plane with a bleeding face. The whole situation was recorded by fellow passengers on the flight and immediately posted online.

A video of the incident went viral on social media, stoking anger over the violent action. One such video was shared 87,000 times and viewed 6.8 million times in less than a day.

Many politicians expressed concern and called for an official investigation. President Donald Trump criticized United Airlines, saying the airline's treatment of the passenger was "horrible."

Where this brand went wrong:

The following day, the then-CEO of United Airlines, Oscar Munoz, issued a statement that appeared to justify the removal of the passenger. And it gets worse.

After that, Munoz sent an email to United Airlines staff that was obtained by the media. Munoz said the passenger was "disruptive and belligerent" and that employees "followed established procedures."

The email contained utterly different information from the official statement. This caused more online fury. United shares plummeted in value dramatically.

How this problem could have been prevented:

A coherent, sincere message at first. The airline should have responded to each and every comment with complete respect. There was no reason for them to blame a passenger whose safety they should have been prioritizing. The whole situation should have been explained.

Retaining Outside Assistance

While the writing of social media posts is generally best handled by the organization or its retained PR consultant, there may be times when a social media specialist may provide strategic insight and assistance. For instance, you may want to hire someone to help draft or update your social media strategy, or you may want to work with a social media monitoring and measurement organization to measure your effectiveness. This can provide information data points to update or improve what you are doing as well as provide important metrics to demonstrate that you are reaching organizational objectives.

Summary

In summary, social media is an important strategic tool for the strategic public relations writer. It is an effective tool for communicating directly to your key audiences, as well as working with journalists and influencers. That is why strategic organizations create a social media strategy and update it as social media itself changes, as well as to reflect changes in goals and objectives.

An effective social media strategy can also boost your earned media efforts. It can support your media relations efforts and relationships with journalists and news organizations. Used correctly, social media can be a powerful tool before, during and after a crisis. However, if social media is not monitored and handled correctly, it can also be the source of a crisis it. In short, social media is a powerful tool.

Exercises

1. Read the most recent Pew Report on social media use. What are the key trends? How would you use these trends from a public relations perspective?
2. If you were tasked with creating a social media campaign to reach Hispanics, based on the Pew research, what social media sites would you use?
3. Pick an organization that interests you and create a social media strategy for it.
4. Imagine you are hired by the American Red Cross. Create a social media calendar for the organization.
5. Review either the Facebook Awards (www.facebook.com/business/news/face-book-awards-winners-announcement) or the Shorty Awards (https://shortyawards.com/). Pick an award winner that you think is interesting. Explain what they did and why you think it is so innovative.
6. Assume you have been hired to provide PR for a new app to sell children's sports equipment to parents. Write content for it on LinkedIn, Facebook, Twitter and one other social media platform of your choice.
7. Study the Elf campaign on TikTok and explain how you can apply it to other brands.

Glossary

A **click-through** is the action or facility of following a hypertext link to a particular website.

SMART refers to goals and is an acronym that stands for specific, measurable, attainable, relevant and time-bound.

References

Examples of Social Media Crises that Could Have Been Prevented Mediatoolkit. www.mediatoolkit.com/blog/social-media-crisis-examples/

Social Media Content Writing Tips | Social Media Today. www.socialmediatoday.com/news/7-social-media-content-writing-tips/555805/

Social Media Best Practices for 2021: Tips for Each Platform | RingCentral. www.ringcentral.com/us/en/blog/social-media-best-practices/

About Nextdoor. https://about.nextdoor.com/

Benefits of Facebook. www.businessnewsdaily.com/2534-facebook-benefits.html

CDC Guide to Social Media. www.cdc.gov/socialmedia/tools/guidelines/facebook-guidelines.html

Facebook Awards for Social Media. www.facebook.com/business/news/facebook-awards-winners-announcement

The Georgetown University Center for Social Impact Communications Points. https://csic.georgetown.edu/magazine/public-relations-play-role-social-media-marketing/

Hootsuite. https://blog.hootsuite.com/how-to-create-a-social-media-marketing-

How to Use Nextdoor. https://blog.hootsuite.com/how-to-use-nextdoor/

Meltwater Templates. www.meltwater.com/en/resources/content-calendar-template

Pew Research Center. www.pewresearch.org/internet/2021/04/07/social-media-use-in-2021/

Pew Research Center Fact Sheet on Twitter. www.pewresearch.org/internet/2019/04/24/sizing-up-twitter-users/

Shorty Awards for Social Media. https://shortyawards.com

TikTok Campaign. https://moversshakers.co/elf-tiktok-challenge

What your Business Needs to Know About Instagram. www.cision.com/resources/white-papers/what-your-business-needs-to-know-about-instagram/

Why YouTube Should Be Part of Your Public Relations Strategy. www.pushkinpr.com/blog/why-youtube-should-be-part-your-public-relations-strategy/

For Further Reading

7 Best Practices for Using Hashtags. www.searchenginepeople.com/blog/16031-hashtag-how-to.html

9 Ways PR Pros Can Use Social Media to Connect with Journalists – PR Daily. www.prdaily.com/9-ways-pr-pros-can-use-social-media-to-connect-with-journalists/

Best Practices for Working with Instagram. https://sproutsocial.com/insights/instagram-best-practices/

Inspiring Social Media Case Studies from Reputable Brands and Digital Agencies. digitalagencynetwork.com

Neighborhood Social Media Network Raises 123 Million. https://venturebeat.com/2019/05/14/neighborhood-social-network-nextdoor-raises-123-million-at-2-1-billion-valuation/

Pew Social Media Fact Sheet. www.pewresearch.org/internet/fact-sheet/social-media/

PR Tips for Using Pinterest in Your Public Relations Campaigns. https://newsmakergroup.com/pin-your-pr-tips-for-using-pinterest-in-your-public-relations-campaign/

Shorty Awards for Social Media. https://shortyawards.com/archive/brands-orgs/13th/all-categories/winners

Six Reasons You Need a Social Media Strategy. www.smartinsights.com/social-media-marketing/social-media-strategy/social-media-strategy-planning-essentials-6-reasons-need-social-media-strategy/

Snapchat for Business. www.businessnewsdaily.com/9860-snapchat-for-business.html

Social Media Case Studies – Apple Is a Good Example.

Social Media Marketing Strategies. www.smartinsights.com/social-media-marketing/social-media-strategy/new-global-social-media-research/

Ten Reasons to Use Instagram. https://www.business.com/articles/10-reasons-to-use-instagram-for-business www.businessnewsdaily.com/7488-twitter-for-business.html

This Surprising Reading Level Will Change the Way You Write. https://contently.com/2015/01/28/this-surprising-reading-level-analysis-will-change-the-way-you-write/

Three Major Ways Social Media is Changing Journalism – Kurt Wagner '12. www.scu.edu/illuminate/thought-leaders/kurt-wagner-12/three-major-ways-social-media-is-changing-journalism.html

TikTok: The Story of a Social Media Giant. www.bbc.com/news/technology-53640724

Why Yelp is Important to Your Business. www.socialmediatoday.com/content/why-yelp-important-your-business

www.searchenginejournal.com/social-media/biggest-social-media-sites/

10 SCRIPTING VIDEOS AND PODCASTS

Learning Goals for This Chapter

After reading this chapter, you should be able to:

- Discuss the growth and power of video in communications.
- Describe the uses and goals of video and podcasts for public relations.
- Explain how strategic videos and podcasts advance organizational goals.
- Identify situations where scripted storytelling may be most effective.
- Discuss technical requirements and options for podcasts.
- Talk about the potential PR value of podcasts, VNRs, YouTube and corporate videos.

Video has become a clear winner for public relations. It is used – even expected – by journalists and other communicators, as well as by consumers. It is also an important strategic choice to enhance other tactics. The "State of Social" report by Buffer.com, based in San Francisco, and German firm Social Chain AG, shows that almost 50% of businesses surveyed broadcast live video – a number that is very likely to grow. More than one-third (36%) publish video content monthly, with around one-quarter (24%) publishing video content weekly.

Michael Sadowski (2018), public relations manager at the Intrepid Group, wrote this in Forbes on the use and flexibility of video:

> One of the most important lessons we've learned is that good video content isn't about creating a single piece of content for distribution on a single channel. Rather, the most effective video content will have the ability to live in many different places in multiple formats.

Facebook and YouTube are the most widely used platforms for video distribution, according to the survey of 1,842 marketers by Buffer and Social Chain. You can find the report here: https://buffer.com/state-of-social-2019.

DOI: 10.4324/9781003248330-10

SEO Inc. (2020, www.seoinc.com/seo-blog/seo-statistics-youtube-2020/) reports this about the power of video: Video results are 50 times more likely to be organically ranked in Google than text-based results. And that video has a ratio of 11,000:1 probability of making it to the first page of a Google search. Text-based results have a 500,000:1 probability of making it to the first page.

For media relations, video is essential. When the authors of this book interviewed journalists about when to include video with other press tactics, the universal reply was "when you want a journalist to cover your story." All media outlets want and need video. It is not just used by broadcast television and cable or web-based news outlets such as BuzzFeed or the Huffington Post.

Legacy publications that have prospered all have online versions of their publications. For instance, the New York Times, the Wall Street Journal and the Washington Post all have deep, detailed websites. Magazines such as Vogue and Vanity Fair have robust digital versions. And other magazines, such as Self and Teen Vogue have reinvented themselves as online publications. They all have a voracious need for video, and because journalists are required to produce more work with fewer resources than in the past, a story that has video support to its pitch is more likely to be successful with journalists or bloggers and other outlets.

Video also makes it easy for the most people to understand many types of content.

In its 2021 report on video in business, Buildscale Inc., which operates as Vidyard, estimated that video production for business increased 135% from a year earlier. The study was based on data about videos created by Vidyard customers, representing more than 760,000 videos in 2020.

The company noted in its report (available here: https://awesome.vidyard.com/rs/273-EQL-130/images/2021-Vidyard-Video-in-Business-Benchmark-Report.pdf) that the leading industries in producing videos were high tech, professional services, financial services, and manufacturing and distribution.

In the high-tech industry, an average of 583 videos were created per company in 2020. Of that total, about 60% were generated in-house, with others being created externally by professional video firms. The growth in **user-generated content** from companies has accelerated, Vidyard clients report, based on ease of production and effectiveness of communicating with video for demonstrations and one-to-one messages to journalists, consumers and other members of key audiences.

Video continues to grow and become central to communications tactics among companies of all sizes. Vidyard noted in its 2021 report that 91% of brands in its study were maintaining or increasing their video content production budgets.

Most video is intended to put an organization in a good light, to advance its mission or vision, or to share news, such as new products or a partnership or promotion.

However, there may be less than positive situations where companies and other organizations need to produce video to explain their points of view or to set the record straight.

When a company conducts a media interview that has the potential to be contentious, it is customary to record it. If the company is not pleased with the resulting media coverage, it can put its recording of the interview on the company website and explain why the media interview was not balanced or fair and provide a factual narrative.

On the other end of the spectrum, user generated or produced content can create a downside as well. If a company has done something that is less than honorable – in terms of environmental or product issues – videos from cell phones can readily be posted on social media and can go viral.

For example, when two employees of Domino's Pizza videotaped themselves adulterating food, the company had to act immediately and forcefully (Clifford, 2009). The PR department for Domino's first decided to try and downplay the incident. But the video had gone viral and Domino's pivoted its strategy by creating a Twitter account to respond and provide its own factual information.

Within another day, the company had put out a video with the chairman forcefully responding to the situation and noting that the employees had been fired and arrested and that the local health department had been called and had told the company to throw away most of the food in the affected kitchen.

Other ways that videos can be used may include:

- Visual assets of spokespeople, products and background information
- Video news releases (VNRs)
- Developing b-roll
- Producing informative or documentary-style YouTube videos
- Live streaming events
- Producing short and engaging videos specifically designed for social media platforms (e.g., Instagram, Facebook, TikTok)
- Documenting speeches and special events

Creating Video News Releases or VNRs

In recent years, VNRs have been used less and less in favor of providing outlets with materials that journalists and editors can use to fashion their own presentations. Because VNRs have clearly stated that they were provided by an organization, journalists have come to dislike using them.

Like any PR tactic, a VNR should have firm goals in mind, present information clearly and concisely, and be carefully developed for ease of use by the intended audience.

When planning a VNR or any informative video, you should take on the role of a movie producer, keeping an eye out for visually powerful images, moving images that are difficult to describe in text, and powerful, insightful or meaningful quotations from principals in the story being told.

One key decision is about having a narrator or anchor person. Many news organizations want to insert their own narrator or rewrite scripts for VNRs and will not use products that have a company spokesperson doing the voice-over work. It is a good practice to provide video with narration only on one audio track, which permits a news organization to record its own narration and commentary on another audio track for its own use. Enabling closed captions in various languages can also be helpful for broad dissemination purposes.

In developing a VNR, however, there are other considerations to keep in mind: editing or changing a VNR is much more complex than editing a digital document. If a journalist does not find worthwhile information very quickly, it is likely that the VNR will be discarded in favor of other information that is more interesting or newsworthy and more readily used.

The production of a VNR should never be left to the last minute because of the additional requirements of editing, keeping a level of quality in video and audio throughout, and the additional steps needed in uploading and linking or distributing. It's much easier to send an electronic news release than a video release.

In that light, it is important to make sure the correct and adequate video production equipment is available. While video can be edited on a laptop or phone, the process is much easier and faster on specialized software and powerful computers because video files are so much larger than other types of digital material.

By the same token, distribution of a finished VNR may require specialized uploading software or networks or drop boxes. And it is wise to connect with possible recipients to make sure there is equipment at the receiving end that functions with your transmission technologies and standards.

When strategically created to announce, demonstrate and explain products or processes or even people, video and audio tactics can win hearts and minds.

The power of well-crafted video presentations by persuasive, knowledgeable spokespeople can hardly be overstated.

When a new computer, video game or even an advanced airliner is unveiled, video has the power to show off functions, go in depth into features and give the viewer a seemingly personal experience. Companies routinely stream announcements of new products and presentations by executives and include videos in multimedia announcement packages.

Livestreaming Video

Livestreamed events have become commonplace with the growth of video services and technical changes that make production faster, less expensive and more readily transmitted.

During the worldwide pandemic of 2020 and beyond, live video meetings became daily events and the success of video streaming opened up new opportunities for providing materials and even for interviews with newsmakers by journalists and podcasters.

Berkshire Hathaway Inc., an iconic and highly successful conglomerate run by famous investor and billionaire Warren Buffett, was a leader in streaming its annual meeting. Here is a link to the 2021 annual meeting on Yahoo Finance: https://finance.yahoo.com/brklivestream/.

Apple Inc. has been on the leading edge of this use of active media. Co-founder Steve Jobs was famous for his presentations of new products; he stood on a minimalist stage in his turtleneck sweater and jeans, and new products were projected on a giant screen behind him as he was showing them in his hand. The videos of his presentations became famous and expected; Apple executives who followed him have taken the same tack, as have other company executives.

See a classic Jobs presentation – introducing the iPhone – on YouTube here: www.youtube.com/watch?v=MnrJzXM7a6o.

Of course, Jobs was unique and a pioneer – a visionary technologist and a demanding executive. Few executives or people in general have his presence, knowledge and vision. He also knew Apple products inside out and spoke without notes. A most unusual executive.

Well-run, sophisticated organizations have learned to take advantage of video, whether for fundraising or building links with customers by demonstrating products and explaining best ways to use them.

Walmart Inc., for example, has created an online video program under its Facebook page. It's here: https://one.walmart.com/content/walmart-world/en_us.html. The program, titled "Walmart World," says by way of introduction, that it is designed as a place "where you'll find inspiration, entertainment and innovation from Walmart and Sam's Club associates around the world." The site includes interviews with Walmart executives and user content about interactions with company employees and a variety of other topics. It also is listed as the home of Walmart and Sam's Club Radio.

When Microsoft Corp. introduced Windows 11, it created a special section of its corporate website for the new operating system. The site included a variety of videos, motion graphics and interactive clickable links to show off the features of Windows 11 and to explain how it would provide value to users and how users of previous Windows operating systems could upgrade.

The new site section was highly produced, with clear, compelling graphics and demonstrations of new functions that define the system. The company streamed a 45-minute program, live and recorded, to introduce Windows 11. You can see it here: www.microsoft.com/en-us/windows/event.

When a consumer wants to understand how to use a product or solve a technical issue, the internet and video are often the first place the consumer turns. And if a company has had the foresight to produce and post videos that are easily found and show the best solutions to issues or "hacks" of products, the company can win loyalty and gratitude from consumers.

In the same vein, if a company is in a crisis situation, one of the most effective approaches to address concerns of consumers and shareholders is to create video with a credible spokesperson – preferably the senior executive if she or he has a good, calming presence.

Further, companies can ameliorate bad situations with videos that have been produced ahead of time to fit potential situations – whether an illness on a cruise ship or an oil spill or some other unfortunate incident. The caution about responses taken off the shelf is that they may be too generic and not address the specific situation that has arisen. Such products can be valuable as background information, but if not right on target or addressing the issues at hand, they can seem less than credible and out of touch.

Another option for live video is the satellite or internet-based interview. Such a series of interviews with media outlets is valuable because of the reduced time and expense compared with having personnel travel and meet with various news organizations. Satellite connections have largely given way to internet meetings, but for quality and control, satellite connections are preferred.

Here is a sample of a real satellite interview confirmation that was conducted by one of the authors.

Interview Confirmation Materials

Date:	Thursday, August 27	
Time:	6:00 a.m. – 12:00 p.m. ET	
Title:	Mother Nature: Public Enemy #1	
Interview With:	Dr. Robert Hartwig, CPCU – President and Economist, Insurance Information Institute OR Jeanne M. Salvatore, SVP, Chief Communication Officer Insurance Information Institute and Consumer Spokesperson	
Satellite:	Ku Digital: Gal 17 Downlink: 12091.0(V) FEC: ¾	Transponder: 20K Audio: 6.2 & 6.8 Symbol Rate: 12.8
Number of Cameras:	One	
Studio Location:	New York, NY	
Director/Producer:	Alex Cole	
Trouble Phone:	212-485-5166	
On-site Staff Cell:	224-715-7715	
Additional Information:	D S Simon Productions 212-736-2727 Overnight Hotline: 848-448-1317	

SUGGESTED ANCHOR LEAD-IN: SEVERE WEATHER EVENTS CAUSE BILLIONS OF DOLLARS IN DAMAGES. ON AVERAGE, DISASTERS COST THE U.S. $29 BILLION PER YEAR. HOW DO YOU KNOW IF YOU ARE READY FOR THE NEXT DISASTER? JOINING US THIS MORNING IS JEANNE SALVATORE, FROM THE NONPROFIT INSURANCE INFORMATION INSTITUTE, TO SHARE WHAT YOU NEED TO KNOW TO MAKE SURE YOU ARE COVERED. WELCOME, JEANNE!

Suggested Interview Questions:

- What are the primary lessons learned from big disasters (e.g., Hurricane Katrina, Superstorm Sandy, wildfires and earthquakes)?

- Are there any disasters not covered in standard homeowner's and rent insurance policies?
- What are the key things to consider when buying a homeowner's or rent insurance policy?
- Can you provide a disaster checklist for a small business?
- How can I save money on my homeowner's or rent insurance policy but still be properly insured?
- What do I need to know about deductibles?
- What is a home inventory and why do I need one?
- Is it ever "too late" to get more insurance or amend my current insurance policy?
- Where can I go for more information?

Station note: This segment is brought to you by the Insurance Information Institute.

Used with permission of the Insurance Information Institute.

Developing B-roll

Television and cable networks value what is called **B-roll video**. B-roll is often a series of scenes with natural sound or, in industry lingo, "nat" sound. There is no narration. It can be used to link elements of a breaking story by showing scenes that represent scenes that a bystander might see near the site of an event. B-roll can help explain operational activities of a company such as production lines or even the fronts of stores or corporate headquarters.

B-roll is often used in situations where it would be difficult, dangerous or expensive for a news organization to get their own coverage. It can also be used when the news organization is on a very tight deadline and has asked for filler footage.

Wise PR people make b-roll available so that news producers do not need to find or shoot video that might be unflattering or may even not represent the real operations or locations of a company. B-roll should be produced with and without narration so producers and editors can have a range of options when inserting it. The video without narration should include a description of what is included and specific information that can be used by a newsperson or that can be displayed as text with the video. **Note:** If there is narration, it is not B-roll; it is narrated video. Both are used by news outlets to fill out stories. Both are important tactics.

A B-roll archive is a good opportunity to review historic video and put in historically significant video for use as background or generic filler material by news organizations or others, from documentary producers to podcasters.

If creating such an archive, it is important to make sure that any footage is marked as such and contains a date so it will not be seen as current or badly produced.

Veteran journalist Grant Winter, who works for the Black News Channel (https://bnc.tv/), offers these best practices for B-roll:

- There is no narration. However, there should be natural sound, or "nat" sound. This means that if you are shooting B-roll in a park, there may be birds chirping or car horns in the distance. Inside buildings, there may be the background hum from the air conditioning or heating system.

- B-roll should be professionally shot. It is not simply something that can be recorded on your smartphone unless you have been trained in the technology. If you do shoot on a smartphone, it is important to use the landscape or portrait orientation. Use an attachment such as a gimble to keep the phone steady.
- Provide a variety of shots, including close-ups and wide shots. Each shot should be a minute long. There should be no music and no chyrons or other wording.
- Make sure to include a variety of ethnicities and genders.
- Include a shot sheet that describes what everything is and where it is happening.
- If you are shooting people, it is important that they sign releases. And, if it is a group shot, provide 24-hour notice so that anyone who does not want to be taped can be left out.
- When shooting in a factory, make sure that everything in the video is OSHA compliant. It's best to have the OSHA compliance officer at the company review what you are planning to shoot so that everything is in compliance with the law and regulations. For instance, if employees are required to wear protective gear, they should be wearing the appropriate gear in the video.
- Offer three different resolution sizes. A blogger will need a lower resolution than a broadcast station.
- Save B-roll on a company website so that a link can be emailed to a reporter. It is also okay to save B-roll on YouTube, but remember that some news organizations block access to this site. It is smart to have a Dropbox account set up to make it easy for a news outlet to access your video. And, if you are offering B-roll at a press conference or trade show, consider saving it on a thumb drive. This makes it easy for reporters to use the video and avoids Wi-Fi issues that can occur at hotels and convention centers.
- If you are looking for professional examples of how video and B-roll is best presented to journalists, look at the press rooms of car companies. BMW, for example, has a great site. You can view it at www.press.bmwgroup.com/global.

Producing YouTube Videos

YouTube has become a central marketplace of ideas and images and a visual encyclopedia. Videos on the Google-owned service cover an almost unimaginable range of human activities, from replacing a bathroom faucet to historic lectures by presidents, kings, outlaws and despots.

It's a natural place to put information and news about an organization because interested audiences may turn there before turning to the website of the organization. Further, with a free YouTube account, it is easy and fast to upload new information.

The standards for YouTube productions vary widely, but the standards for a professional communicator should always be high and fit with the organization's graphic and communications standards. It's important to remember that anything in the public domain should meet the high expectations of customers and other stakeholders. Your organization will be known for what it produces.

Documenting Speeches and Special Events

When executives make speeches or appear in pop culture situations such as podcasts or awards programs, those appearances can be added to the mix of brand building and interest-generating tools. An occasion like an executive speech at an MBA class can provide valuable information and raise the profile of the executive and the company. When such an invitation is accepted, it is important that the PR staff review the circumstances and understand who will be in the audience in addition to students and faculty and whether the sponsoring organization is planning to tape the presentation and question-and-answer period and to make the tape available.

It's wise to ask for a review of the tape before it's released to make sure there can be no misunderstandings. Often, you will be allowed to review such presentations, but occasionally not.

Strategic PR writers use the power of video to demonstrate products and services and to promote influencers and announce new options as well as fire off competitive notifications.

Writing for the Ear and Eye

When creating videos, multiple elements need to be managed for a successful project. A script is generally the basis for the planning. It contains the key messages and the structure of the project and is usually written as the basis for creating the whole piece.

Writing for hearing and listening is a different kind of skill than writing for reading. Sentences are shorter. The form is more circular. The importance of being focused, detailed and with the audience in mind are still paramount.

Then the recorded elements need to be carefully and professionally created. Any corporate video will be compared with the production values of network television and so must be well lit and carefully shot, and the audio must be clear and linked precisely to the action on the screen. Even though full-length movies have been shot with cell phones, it is best to use more traditional professional equipment and often it is worth the expense to hire professional staffers.

Even then, it is not likely that video created by a corporation or nonprofit will be a draw online or at the box office. But it may very well meet the goals of the PR campaign and improve the public opinion of the organization.

Despite the ease of creating video digitally – on smartphones or small video cameras or combination cameras that can shoot photos as well as video – there is still a requirement for skill and experience in developing and finalizing a video production.

When a production is being contemplated, one of the first decisions to make is how strategically important it is going to be. If it has the potential to reach a large audience and impact the image of the organization, serious consideration should be given to bringing in professional video producers.

If professional producers are on the ground floor, they may provide insights about how to be most effective, how to be efficient and even how to spend money wisely. Experience counts in areas from writing an impactful script to hiring supporting crew to finding the right studio or locations for the production.

When seeking professional expertise, be sure to look at work samples that parallel the project you are putting together. Some producers and directors may be very creative and innovative, but that expertise may not be required for a business production. Or it might be.

Using seasoned pros can leave the organizational communicators to do what they do best: think about the language and audiences for the tactic and not about logistics and technical details.

Podcasts

Another digital medium, podcasts have exploded on topics ranging from genealogy to auto repair. The Podcasthosting.org overview site estimated in 2021 that worldwide there were more than two million podcasts and more than 48 million episodes (podcasthosting.org/podcast-statistics). Many mainstream media outlets, including the New York Times, produce daily podcasts where they provide listeners the news of the day in an audio-focused format.

The definition of "podcasting" can be fluid, ranging from a recording on a smartphone to a highly produced audio show with multiple speakers spread across the globe to video podcasts.

The chief executive officer at PayPal has his own podcast called "Never Stand Still" where he interviews other leaders about variety of issues. See it at https://podcasts.apple.com/us/podcast/never-stand-still/id1394307884.

The head of PR for a New York City real estate firm suggests that appearances on industry-specific podcasts can be positive for organization image and branding. Before recommending that a representative accept an invitation to appear on a podcast, it would be important to understand the parameters of the planned discussion.

National Public Radio has even put out a book recounting the staff's experience with podcasts and offering advice to would-be podcasters. Here's a quote:

> Well before we launch any new podcast, we at NPR ask ourselves a long series of questions that hit on every aspect of what the podcast will be – format, length, tone, intent, originality, audience, sound design, budget, staff and so on. These questions get asked and answered over months in meetings.
>
> Weldon, NPR's Podcast Start Up Guide, 2021

Ask questions like:

- Is the invitation only for the organization's representative or will there be others – even competitors or gadflies who have a negative point of view about the organization or the industry in general?
- What specifically are the topics to be discussed? Can you get a draft of the questions?
- How long will the interview last?
- Will this be a standalone program or one segment of a multiple-topic edition?
- Where is the podcast distributed (e.g., Spotify, Apple Music, web only)?

- Is there any information about the number of listeners and a demographic profile of them?
- Is there any opportunity to listen to the interview before it's published or posted? This is not often permitted, but it never hurts to ask.
- Who will be the interviewer? What is this person's background?
- Who else has participated in this series before?

In 2021, Nielsen Holdings PLC launched a highly focused measurement function for ads in podcasts, in a sense showing the impact of this communications tool and giving it a tacit seal of approval as a mass media option for organizations (Nielsen Podcast Effectiveness, www.nielsen.com/us/en/solutions/podcasting/podcast-ad-effectiveness/).

Nielsen's new tool, while created for advertisers, is called the Podcast Ad Effectiveness solution. It's designed to measure the effectiveness of podcast advertising, including brand lift and memorability across podcasting audiences (Podcast Content is Growing Audio Engagement, www.nielsen.com/us/en/insights/article/2020/podcast-content-is-growing-audio-engagement/).

Podcasts for public relations can help build an organization's reputation for expertise, innovation and openness. A well-planned, well-executed podcast can build an audience over time and help establish a positive environment where the organization operates – brand building, in essence.

If a podcast is going to cover a current topic in the news or to break news, the PR team should contact interested outlets and journalists and even offer previews or access to the newsmakers.

There are some technical and production standards that should be observed for best outcomes. If you are not an experienced audio editor, it may be worthwhile to hire a company or an experienced editor to do the technical work or to help you until you gain the skills. There may be people in the technology department of your organization or the client's IT group who can perform these tasks.

Here are some areas to remember when planning and creating a podcast:

1. Focus: Audiences are pressed for time. It goes without saying. And despite the fact that podcasts are portable and readily accessed, people will not seek them out if the topics are not valuable and not timely. It is best to limit the topics in each episode. The number will depend on how much information is needed to cover a topic and the estimate of how informed the audience is about the topic.

2. Length: Again, the length of time for the podcast will depend on the topic. But more than half an hour is probably too long on a regular basis. It is wise to create two or three episodes to practice pacing and interactions between hosts if that is part of the design and to iron out technical hiccups.

3. Audio quality: Audiences will not tune into a spoken word – versus music or other special effects – for the quality of the sound, but listeners likely will not put up with seriously deficient sound quality. It is a good idea to buy USB microphones for all people who will be talking – don't forget that you may have guests. And try to establish your recording space where you have strong,

consistent internet connections if not all of the participants are together. Encourage speakers not to try to participate from their phones.

4. Frequency: Launching a podcast should not be done without a commitment to creating one regularly. And a general approach should be once a week or every two weeks. Any less than that makes your podcast too easy to forget and may show the audience that the organization is not very active and does not have much new to say. Once the podcast is launched, it should appear at approximately the same time every time it's due. In other words, when launched on a Monday, future episodes should appear on Mondays.

5. Technology: Podcast technology is not complicated and there is a wide range of software applications that can record voices, even from multiple sources, and then can provide basic editing functions. Most work with computers of all types, including smartphones. Software such as Audacity or GarageBand will help you save the audio file as an MP3 for widest distribution and upload it to a site where you want to make it available. That can be on a dedicated segment of the organization site, linked from the home page or on a podcast aggregation site, which range from Stitcher to iTunes to Spotify and many others. You can upload to all of the options for widest access, or you may want to only appear on certain sites that are favorites of your audience.

6. Branding and appearance: Because podcasts are audio, it's almost an after-thought to create a visual identity for them. But when they are posted to a podcasting site, a graphic may be the first element that a potential listener sees or is attracted to. Lack of one certainly reflects a lack of attention to details and is a serious missed opportunity. Like any good graphic, the "slate" for your podcast should carry minimal words – just the title and a corporate or personal ID. Resist the temptation to include a microphone photo or graphic – it's obvious. And it's a good idea to review the art of competitive podcasts and make sure yours is different and stands out. Different podcast sites may have different standards for graphic file types and sizes. Be sure to check the requirements for the places you want to have your podcasts appear.

7. Podcast directories: Here is a list of some of the major directories where podcasts can be uploaded and where potential audiences can find podcasts on a wide variety of topics: Apple Podcasts, Spotify, Google Podcasts, Stitcher, iHeartRadio, TuneIn, Alexa, Overcast, PocketCasts, Castro, Castbox, and Podchaser. While it is possible to approach each directory, there are services that will take your recording and distribute it to the outlets of your choice and make sure it matches the technical requirements of the chosen sites.

8. Preparation: Similar to a video interview where your intent is the conversation to flow naturally and comfortably, it is best practice to set time for the interviewer and interviewee to connect prior to the recording or the podcast so they can familiarize themselves with each other, get comfortable with the nature of the discussion and go through specifics on any particular questions in advance.

9. Another tip: To make your podcast even more valuable and increase the opportunity for search engines to find the information you have created, you may want to consider having the whole program transcribed and posted, either on the organization site or elsewhere that you can access.

Writing for Podcasts

Podcasts by their nature are conversational and can be open to spontaneous thoughts and comments.

In that light, scripting can reduce the effectiveness by reducing the interest and creative conversations.

That doesn't mean that each episode should be done by the seat of the pants. Planning to define topics, some research for data and facts will improve the outcome by keeping the discussions on track and valuable for listeners.

The role of the host (it's recommended that there be a lead person even if only two people are talking) is to keep the conversation on track and to keep an eye on the clock to bring segments or the whole episode near the planned episode limits.

Writing for a podcast is similar to writing for video – the sentences and phrasing is straightforward and clearly focused. It often is best to set out the key points for the program in the beginning and then remind listeners as you move through the steps. At the end, sum up using those same key focus areas.

Many podcasts are relatively unstructured and resemble conversations. Even these need to be planned so they don't become random and disorganized. At minimum, the host should have introductory remarks that explain the topic, the background of the guest or guests and demonstrate the order of the discussion. At the end, a summary should be given with any information about getting further information on what was discussed.

Another podcast option is to have a spokesperson record information and make it available on the organization website. The spokesperson will simply state their name, spell their name and say what they can talk about. The recording is best if video. Many syndicated radio programs are including video links so that the show can be viewed as well as heard.

Producers want to see someone before they will put the person on air. Also, many interviews are now conducted by computer. TV stations now will interview someone through WebEx or Zoom. And big companies are set up with satellites to make it easy to interview executives and spokesperson. Lastly, newsrooms also provide audio.

Chapter Summary

- Electronic communications can be powerful tools in strategic PR programs.
- Video in particular has enormous power to demonstrate functionality and to show off individuals.
- The possible downside of video is that people are used to watching good television, so amateurish products reflect badly on the sponsor.

- The internet and social media have made video a potential damaging factor for company detractors or disgruntled employees. More and more organizations are using video regularly for major and minor communications inside and outside the walls of the organization.
- It is wise to explore using proven video production teams when a video production is designed to have significant impact on target audiences.
- Podcasts can provide another powerful tool for organizations to provide information in a convenient, conversational style. They may be interactive with listeners when online live or to answer submitted questions.

Exercises

1. Go to the newsroom of a Fortune 500 company and see if videos of products or announcements or executive presentations are posted. Watch one and analyze the messaging. Is it effective? Who do you think it's aimed at – what audience or audiences? Do you think it represents the brand of the organization well? Is the language readily understandable?

2. Go to the newsroom of a major nonprofit or nongovernmental organization. See if videos of activities or executive presentations are posted or linked. Watch one and analyze the messaging. Is it effective? Who do you think it's aimed at – what audience or audiences? Do you think it represents the brand of the organization well? Is the language readily understandable?

3. Try writing a video script based on a news release your professor provides or that you have found at an organization you are interested in. Follow the precepts of the chapter.

4. Search for business or public relations podcasts on Spotify or iHeartradio or other podcasting sites. Listen to two or three of them. What do they have in common? How do they differ? How would you improve the presentation to help the company image or to build loyalty?

5. Look across a company's various owned channels where they share video content. Can you find examples of content focused on the same topic but produced in a different way to best meet the needs of the forum in which it is being shared and the audience? (Does a company post different kinds of content announcing a new product or service on its newsroom versus YouTube versus Instagram? How are they different?)

References

Apple Computer Inc. via YouTube. www.youtube.com/watch?v=MnrJzXM7a6o

Berkshire Hathaway, Inc. Live Stream Video via Yahoo Finance. https://finance.yahoo.com/brklivestream/

Buffer. https://buffer.com/state-of-social-2019

Clifford, S. (2009). Video Prank at Domino's Taints Brand. *The New York Times*, April 15, 2009. www.nytimes.com/2009/04/16/business/media/16dominos.html

Nielsen Podcast Effectiveness. www.nielsen.com/us/en/solutions/podcasting/podcast-ad-effectiveness/

Pay Pal CEO Podcast. https://podcasts.apple.com/us/podcast/never-stand-still/id1394307884

Podcast Content is Growing Audio Engagement. www.nielsen.com/us/en/insights/article/2020/podcast-content-is-growing-audio-engagement/

Sadowski, M. (2018). Five Reasons Why Video Will be Crucial for PR in 2018. *Forbes*, January 5, 2018. Five Reasons Why Video Will Be Crucial For PR In 2018 (forbes.com)

SEO Inc. (2020). *Video is 50x More Likely to Get Organic Ranking than Plain Text Results*. www.seoinc.com/seo-blog/seo-statistics-youtube-2020/

Walmart World Website. https://one.walmart.com/content/walmart-world/en_us.html

Weldon, G. (2021). *NPR's Podcast Start Up Guide*. Ten Speed Press.

Worldwide Podcast Estimate. www.PodcastHosting.org

11 SPEECHES FOR MEETINGS, CRISES AND OTHER SITUATIONS

Learning Goals for This Chapter

After reading this chapter, you should be able to:

- Discuss how presentations fit into PR programs and planning.
- Describe the role of PR professionals in developing spoken communications.
- Explain the differences between written and vocalized public relations products.
- List and analyze various speaking opportunities and how they relate to public relations.
- Demonstrate the ability to analyze and create PR materials for presentation.

Spoken communications have power that is different from words on a page. It's more personal and carries nuances that printed words don't.

A well-written and powerfully presented speech can be an unmatched tool in the public relations tool kit.

When people see and hear a speech, they feel as if they are living in the moment, that the speaker is addressing them. Add to that the fact that speeches often mark important events or notices. Think of these speeches:

- President Bush telling U.S. citizens that thousands of people had died on September 11, 2001, the victims of a terrorist attack, and his subsequent visit to the smoking ruins in New York City where he declared "I can hear you. I can hear you. The rest of the world hears you. And the people who knocked these buildings down will hear all of us soon." See it here: www.youtube.com/watch?v=zi2SNFnfMjk.
- President Obama announcing the death of Osama bin Laden, the leader of the terrorist group responsible for the 9/11 attacks. See it here: www.youtube.com/watch?v=ZNYmK19-d0U.
- Martin Luther King, Jr. giving the "I Have a Dream" speech on the steps of the Lincoln Memorial, which was ranked first among the 100 most significant

DOI: 10.4324/9781003248330-11

American political speeches of the 20th century by scholars polled by the American Rhetoric website. See it here: www.youtube.com/watch?v=vP4iY1TtS3s.

Drafting remarks for a wide variety of situations is a core strategic communications task.

Preparing presentations at conferences and meetings is an important strategic writing skill. The PR writer may be writing for himself or herself. But, in most cases, they will be writing for clients or company executives. This means that they not only have to write for the format but they need to write in the voice of their "client" to a very specific audience.

Such writing requires a special, conversational skill as well as the ability to adopt the speaker's style and key phrases. It's a unique skill, but it can be done effectively by using fundamental writing skills: know the audience; know the speaker; write coherently, with specific goals in mind; and be extra careful to be precise and factual.

These same guidelines apply in media interviews but with a key difference. Strategies for media interviews should focus on short, interesting, factual quotes. Media outlets and media consumers have little patience for long, meandering explanations.

Make the main point of an answer very near the beginning, not toward the end. Be conversational and natural, but not too comfortable or folksy.

Personal presentations have influence that can have enormous positive results. Memorable speeches by chief executives often become part of the brand and the public personality of the organizations they head. Steve Jobs, the late chief executive and co-founder of Apple Inc., was well known for his presentations in a dark turtleneck at yearly product introductions. He was a unique leader, completely at home with technology and business and eager to take the stage.

Few PR people are so lucky as to work for such a charismatic and knowledgeable boss.

Nonetheless, creating messages for formal speeches, congressional testimony, product introductions, media interviews or crisis situations – among many, many situations – is one of the roles the PR writer plays.

The Craft of Writing for Someone Else

Putting words in someone else's mouth is a delicate and sometimes tricky process.

There are multiple considerations in developing **"talking points"** for others to use. At the highest levels of organizations, speechwriters are highly focused, highly literate, business savvy and adaptable. They often work closely with their clients, learning everything from types of humor enjoyed to what words are difficult for a person to pronounce and should be avoided.

Some executives appreciate a well-turned phrase and will gladly take well-written, well-researched material that has been adapted to their personal style and desires.

Others may be very comfortable with the material – like Jobs – and only need a set of bullet points that provide details and nuances for the specific situation and audience.

The majority of executives, however, will probably want the comfort of having a script, which will keep them organized and help them get complex ideas across. It is the responsibility of the communications professional to make sure that executives are given proven, double-checked information and that it is crafted so that the intent and the direction is clear and obvious.

Writing a speech calls for discipline. It is tempting to use great-sounding quotations from Shakespeare or the Bible or even from contemporary culture. But it is the responsibility of the writer to make sure that any references or quotes are right on target and that the speaker is familiar with them and comfortable using them. For example, if a name or place can be misconstrued or easily mispronounced, the writer must spell it out phonetically to ensure that it's pronounced properly.

At the same time, the goals of the organization must be kept in mind. For example, there may be specific strategic messages that need to be included in virtually every communication and be synchronized with other communications activities – from advertising to speeches that are happening concurrently and all other materials being generated.

For the most part, creating materials for presentations will parallel the processes and requirements of other PR activities:

- An understanding of the strategic goal or goals of the presentation
- An analysis of the audience and an understanding of any pending issues or expectations
- Confirmation and knowledge of specialized or arcane legal, technical or financial situations or announcements
- Specialized intelligence about potential disruptors or competitors

In addition, personal appearances require other information such as times, addresses and specific room numbers, any audio/visual requirements, and knowledge about others who may be speaking or who may be introducing the speaker. The PR person is often responsible for gathering background information about organizations, other executives, current issues or conflicts, and, if possible, the topics being covered by others as well as recent presentations by others from the same company to reduce overlap or repetition.

Specific Presentation Situations

Annual meetings. Like the name suggests, most publicly traded companies hold annual meetings of stockholders where the top executives are expected to talk about the company performance for the previous year and give some indication of the future – though such information is limited by regulations and by worries about not living up to expectations.

Other business that often comes up at annual meetings are issues that shareholders or corporate gadflies want to raise at annual meetings, which they see as an opportunity to confront executives and board members with complaints and other topics. At the annual meeting, there also are announcements about changes to a company's board of directors and other governance issues.

The speeches at the annual meeting by the CEO and chief financial officer are closely watched by security analysts and journalists for hints or suggestions about the future performance of the company. Some firms record the speeches and make them available to the media, shareholders and general public. You can find them at the Investors section of major companies.

Also at annual meetings are periods when executives, generally led by the CEO, take questions from the audience.

In preparation for what could be a very broad range of questions, some CEOs spend a good deal of time going over literally hundreds of questions on topics ranging from finance to human resources to good corporate citizenship. All of the answers to those questions as well as the speeches for the meeting need to be perused by the PR staff – which may also write many of them – for possible communications issues and to make sure the answers are consistent with current strategies and branding and positions on issues.

Typical questions may include:

- Why do the executives make so much more money than the average employee?
- Why does the company do business with some country?
- What is the organization doing to recruit minority employees and executives?
- When will the company become carbon-neutral?

Crisis Situations

Crises are a fact of life for modern organizations – whether product recalls or environment-damaging events or social issues or alleged criminal activity. Executives must be prepped to handle public and media interactions in tense and emotional situations.

Press relations and presentations are vital and can make the difference between a huge, brand-crushing disaster and a situation in which an organization can receive empathy and admiration for its response.

As mentioned in Chapter 3, in June of 2016, when a 2-year-old boy was dragged into a lake by an alligator at the Disney Grand Floridian Resort and Spa, the company could hardly have faced a more emotional and heart-wrenching situation.

The child was found soon after, drowned after being taken under the water by the alligator, and media from around the world focused on the company that offered "the happiest place on earth."

The PR actions of the company were quick and professional. Even though CEO Robert Iger was in China at the opening of a new park, he was kept informed of the events and issued this statement: "As a parent and a grandparent, my heart goes out to the Graves family during this time of devastating loss. My thoughts and prayers are with them, and I know everyone at Disney joins me in offering our deepest sympathies." He also spoke with the parents of the dead boy (DiPietro, 2016).

The head of Disney theme parks was sent back as quickly as possible. In the meantime, press relations went to work and provided access to the press and frequent briefings as the search for the child progressed.

The company showed concern for the family and immediately closed parts of the park for other visitors. Gamekeepers cleared the lake of alligators and the situation was managed as well as could be, given the sad and virtually unimaginable situation.

It is difficult to imagine all possible crises that might befall an organization, but professional PR people take time to game out the ones that are most likely – an oil spill at a petroleum company or recalls at grocery suppliers, toy manufacturers or car companies, for example. And plans should be put in place in case the worst case happens.

Such plans and crisis kits can include such items as:

- Lists of critical personnel with all contact information (crises don't just happen during working hours)
- Drafts of releases for various kinds of crises, based on history and experience of other organizations in your industry or area of operation
- Lists of questions and answers based on the situations and what could happen in various scenarios
- Contact information for media representatives who cover the organization and can be brought in for briefings and visits as appropriate

Media Interviews and Press Conferences

In the current environment of the 24-hour, worldwide news cycle, executives are often called to give their views on news or trends, not necessarily related to events or announcements. Even spur of the moment interviews need to be managed because they can be turned into unwanted news if a comment is made that is either misinterpreted or does not represent the most current information.

The chairman of BP was captured on video after the Deepwater Horizon explosion and oil spill in the Gulf of Mexico where 11 workers were killed. He unfortunately said, "There's no one who wants this thing over more than I do. I want my life back." He later apologized, but his words and demeanor went viral and severely damaged the company's reputation.

Press conferences require careful planning and organization. The goals and the talking points need to be carefully defined and there should be written notes even if the presenter or presenters are skills and experienced at public interactions. The PR staff should define the parameters with invited media and establish ground rules on how long the conference will run and often will act as moderators to introduce speakers and acknowledge the questioners to maintain order.

Product Introductions

The unveiling of new products can be exciting and nerve wracking. As the saying goes, you only have one chance to make a first impression.

When an organization does something new, especially announcing a new product or a major upgrade to existing products, the announcement provides an opportunity to demonstrate leadership, to support the company brand and direction, to talk about particular expertise and at times to introduce personnel to the public.

In other words, the overall strategic communications direction should be the guiding framework for introductions of products or such strategic actions as acquisition of another company or a partnership or even the announcement that a segment of a company is being sold.

Some occasions require or suggest executive presence and presentations. At those times, a public relations person should be the host or emcee of the meeting and act as the linkage between parts of the program, guiding the audience to various activities from demonstrations to executive speakers to celebrities who are endorsing the product. The PR person also will manage the press conference, calling on media members for questions and defining the rules of the engagement – keeping the focus on the announcement and calling an end to the conference when time is up.

Guest Lectures, TED Talks

Corporate executives and professionals such as researchers or marketing heads are popular speakers at business schools, and while meeting a classroom full of MBA students may sound pretty mundane, it can be a PR situation. Universities sometimes invite the press to cover a celebrity executive and students may generate questions that go beyond the stated topic of the lecture or discussion.

For these reasons, PR should be aware of any outside speaking engagements and should usually be involved in preparing the remarks to ensure that the discussion does not lead to topics that the speaker is not involved in or capable of discussing. For example, if a computer software executive were to be asked about a company's policy for selling products to a country in the news, he or she would not be likely to have the latest information or to have a detailed and nuanced answer – if the company has a position and an answer for such a question.

Another powerful and widely viewed type of executive presentation is a **TED Talk**. The TED organization is a nonprofit that has been around since 1984 when it started as a meeting of creative people who wanted to share ideas in punchy, concise talks. Short was the defining concept. Most talks were 18 minutes or less and focused on a single topic. TED, by the way, stands for technology, entertainment and design, but the talks have evolved to cover virtually any topic in the human imagination – from science to business to global issues, in more than 100 languages.

The TED.com website puts it this way:

We're building a clearinghouse of free knowledge from the world's most inspired thinkers – and a community of curious souls to engage with ideas and each other, both online and at TED and TEDx events around the world, all year long.

Competition to be on the stage is tough; many apply and few are chosen. *Inc.* magazine wrote:

Everyone wants to speak on TED's stage – doing so automatically establishes you as a thought leader in your industry. Because TED wants ideas worth sharing, the chance of your talk going viral makes it the modern equivalent of the printing press.

In addition, being a TED speaker opens up multiple opportunities for cross-promotions and for further speaking and writing engagements. It can be a real promotional bonanza.

Introductions of Speakers

At times, an executive may be asked to introduce another speaker, whether as a guest of the organization or at an association meeting where the executive has a role. In those situations, unless the executive has personal knowledge of the person being introduced, it may be up to the public relations department to do background research and create the introductory remarks. PR is often the chosen function for these kinds of tasks because PR people are focused outside of the organization and are aware of issues that might be looming and that may affect even the most mundane task. For example, if asked to introduce a potential political candidate, an organization executive should be aware of the possibility that the introduction could be seen as an endorsement or that he or she might be linked with the politician in the future.

By the same token, introductions should be straightforward and lack any attempts at humor or contemporary pop culture references that could be misinterpreted or embarrass the person being introduced. A sophisticated PR person will be aware of issues like these and will caution executives to err on the side of understatement.

Panel Discussions

It might be concluded that sitting on a panel is easy and doesn't require much more than showing up.

As previous examples have demonstrated, many different scenarios can spiral into a PR quagmire if proper care and research are not exercised. For example, the PR person should examine the context for the panel and who the other members are. Do they or the sponsoring organization have a history of being controversial on topics that your organization does not want to discuss or be associated with? Has the invited executive had previous interactions with any of the other panel members? How much time is going to be given to presentation and how much to discussion or questions from the audience?

Scripts for panel discussions are typically abbreviated and don't last more than five minutes or so and as such need to be highly refined and edited. The amount of time available for making your point is small and the stage is being shared. Preparation for such events should also include a list of expected questions with suggested bulleted answers.

Chapter Summary

Live presentations can be powerful communications actions but require special, careful preparation, not only in writing but in understanding the circumstances and expectations.

PR people should be involved in planning and vetting appearances by executives no matter how mundane or seemingly harmless.

Writing for others is a specialized skill, but the words must reflect the overall goals and branding of the organization.

PR people are good choices for understanding the implications of public presentations because they are focused on the word outside the organization and current climate.

Exercises

1. Go to the American Rhetoric website and listen to one of the top ten speeches of the 20th century. What elements made it special or distinctive? Write a news release as if you were promoting the speech and it had not been given yet.

2. Find a product announcement on a company website or on YouTube. Analyze the presentations for effectiveness, clear presentation of ideas, support of the organization brand and overall coherence. Was the presenter prepared and did she or he seem to know the material well? Did the overall presentation hold together and were transitions smooth and logical? What do you think could have been done better?

3. Take a news release from BusinessWire or an organization you are interested in and write talking points for a news conference introduction. Write a paragraph about who you imagine the audience to be and the level of knowledge that you estimate members of the audience will have.

4. Go to the TED Talks website (TED.com/talks) and choose a business or nonprofit talk to watch. Write a news release as if you were working for the speaker and the speaker's organization. Create a promotional plan for the talk. What news outlets or other platforms would you send it to? Where else might you send notifications and links to the talk for the greatest promotional impact?

Glossary

Talking points – key messages that need to be the focus of a presentation. They should emphasize the strategy of the public relations activity. May include press discussions, speeches or employee meetings.

References

American Rhetoric Website. https://americanrhetoric.com/newtop100speeches.htm
BusinessWire Current Releases. www.businesswire.com/portal/site/home/news/
President Bush at Ground Zero. www.youtube.com/watch?v=zi2SNFnfMjk
President Obama Announcing Death of Osama bin Laden. www.youtube.com/watch?v=ZNYmK19-d0U
Rev. Martin Luther King "I Have a Dream" Speech. www.youtube.com/watch?v=vP4iY1TtS3s
TED.com. www.ted.com/about/our-organization

12 BLOGS, VLOGS AND NEWSLETTERS

Learning Goals for This Chapter

After reading this chapter, you should be able to:

- Discuss the strategic functions of blogs, vlogs and newsletters.
- Determine which tactic is best for your communications goals and objectives.
- Know how to produce each tactic.
- Talk about production issues that can accompany each of these.

Blogs, vlogs and newsletters have one essential element in common: they are long-term forms of strategic communications for all types of organizations from small to huge, from nonprofits to powerhouses of industry, from private to publicly traded. They have another common element: they are products of planning, strategic writing, careful and detailed execution, and, typically, digital distribution.

Unlike producing a video for a specific event or creating an infographic to explain a complicated issue, these tactics should be launched with the intent of producing them regularly from weekly to monthly.

All three can be powerful and effective communications tools. But clear goals need to be in place for producing them. The goals must fit into the strategic direction and planning for the organization, focus on specific target audiences, be specific and clear in presenting information and messages, work within the accepted standards and protocols of the medium, and be developed with an eye toward measurable effectiveness.

It is important to remember that the decision to launch a specific PR tactic should never be based simply on what is new or simply dismissed out of hand for being an older form of communication. Instead, it is important to understand exactly what these tactics can do, who they can reach and the resources it will take to make them successfully.

This chapter details how to decide if blogs, vlogs or newsletters fit into a strategic communications plan. It also provides tips on how to produce these important tactics.

DOI: 10.4324/9781003248330-12

Some definitions:

- **Blogs** started as online diaries or journals and were originally named weblogs. Early adopters of internet communications often kept a weblog to keep track of projects or to share information with a select group of people or just to have a handy way of maintaining a personal account with private observations. Today, blogs range from personal memoirs to powerful online publications from organizations and individuals who have products or points of view to promote and share.

  In 2020, 89% of companies that were selling to other businesses – business-to-business companies – that were surveyed were blogging as part of their overall communications and marketing strategies. This was the conclusion of a study called B2B Content Marketing 2020: Benchmarks, Budgets and Trends – North America produced by the Content Marketing Institute and MarketingProfs.

  According to the survey by the Content Marketing Institute (https://contentmarketinginstitute.com/2020/09/b2b-industry-benchmarks-budgets-trends-research/), 86% of companies distribute content on blogs linked to their websites.

- **Vlogs** are very similar to blogs but have the added dimension of being video enhanced. Their creation and expansion grew out of blogs and paralleled the ease of producing video and the explosion of video uploads. Vlogs and video podcasts can easily be lumped together. Video, as in other applications, has the value of being highly credible and can be used to demonstrate all kinds of products or materials or documents and even other videos. The great growth of Zoom, Microsoft Teams, Slack and other video streaming services during the COVID-19 pandemic has increased the comfort with using video services and spawned many new approaches and vlogs for learning and communicating. Blog posts with videos exhibit a 157% increase in search traffic compared with blog posts that are solely text based, according to a posting by Brightcove Inc., a technology company (www.brightcove.com/en/resources/blog/create-compelling-video-experiences/).

- While blogs and vlogs are newer PR tactics, **newsletters** have been used by PR departments and for other communications functions for decades.

  In fact, writing and printing company newsletters was one of the primary functions of many PR writers, especially those working for corporations. Today, most newsletters are electronic and are designed to be distributed via email and easily viewed on mobile devices.

  A well-written newsletter can be used for marketing purposes, for internal communications or to update important audiences about issues, products and new ideas. Newsletters can be powerful and effective communications vehicles. But, like blogs and vlogs, there must be a clear reason for producing them. They also have to be designed and written with a specific target audience in mind. Newsletters also should be published on a regular basis. They can be daily, weekly, monthly or quarterly. You need to commit to the regular publication of a newsletter with new and valuable content for it to be successful.

Strategic Blogging

The information carried on an organizational blog can be vital and instructive for persons interested in the industry or specifics of the organization. The blog can be a kind of "information, please" tool for any person looking for information. And because blogs are generally written in a conversational but professional style, they may be more approachable and attractive to readers.

Even more than the "About" boilerplate on a website, though, blogs have come to be contemporary, timely sources of information. They carry updates about everything from a new product to insights into corporate good works and social responsibility.

Here is a screenshot of the blogging site created by McKinsey & Company, one of the world's leading management consultants. You can see how it is friendly and inviting even though the topics are serious issues that are faced by major organizations. It clearly has been designed to attract readers – as suggested by the comment in parentheses.

≡   McKinsey
     & Company   Industries   Functions   Featured Insights   Locations   Careers   About Us   McKinsey Blog

‹ Back to McKinsey Themes

Get up to speed with McKinsey blogs

November 13, 2021 - In an era of information overload, "short and sweet" can be refreshing *and* informative. On National Blog Posting Month, or #NaBloPoMo, get up to speed on the business and management issues that matter with the latest

Figure 12.1 McKinsey screenshot
Source: www.mckinsey.com/about-us/new-at-mckinsey-blog

However, the blogs must have clear goals and be directed to a specific target audience. If you recommend that your client or organization launch a blog, there must be a strategic decision regarding "authoring" the blog. A blog can have multiple writers, each with a distinct personality and style, but those distinctions should be clearly delineated with bylines and a unique title.

Because blogs are online and readily updated and posted, they can be as current as today's news and can be readily used by the communications function to carry messages and support branding and strategic initiatives of the organization.

In addition, bloggers can be creative and quick at the same time. Blogs can carry examples of video showing newly announced products or projects that the organization is supporting – complete with video and other supporting digital materials.

For example, Home Depot, a nationwide seller in the United States of home products and services, used blogging as a key element of its campaign to increase rentals of specialized equipment by both professional contractors and experiences do-it-yourselfers – labeled DIYers – who do their own renovations. The campaign won a Silver Anvil Award from the Public Relations Society of America.

After doing detailed research about the target audiences, Home Depot, according to its Silver Anvil Award submission, created separate lines of communication for the two groups.

As stated in the Silver Anvil application, a central point for both groups, however, was the importance of online searching for information on where to find specific products and specialized equipment. The agency supporting Home Depot concluded that demonstrations in the form of videos and stop-action presentations would be valued by pros and DIYers, so a series of productions was created.

In addition to using paid social media ads and information, Home Depot used a blogging strategy to support its efforts to build awareness and to drive web traffic. Every month, four blog posts were generated – three of which targeted pros to encourage rentals of the equipment featured and one aimed at DIYers that highlighted seasonally relevant projects. The blogs included topics such as equipment highlights and specific features, how-to projects and project tips.

The campaign was a large success and resulted in a series of record weeks of tool rentals and a concurrent increase in revenue. Brand awareness for Home Depot also increased.

Another phenomenon has emerged as organizations support and depend on blogging as a friendly, accommodating communications method. Many bloggers have become influential voices in their fields. In other situations, senior management often feels the need to launch a blog to voice an opinion or to demonstrate thought leadership in the organization's field or industry.

Organization blogs should be written in a conversational, virtually personal style. They often link to articles on other websites and can be useful tools for boosting SEO – search engine optimization – on a company's website. Most blogs focus on a particular topic for a specific audience. They also can be useful for internal communications, thought leadership or even marketing purposes.

Using a blog is much more timely than waiting for an opportunity to make a speech or writing an op-ed for a general-purpose or industry-specific publication. The organization has control of the timing, the language and the promotional activities and can merchandise the blog with other forms of communication from tweets to media alerts to messages to key shareholders.

From a cost point of view, blogging is much less expensive than advertising or even sending news releases through a distribution service. That lowered cost factor makes blogging attractive to nonprofit organizations of all kinds from universities to professional associations to special-interest groups that focus on specific diseases or social problems.

For instance, it may make sense for a CEO to blog to employees about the direction of the company. However, most CEOs don't pen their own blogs. Instead, the PR writer at the company will write in the CEO's voice for his or her approval. Decisions will also need to be made about how often to blog and what other blogs or websites will be linked to or mentioned. Done right, a blog can successfully communicate key information to important audiences. Done wrong, it be an embarrassing waste of time and money.

Vlogs – Video As the Foundation

A vlog, which should have the same informal tone as a blog, can also be an effective tactic. Video is very engaging and can easily be sharable on social media. Producing video keeps getting easier. But there must be a clear reason for communicating with video. And it must be a medium that is going to appeal to your target audience. And, like a blog, you must commit to producing new content on a regular basis.

Although creating videos has become routine, creating videos for posting and to represent yourself, your boss, the big boss or your organization is not a project to be taken lightly. Creating videos for public consumption requires you to plan, shoot, review, edit and finalize before posting. You have to spend time and energy and make sure your final product is something you are proud of and meets your communications goals.

Remember, you are in competition with huge organizations and with experienced producers. Viewers have little patience for videos that don't immediately attract them or that are technically unsophisticated or low quality.

Here are some items to keep in mind:

- What kind of video equipment do you have access to? For the most basic projects, a good smartphone may suffice. But it won't be forgiving in low-light or noisy situations. It may be worth renting a professional camera with good sound equipment.
- Do you have an interesting, newsworthy topic? Have you checked the competition for similar vlogs on your proposed topic? It's never a good idea to be repetitive.
- What kind of editing equipment can you access, and do you know how to use it? Phones and video cameras have limited editing capabilities, but more sophisticated effects and quality are more readily available on computer-based software. In addition, the software can support the addition of graphics and improve sound quality and the addition of music.
- You definitely should edit and polish your video before uploading to the internet, where it will compete with many other productions for eyeballs.

The Continuing Value of Newsletters

While blogs and vlogs are newer PR tactics, newsletters have been used by PR departments for decades. In fact, writing and printing company newsletters was one of the primary functions of many PR writers – especially those working for corporations. Newsletters are sometimes dismissed as being old fashioned. Different audiences appreciate having a document that is received in the mail or that can be downloaded.

Today, most newsletters are electronic and are designed to be distributed via email and easily viewed on mobile devices. Some are developed by professional designers who create a set of branded templates that can be put together for specific topics – such as calendars or celebrations – or can be used for text and photos about organizational events and promotions.

If an organization has a set of design guidelines, there is a wealth of cost-free templates and formatted structures for creating newsletters available online or in Microsoft Word or Publisher or from the Google Docs template gallery.

Lauren Young, an editor for Digital Special Projects at financial news outlet Reuters, writes and edits a biweekly digital newsletter aimed at people who are relatively new to managing their own money. It's called "Young Money" and addresses issues of salaries, savings, investing, workplace situations and a wealth of questions. She writes about a number of topics in each newsletter but adds the option for readers to send her questions, which she often poses to financial experts. See her blog here: https://twitter.com/Reuters/status/1430204622715723780

Those questions can include topics such as the amount of money to have when thinking about quitting a job or taking a year off from work, the value of spending a semester or year studying outside the United States and the outlook for the price of houses.

The newsletter is purely digital and is published via LinkedIn, the professional networking and collaboration site, which hosts newsletters as part of its service. It has almost 4,000 subscribers and is clearly aimed at younger workers and focuses on both timely issues like the outlook for inflation and time-tested topics like how much money should be in a rainy-day fund.

One of the authors consulted with a youth organization that had been using a printed newsletter format as the primary method of communicating with parents and the adolescent clients who engaged in a wide range of activities each year from campouts to door-to-door sales and summer camps. The newsletter was designed and edited using desktop software; it was printed on a color printer, stapled and mailed to the homes of participating young people.

The newsletter had accumulated a variety of sections over time and did not have a consistent look and feel – as would be expected of a sophisticated, branded organization. Further, the production process took most of the month to design, copy-fit and read both for content and for approval by various staff members. As a result, some material was dated when the newsletter arrived at homes.

A survey of parents and youth was conducted, and the results were not surprising: the newsletter was not widely read or used. Most of the parents and youths were digitally literate and wanted timely information and reminders via email or text or on the organization website.

The management took the feedback and consulting advice to heart, revamping the website and creating email blasts that were timely, allowed for planning and even could be linked to the individual calendars of recipients.

Positive feedback came rushing back from recipients, and the organization saved important funds that were then directed into programs and events that were valued by the clients. The newsletter itself was not entirely discarded but was moved online and served as a repository of information, a photo album of activities and a planning document for people who wanted a month-long view of activities and future events.

Here is a checklist for deciding if a blog, vlog or newsletter is the correct PR tactic:

- What is the goal for the tactic?
- Does the client have access to technology or the budget to hire professionals to manage the technology of recording, editing and distributing blogs or vlogs?
- Does the client have expertise to create brand-worthy newsletters? Does it have the budget?
- Which tactic is best for the target audience?
- What is the estimated level of understanding of the issue by the target audience or audience segments?
- Does the audience know and understand jargon or specialized language used by the client or organization?
- Are the resources available to produce these tactics on an ongoing basis?

Exercises

1. Look up a company or an organization that you admire and see if and how it uses blogs, vlogs or newsletters. Based on the information is this chapter, analyze the tactic. How well does it fit other communications from the organization? How timely is the information? Who is the author? Do you think it is strategically in line with what you see about the organization in its other activities or communications?
2. Write a strategy for a blog for your college. Focus on a long-term approach by listing the topics you would cover if blogging once a week for six months. Be sure to take into account current events affecting the school and any recent awards or celebrations. Are there any of your professors or other thought leaders on campus that you would blog about?
3. Pick an organization that you might like to work for. Based on a current news release or story in a news publication, write two or three pages of a blog that would support the strategy of the organization and fit with its current direction as you see it. Be sure to include facts and data that you find through research on company sites and in the business press.
4. Create a script for a vlog that you might find interesting. For example, if you are a football fan or a fashion fan, imagine yourself talking to a prominent person in the field you like. What kinds of questions might you ask? What conclusions and observations could you include in your vlog? If you had such an opportunity, where would you promote the production and why?
5. Write a plan for a newsletter about a topic that interests you – from a hobby to a professional area. You might write a newsletter about fishing or cooking, for example. What would you include in an eight-page newsletter? Think about your audience and what people like you would be interested in.

Glossary

Blog – a conversation or informational website created, posted and established on the internet on a routine schedule. Blogs can take many forms. The tone can range from very serious to humorous. Originally started as online diary-like reflective writing, blogs have changed and expanded in type, topic and importance. Organizations use them to put out information quickly and in their own formats and language. Entries typically show with newest on top.

Vlog – a video blog or video log. They are essentially blogs but done using video, taking advantage of less expensive and accessible video-capture and editing tools that have become common. In addition, video distribution has become very inexpensive, making YouTube a highly valued platform for vlogs. Vlogs may be enhanced with other forms of digital content, from video links to graphics and interactive images.

Newsletter – a small publication containing news of interest to a particular group. Newsletters have a long history of production by organizations of all types, from clubs to large commercial enterprises. They range in production value from copier versions of computer documents to highly designed and professionally printed editions rivaling magazines or catalogs. The concept of collected news articles and informational notices has transitioned from print to online, with organizations both distributing newsletters digitally and making them available for download on websites.

References

Brightcove Inc. www.brightcove.com/en/resources/blog/create-compelling-video-experiences/
Content Marketing Institute. https://contentmarketinginstitute.com/2020/09/b2b-industry-benchmarks-budgets-trends-research/
New at McKinsey Blog. www.mckinsey.com/about-us/new-at-mckinsey-blog
Reuters Young Money by Lauren Young on Twitter. https://twitter.com/Reuters/status/14302046 22715723780

13 INFOGRAPHICS AND DATA DISPLAYS

Learning Goals for This Chapter

After reading this chapter, you should be able to:

- Describe the attributes of effective graphics for strategic public relations.
- Explain how graphics may be included in a news release kit for maximum exposure.
- Discuss various methods of developing and transmitting graphics.
- Create basic data graphics using readily available software packages.
- Understand when it is appropriate to create an infographic.
- Describe the differences between an infographic and data graph.

Infographics and data displays are very popular and eagerly accepted by journalists and others who make decisions about publishing or broadcasting.

For good reason.

Both infographics and data displays – when done well and with the chosen audience in mind – can convey complicated information in simple, engaging and even striking ways.

And, while they are both tactics that have shown explosive growth in the digital era, graphic representations of information can be tracked to prehistoric cave drawings and hieroglyphics.

Professor Edward Tufte of Yale University summed up data displays this way in "The Visual Display of Quantitative Information" (1983): "At their best, graphics are instruments for reasoning about quantitative information. Often the most effective way to describe, explore and summarize a set of numbers – even a very large set – is to look at pictures of those numbers."

That sounds like what today's journalists and readers are looking for – information easily and quickly understood.

Infographics work in a similar way.

They use pictures or graphical representations to communicate information.

DOI: 10.4324/9781003248330-13

Infographics and data displays are important tools in strategic public relations and in integrated marketing communications. They are powerful and highly impactful communications tactics. But while they both rely on pictures more than words, they are very different in purpose and intent.

The goal of creating an infographic is to tell a story and to guide the audience to a very specific conclusion. An infographic is also useful when you are trying to point out the relationship between facts and figures.

A data display or data visualization, on the other hand, lets the audience draw their own conclusions. They are ideal for communicating data at a glance. They are also more objective than an infographic. In other words, they communicate just the facts and nothing but the facts. Examples includes charts and graphs. They have been used for many years to illustrate data in textbooks, news articles, annual reports and newsletters. They are particularly important when communicating technical, financial or scientific information when there are large numbers or the information is complex. In most cases, they are surrounded by text or embedded in a news release.

Most people would rather look at an infographic, chart or graph than read lengthy, complicated text. They can portray relationships between facts and figures more quickly than words alone. In fact, in many cases, visuals help readers process information more efficiently. The decision to create an infographic is an important strategic choice for the public relations writer. There needs to be a compelling reason. Over the last few years, there has been an explosion of infographics – many of them poorly done. You should only create an infographic if it is going to help enhance the story or key message you are trying to communicate. Like all successful PR tactics, you should design the infographic with a very specific audience in mind. You should also have a goal for the infographics. Ask yourself:

- Would an infographic enhance understanding of the subject matter?
- Can it stand alone as a source of information?
- Would it help pitch a story to a journalist?

If you can answer "yes" to these questions, go ahead and create an infographic. Infographics can portray information in powerful ways and provide a lead-in to a story that may be otherwise overlooked. Quite simply, they can save busy writers, reporters and bloggers a lot of time by giving them key takeaways from a report or news release. Frequently, the infographic or chart itself can also be pitched directly to a magazine or newspaper. For instance, the snapshot section on the front page of *USA Today* is a coveted placement for the PR pro. When embedded in a news release, infographics can also boost the SEO of a website.

Due to infographics' attractiveness, the capacity for them to be shared on social networks and become viral is much higher than ordinary text content. If you embed an infographic with your logo, it is also a powerful way of creating brand awareness. It is critical to view graphics from the target audience point of view – is the impact or impression something that is important to the audience and the takeaway something that can be useful or valuable? PR writers need to ensure that the data or information portrayed is consistent with the more cogent points of the release and ultimately supports the position and brand of the organization.

Infographics are most effective when their message is clear and when the information is presented in easily accessed and understood bites that follow a clear path from start to finish. They need not be highly artistic, but it is vital that the typeface is easily read and distinctive, following closely the graphic standards of the sponsoring organization.

Figure 13.1 shows a great deal of information about caregivers – people who have full or partial responsibility for the care of others. It's a growing issue around the world as populations age and there are fewer children being born.

This infographic was created as part of a much larger set of materials from a survey the Pew Research Center performed on this topic. To provide the most amount of information in the least amount of space and make it interesting, it was designed in segments, each of which covered a specific topic – the demographics of caregivers and household income, for example.

Who Are Caregivers?

Among all adults, the percent within each group who care for someone.

All adults ages 18+

39% up from 30% in 2010

WOMEN	MEN
40%	37%

Household Size

1 ADULT	2 ADULTS	3 OR MORE ADULTS
32%	40%	41%

Race/ethnicity

NON-HISPANIC

WHITE	BLACK	HISPANIC
39%	40%	32%

Educational Attainment

NO HIGH SCHOOL DIPLOMA	HIGH SCHOOL GRAD
31%	36%

SOME COLLEGE	COLLEGE+
44%	40%

Parent of Minor

PARENT	NON-PARENT
46%	36%

Household Income

$75,000+	43%
$50,000-$74,999	46%
$30,000-$49,999	38%
LESS THAN $30,000/YR.	36%

Age

18-29	30-49	50-64	65+
36%	42%	44%	30%

Figure 13.1 Pew caregivers infographic

Source: Pew Research Center, Pew Internet Health Tracking Survey, 2012, pew.org

Further, infographics should include source information or internet links that allow a viewer to gather more insights into the message to take further steps.

For example, the National Oceanic and Atmospheric Administration, or NOAA, successfully uses infographics to communicate complex scientific data in its press and public communications. In fact, the NOAA PR people have an entire section on their website – noaa.gov – dedicated to their infographics with accompanying articles and news releases. Every infographic is designed to be shared on social media or easily embedded in an article.

Another example of an interesting infographic is this one from the American Society for the Prevention of Cruelty to Animals (ASPCA). It includes its logo. This one addresses the issue of what plants are safe for pets. They could have, of course, just listed the plants, but this infographic not only has the name but a picture of the plant itself.

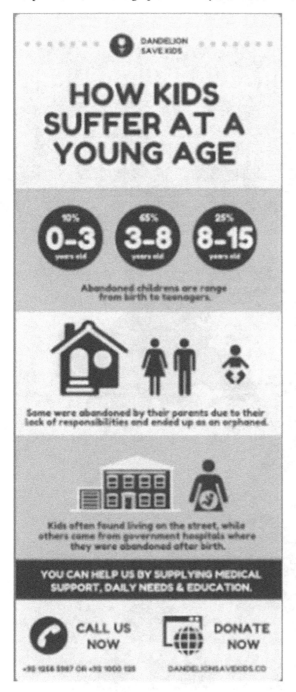

Figure 13.2 COVID poster for kids

Source: By permission of Kazu Kibiushi, boltcityproductions.com

Infographics do not need to be fancy, highly designed or even in color to be effective. This poster from the Washington State Coronavirus Response Infographic Library makes basic information available in a graphical format that is readily understood and reinforced. It was designed by Kazu Kibuishi and made readily available for any organization that wanted materials.

Figure 13.3 CDC severe weather infographic

Source: Centers for Disease Control and Prevention, cdc.gov

The Centers for Disease Control and Prevention developed this stylized infographic to provide people with a checklist of contents that might be contained in an emergency first aid kit. It is monochromatic, which reflects the weather conditions that typically accompany a tornado or severe windstorm. But it does not try to suggest other actions that might be taken if faced with a severe storm; it focuses only on its main goal, which is encouraging people to collect first aid supplies before they might be needed.

Infographics can be farmed out to an external designer, or they can be designed in-house by services such as Canva, Venngage, Piktochart, Easelly or others.

Software packages make the creation of graphics much simpler and faster than ever before, but it is imperative that the strategic PR pro figures out ahead of time what the message is to be sent with the graphic or data display and that the presentation fits with the overall direction of the PR program and is supported by data. Many times, organizations will provide the raw data with the graphic so that news organizations can check the graphic and even create a new format that fits their own transmission methods or other distribution requirements.

Microsoft Excel is probably the most commonly used software for creating business and other data displays. It will take information from a spreadsheet and quickly put it into graphic format. It even suggests options for the user to choose from.

Tableau Public is a powerful, free online product that is popular with many writers and editors.

When to Use Each

In general, both tactics are used when there is a great deal of information that needs to be absorbed quickly or that may be overlooked when presented in detail.

Data displays can be effective when the flood of data seems overwhelming – for example, when a national survey is conducted, with thousands of data points creating a tsunami of information. Creating graphics that compare the findings can suddenly render the results clearly and persuasively. In strategic public relations, the data display may be used in a media kit, emailed to a reporter as part of a pitch or designed to be shared on social media. For instance, a publicly traded company may use a variety of charts and graphs in its annual report to communicate that it had a very successful year financially. If your key message to financial news outlets like the *Wall Street Journal, Bloomberg* or the Financial Times is to communicate the financial strength of the company, a chart or graph that demonstrates this information can be very impactful. It may convince a news outlet to interview your CEO or use the data display in an article about your industry.

Infographics can be used when a graphic simplifies something complex and demonstrates relationships. Info guru Richard Saul Wurman (1997) explained how he led a team that developed a set of graphics for medical students that showed certain conditions – such as a blood clot in the heart – in dramatic colors and shapes rather than detailed medical drawings. The drawings show various treatments in memorable graphics.

No one would suggest that a future surgeon could be guided by such graphics, but they make the points of how to think about approaching a life-threatening situation.

Infographics require a full understanding of the phenomenon, event or situation being described graphically. Skilled information architects or designers may need time

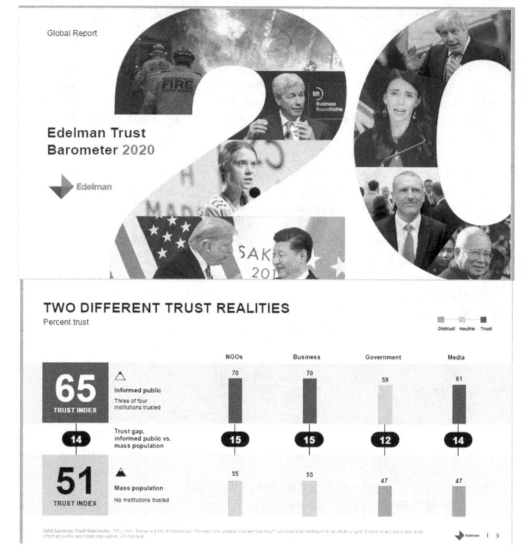

Figure 13.4 Edelman Trust Barometer report 2020

Source: edelman.com

to fully develop ideas and present them to individuals who are deeply knowledgeable about the topic. You should plan as far in advance as possible when suggesting an infographic.

Edelman, the world's largest public relations firm, does a yearly study on trust in institutions around the world. The report is a model of clear reporting of huge amounts of data covering a multitude of topics. The Figure 13.4 summarizes the changes in the gap in trust of institutions between people called the "informed public" – essentially, managers and decision-makers – and the general public. The four institutions studied are government, business, media and nongovernmental organizations (NGOs). In short, the informed people trust those institutions much more than the general public, and the differences in the levels of trust has increased in the five years depicted in this infographic. On the right are the three countries where the gap is greatest, with the most recent difference called out.

Animated Information

Animation of graphics can be powerful in demonstrating processes or fluid situations. If, for example, a major shipping company wanted to depict the efficiency of its supply chain, it could show the links between various modes of transport, from ships to trains to trucks to vans. And with animation, it could show how products are moved through the chain and how quickly it operates. Sound can be added to increase interest and attraction.

Likewise, if a client has an advanced training process that lends itself to movement and animation, that can be shown in action, including video as well as graphics, to clarify and highlight processes and efficiency.

The best animated infographic or data displays are interactive. The reader or viewer can find information by clicking or scrolling over the display. For example, if you had an interactive weather map, you could click on a specific state or city and find out the temperature and possibility of rain, snow or heavy wind.

Here's a checklist for using data displays:

- Is there a lot of data to explain?
- Is the data related to a core question or event?
- Can data be converted to digital form so that it is readily turned into graphic form?
- Is there an expert available to confirm that the graphical display is valid and truly reflects the findings or the story being told?

Here's a checklist for using infographics:

- Is the event or phenomenon not readily explained or demonstrated by itself?
- Is there access to creative information architects who can create a truthful infographic that fairly and completely shows the phenomenon or event?
- Will the infographic be completed in a timely way to support the PR effort?

Chapter Summary

Data can add interest and a compelling face to a PR release.

Any data graphic must support the communications goals of the campaign.

Graphics should be attractive and well labeled so that their message is clear.

Infographics are powerful accents to a strategic PR program and should be used to summarize and present information that may seem complicated to editors or producers.

It is critical to present information credibly so there are no doubts about what is being said.

Exercises

1. Using the data that follows, create a bar chart using Microsoft Excel or another software package.

Person	Grade
1	5.6
2	7.3
3	4.1
4	6.8
5	9.4
6	10.4
7	5.8
8	7.8
9	8.9
10	3.1

2. Take a situation that might arise and try creating an infographic using a software package. You might address a serious incident like how to react to a hurricane warning, or you might be less serious and create a graphic that explains how to register for classes at your university. Think of the goals and the promotional opportunity you are facing and how to be helpful as well as supportive of the organization you are working with.

References

Edelman Trust Barometer Report. www.edelman.com/trust/2020-trust-barometer

Tufte, E. (1983). *The Visual Display of Quantitative Information*. Graphics Press.

Washington State Covid Response Library with Permission from the Artist. boltcityproductions. com

Wurman, R. S. (1997). *Information Architects*. Graphis, Inc.

14 BUSINESS WRITING
Memos, Emails, Etcetera

Learning Goals for This Chapter

After reading this chapter, you should be able to:

- Define primary elements of business writing for internal and external distribution.
- Create strategic business correspondence.
- Describe the etiquette and goals of strategic business writing for PR professionals.
- Explain the value of clear, organized business writing.

Strategic PR writers must not only be able to create winning tactics but also must know how to communicate in writing about these tactics. This includes everything from getting consensus on a strategic approach for a project to updating clients or managers about the progress of a communications campaign. It also includes presenting uncomfortable, sometimes embarrassing, news. Such news can range from a plane crash to an oil spill to closing a manufacturing plant.

In fact, the president of a New York-based public relations agency said this:

> One of the skills that I look for when hiring a new employee is the ability to write a clear, concise memo. She or he needs to be able to communicate strategically with clients and provide written updates internally about the status of projects.

With more and more people working from home and having fewer face-to-face meetings, nuts-and-bolts business writing has become even more valuable than in the past. Talking face-to-face, you get to hear voice intonation and read body language clues. That doesn't happen online or in paper. For the PR writer, knowing how to draft a well-organized memo is as important as writing an effective release or social media post or pitch letter.

As you move to greater responsibility in your career, you will recognize that business writing is the lifeblood of organizations. Day-to-day writing is used in defining

DOI: 10.4324/9781003248330-14

everything from the most mundane, such as announcing the holidays for the year, to the most vital and arcane, like plans for a merger or a revolutionary product.

In the course of a day, a PR writer may generate a proposal for a project, a memo that responds to a question from a client, social media postings, a news release and a speech for a retirement party.

They all share these requirements:

- Deep insight into the thinking and knowledge of the key audience or recipient
- A profound understanding of the goal of the writing
- Some idea of any background or history of the people involved and their relationship or lack of one

Powerful strategic writing is writing with a clear purpose. This means making things happen. It could be getting people to work on a specific project or convincing a client (internal or external) that your proposed project is needed and will accomplish what the client wants.

Every message should have a clearly stated purpose. It also should be organized by topic and have a structure that is clear, whether chronological or by the urgency of the issue. As always, all data and names and assertions must be clearly sourced and checked for accuracy.

Organizations have differing styles and formats. Most organizations will have standardized forms available for use. At times, those formats are highly refined and available to download. In other cases, you may need to ask what is appropriate. Or you may look at examples you have received and use one that is most appropriate for the message, the recipients and the medium.

Email Essentials

When composing an email, check to make sure it has these elements:

Correct addresses: If you have not emailed the person recently, call and check or look in a company database to make sure you have the email address correct. You don't want to have to send a message again or hear from someone that she or he did not get the message you sent.

Descriptive and distinct subject line: If your message sounds routine or contains no specifics about the topic, it may not get noticed or go to the bottom of the to-do list. On the other hand, do not be overly dramatic or exaggerate a situation just to get noticed.

Lead with the goal of the message: Start with a friendly greeting, but when asking for something or a response, make that clear. You can make an urgent request and be polite at the same time. Explain the context and give the reasoning after making the initial request.

Body of the message: Give appropriate details and information in order of importance. If using lists, highlight with bullets or numbers. Group the data about a specific topic together to make the organization and requirements clear. Also, if you are writing to someone you don't work with frequently or someone you just met, remind them of who you are and where you met. Don't assume that a busy person will remember the context of how or when you met.

Closing: Often, it is helpful to repeat the specifics – what you need, the deadline and other issues – at the end of the message. Always include, even repeat, your contact information and offer to answer any questions or explain the requirements in more detail.

Internal messages may be less formal than those that go outside of the organization, especially to clients or potential clients. Further, correspondence is seen as legal communications and when dealing with issues of finances or commitments, you may need to have a lawyer review your correspondence before it is sent.

Remind yourself that anything you write inside an organization represents not only your thoughts and ideas but is a reflection, whether authorized or not, of the organization and your management chain. That doesn't mean you have to have every communications effort approved by your boss, but be sure you have his or her concurrence on a policy or business decision that you are communicating.

For example, if you were asked to take notes in a meeting, check with the leader of the meeting before sending out your notes to make sure you got every nuance correct. It is very uncomfortable and embarrassing to get a note or phone call with suggested changes or comments about misinterpretations. However, that is a lot more valuable and less damaging than hearing from someone that you missed the point and interpreted a comment in the wrong way.

Corporate Culture

Understanding corporate culture is another dimension that you will deal with. Your own organization may have a culture that values initiative and creativity, while other organizations are more reserved and like to follow a series of steps precisely, with little room for deviation. Either approach – or something in the middle – can work, depending on the organization and the situation.

Most organizations will value good, logical thinking based on solid, up-to-date research and minimal suppositions or personal opinions.

Some interpretation is expected, but writers should not go far outside their areas of expertise and experience.

PR professionals write for a living. They should be effective in organizational correspondence because many of the requirements and guidelines are the same.

For example:

- It's always important to remind yourself who your audience is and what the audience knows about the topic, what expectations they hold and what the general attitude will be toward the message: positive, neutral or negative.
- Where in the organization hierarchy does the recipient fit? It is important to understand the pecking order of the organization and not treat the president

or chairperson like a fellow team member. The rules for correspondence have loosened a great deal, but it is still important to treat higher executives and managers with respect. That goes for clients and for members of the media, too.

- Time is valuable. Get to the point. Don't provide a lot of unnecessary detail or explanation. If the message may be better delivered in person, do that. Understand the conventions and culture of the organization. And if you have a question, ask someone.

Primary Ingredients of Business Writing – Internal and External

Organizations of all sizes and purposes have one thing in common: they were established to make something happen. That can range from the obvious, like making money, to the sublime, such as encouraging pet adoption.

To get things done, there has to be direction, planning, execution and evaluation in some form or another. In some organizations, the processes are highly refined – medicine or airplane assembly, for example. In others, the processes are more guided by the circumstances and environment – sales or sports, for example. PR firms, just like other types of organizations, have usually created processes and, at times, step-by-step instructions on how certain work is to be done. You may be following a formula or checklist, but your writing should not be tepid or flabby. It should always be smart, strategic and simply written.

It is safe to say that clear, concise communications – usually in the form of written documents – can aid in the successful completion of organizational goals. Indeed, clear communication can help in developing collaboration among organization members and in clarifying roles and responsibilities. It can also provide you with a competitive advantage because communicating what you do is a valued skill that makes the jobs of your bosses, co-workers and clients easier.

With wide adoption of social media and simple emails and texts or SMS, the distance from the top of an organization to the bottom has been flattened. Some senior executives invite communications from up and down the organization. Others prefer that communications follow the chain of command – going from employee to boss to boss' boss, and so on.

There is a strong temptation just to fire off a letter to the top person; email addresses are not hard to find or figure out. But it also pays to understand the etiquette of the organization – what are expected methods and approaches and that some behaviors are not appreciated or expected. For example, if you think the big boss has made an error, you might be right. But if you tell her or him that without telling your own boss, you might not understand the full rationale behind a decision or you may make your boss look bad by going behind his or her back.

One of the best rules ever developed about emails says that if you feel very strongly about something, you should write the email and then keep the draft for a day and read it carefully before sending.

Among public figures who need to think twice about their choice of words, the unsent angry letter has a venerable tradition. Its purpose is twofold. It serves as a type of emotional catharsis, a way to let it all out without the repercussions of true engagement. And it acts as a strategic catharsis, an exercise in saying what you really think, which Mark Twain (himself a notable non sender of correspondence) put this way: "We write frankly and fearlessly, but then we 'modify' before we print" (Brooks, 2013).

When a memo (short for memorandum) is sent to members of an organizational group, it should include basic information:

- Who is sending it
- Who is receiving it
  There may also be some people copied on it. Emails still use the cc (carbon copy) and bcc (blind carbon copy) designations, which were created when paper predominated. Carbon copying is an outdated, messy and inexact method of making copies, and blind carbon copy denotes that a copy is being sent to someone without the knowledge of those on the "To" and "Cc" lists.
- The primary topic, designated by "Re" for "regarding" or "Ref" for "in reference to"
- Date when it was sent
- Other elements, depending on the situation, including:

  - Attachments
  - References to previous correspondence on the topic (links are commonly used in emails)
  - Deadlines for response
  - A request for confirmation that the message was received

The format for business communication generally follows a pattern that discusses the topic being addressed with some context as to why the correspondence is being sent: a report on a meeting or a response to an inquiry or a standard report on an established schedule, like a monthly sales report.

If more than one topic is to be covered, it is valuable to designate each topic with a number, letter or bullet.

Then each topic will be discussed in further detail as determined by the writer or by convention within the organization, especially if the report is repeated regularly and carries much of the same type of information each time.

It is critical that any new or unexpected information be highlighted at the beginning of the written document. Readers should not have to parse the entire document to find important information. Indeed, putting critical or revealing information deep in a document can result in it being overlooked.

Challenger Tragedy

One of the most tragic examples of a case where the critical nature of a memo was not highlighted and promoted is the memo written by an engineer trying to alert his bosses that a small but essential part of a space shuttle could fail – as shown by some engineering tests.

This was the subject of the memo: "SRM O-Ring Erosion/Potential Failure Criticality."

The part failed – just as Space Shuttle Challenger was taking off. The shuttle exploded 7seconds after liftoff. All seven astronauts aboard were killed (Challenger Explosion, www.history.com/news/how-the-challenger-disaster-changed-nasa).

The engineer warned that something bad could happen if a group was not formally created to address the O-ring erosion issue. He used words like "criticality" and pointed to potential "loss of human life," but the mission went ahead.

In summary, the form and presentation of information are important, but the writing and highlighting of essential information is always paramount.

Amazon and Six-Page Narratives

Amazon, one of the most successful companies in history, has a culture – driven by founder and former CEO Jeff Bezos – that expects and values clear writing – on paper.

Bezos explained the process this way in the 2017 letter to shareholders:

We don't do PowerPoint (or any other slide-oriented) presentations at Amazon. Instead, we write narratively structured six-page memos. We silently read one at the beginning of each meeting in a kind of "study hall." Not surprisingly, the quality of these memos varies widely. Some have the clarity of angels singing. They are brilliant and thoughtful and set up the meeting for high-quality discussion. Sometimes they come in at the other end of the spectrum.

The difference between a great memo and an average one is much squishier. It would be extremely hard to write down the detailed requirements that make up a great memo. Nevertheless, I find that much of the time, readers react to great memos very similarly. They know it when they see it. The standard is there, and it is real, even if it's not easily describable.

Examples of Business Correspondence Formats

The Amazon letter to shareholders demonstrates the company's unique approach to business writing and the profound influence that its founder and chief executive had on its communications practices.

Any written communication going to people outside the organization or to other organizations, including government agencies, shareholders, the media or other stakeholders, will be scrutinized and reviewed before being released.

In part, that's because such output can have legal ramifications and can be highly regulated based on governmental regulations and laws, whether federal, state or local. External communications may have influence and impact on the organization's image and perception among important audiences, which can affect everything from stock prices to donor pledges to standing among neighbors or prospective employees.

The format of such communication reflects the attention and seriousness that an organization attaches to it. For example, company earnings are carefully scrutinized and tracked by investors and security analysts, and it is illegal for information about the earnings to be released to anyone before the official release to all audiences. Because of the legal implications and the potential impact on stock prices, a relatively small group of people in public companies has access to the information and each one in that group has to sign a legal document acknowledging that the information will not be shared in any way – on penalty of being arrested and tried for what is known as insider trading. Further, the written information is closely reviewed and polished by lawyers, accountants and senior executives as well as the communications staff.

Here is part of the earnings release from Facebook for early 2021:

FACEBOOK

Facebook Reports First Quarter 2021 Results

MENLO PARK, Calif., April 28, 2021 /PRNewswire/ -- Facebook, Inc. (Nasdaq: FB) today reported financial results for the quarter ended March 31, 2021.

"We had a strong quarter as we helped people stay connected and businesses grow," said Mark Zuckerberg, Facebook founder and CEO. "We will continue to invest aggressively to deliver new and meaningful experiences for years to come, including in newer areas like augmented and virtual reality, commerce, and the creator economy."

Figure 14.1 Facebook letterhead of news release. Facebook earnings report segment
Source: facebook.com

It is pretty bare bones. The release itself goes into much more detail, all of which reflects the solemn, perfunctory style of these first two paragraphs. This is in strong contrast to the eclectic, free-wheeling attitude reflected by much of the platform and demonstrates the seriousness of earnings reports.

By contrast, here is the top of the General Motors earnings release for the same period:

 general motors

News

For release: Wednesday, May 5, 2021 at 7:30 a.m. ET

GM Reports Strong First-Quarter 2021 Results

DETROIT – General Motors Co. (NYSE: GM) today reported first-quarter earnings driven by strong price and mix performance in North America, strong credit and residual value performance at GM Financial, and the industry recovery in China. The company is highly confident in its full-year 2021 guidance outlined earlier this year as it works to manage through the semiconductor shortage, which is impacting automakers globally. Based on information available today, the company expects to be at the higher-end of the EBIT-adjusted range.

Figure 14.2 GM earnings report segment. GM letterhead of news release
Source: gm.com

The GM release is more descriptive and effusive and provides a broad picture of the company results, including comments about the economy and international sales, while giving a brief description of its outlook.

Take note that both reports have headlines, dates, datelines for the headquarters location. Facebook is quoted as giving the information. GM talks with a corporate voice, noting that GM "reported first quarter earnings."

Two different styles for two major companies with different personalities.

Internal Communications

A peek behind the curtain of most organizations will show that the variety of styles, formats and levels of sophistication and formality is wide and deep.

Some organizations prize speed and responsiveness; others desire a more measured approach, which may include deep research, committee-approved communications and specific citations of information sources.

Here are some of the many types of internal communications:

- Personnel communications – usually classified "confidential" and "to be opened by addressee only." Digital communications may be encrypted.
- Financial reports – detailed descriptions and discussions that can involve spreadsheets and business graphics and are likewise confidential and have limited distribution, at times to the point that copies are numbered and tracked by addressee.
- Informational memos or letters – the differences can be minimal but keep with the history and tradition of the organization.

  - These can include announcements such as promotions, changes to benefit plans, updates to safety or security procedures, or even condolence messages when a relative or former employee has passed away.
  - Some may cover such mundane topics as a notice that certain parking lots will be unavailable when being repaired or the company vacation days for the coming year.

- Organizations often use social media sites such as Facebook for less formal communications such as birthday or service anniversary notices for personnel and at times for more neighborly purposes such as selling items or offering ride-sharing options.

Whatever form the communication takes, it will likely share some common characteristics.

It will reflect the personality of the organization, which can range from highly formal and legalistic to chatty and more personal.

Such communication should be well written, with clear direction and a clearly stated purpose. It also should have a date and often will have a "best by" date or time when it expires.

Importantly, the organization should adopt a common point of view and, in doing so, adopt a vocabulary that is consistent. For example, will terms like "we" and "our" be used to describe people in the organization? And will it be called "our company" (or "association" or "group") as opposed to the formal name (XYZ Co.)?

For example, if you write to an influential journalist suggesting a story that will highlight a client or your company, the document better be clear, concise and persuasive, not to mention short. Just like the business writing described here.

If you work for a PR agency and are writing a letter to a client about a proposed project or campaign, it must be clear, persuasive, logically presented and meet the appropriate etiquette standards as established by your agency with the client.

Further, writing for all of the output from a PR pro has to be exceedingly well done. It must be grammatically correct, without typos, short and to the point, and arrive at a good time for the recipient – at the least busy time of the week, unless the communication is time sensitive or responding to an inquiry.

And it is always important to remember that your work is representing not just yourself, but also your organization and/or your client.

Chapter Summary

Business writing comes in many shapes and sizes, depending on the purpose, audience, organizational culture and other influences, including legal and historic standards.

Emails are the most common method of communicating, whether inside or outside an organization, but should be used judiciously, keeping message importance and audience in mind.

There are still occasions when paper correspondence is appropriate and even required.

Business writing should be well constructed and clearly written with the purpose obvious. All key elements should be included and double-checked.

Exercises

1. Write a memo to the president of your college or university suggesting that more parking be made available for students who attend evening classes. Explain why issues of safety, convenience, and access to facilities such as cafeterias, libraries and laboratories can be facilitated with designated parking for evening students. Use your own experience and other research to flesh out the memo. You might even call the college security office and find out if there are issues in parking and if there have been incidents involving evening students. Write in a clear, concise style. Do not make assertions that are not backed up by observations or facts or opinions from experts such as traffic or security officers.

2. Review the letter to shareholders in the annual report from a company you are interested in. Analyze the style, word use, apparent target audience and visual

presentation. Do you think it is effective? Is the language readily accessible to someone not familiar with the inner workings of the company or its industry? Is it visually appealing? How would you change the language use, the organization of information or the design – if at all?

3. Write a notification to all students and faculty from the president of your university with the following facts. Organize the information to be of most value to your intended audiences and to give them the best opportunity to comply with or adapt to the situation at hand:

- The main cafeteria will be closed for two weeks.
- A grease fire in the bakery area two nights ago left the wall scorched and the ceiling close to falling down.
- Firefighters did their best, but a lot of water was required to put out the fire.
- Food trucks are being invited to park in college parking lots to provide food from 7 a.m. until 9 p.m. It is not yet clear how many will be available.
- Students will receive refunds for meals missed by the end of the semester.
- No one was hurt in the fire.
- The president, Dr. Smith, said, "We are very distressed by this situation and are working hard with facilities and outside vendors to get the cafeteria back in working order."
- The college is also asking local restaurants and groceries to stay open longer to serve college citizens.

4. Go online to two public companies and find the most recent letter to shareholders or the most recent news release on a policy topic – something that reflects a position or decision the company management has taken. Compare the styles of the two documents: look for evidence of the intended audience, the purpose of the communication, the use of industry-specific language, the use of inclusive pronouns such as "we" and "us," and other distinguishing features. Which do you think is more effective? Be specific.

References

Bezos 2017 Letter to Shareholders. www.aboutamazon.com/news/company-news/2017-letter-to-shareholders, July 2021.

Brooks, Van Wyck. (2013). The Ordeal of Mark Twain. *eBook #42225*. www.gutenberg.org/files/42225/42225-h/42225-h.htm, July 2021.

Challenger Explosion. www.history.com/news/how-the-challenger-disaster-changed-nasa

For Further Reading

Writing a Basic Business Letter. https://owl.purdue.edu/owl/subject_specific_writing/professional_technical_writing/basic_business_letters/index.html

15 KEY ELEMENTS OF A PR CAMPAIGN

Learning Objectives for This Chapter

After reading this chapter, you should be able to:

- Explain and demonstrate how to use multiple tactics as part of a PR plan.
- Exhibit proficiency in creating a strategic public relations plan.
- Describe how to decide which tactic is best for the strategic organizational and programmatic objectives.
- Use a creative brief template to define a campaign and its elements.

Putting all the pieces of a PR campaign together is the ultimate goal – and where some of the real creative, interesting work begins.

Until this point, the text has presented various pieces or tactics of a PR campaign. Your communications plan or template is the architectural guide for your campaign. It starts with a foundation – much like a house – that includes the fundamentals:

- Client (internal or external; may be someone from your company or organization or a client of an agency) and assignment
- Goals for various parts of the campaign
- Key audiences in discrete segments
- Messages by audience segment
- Media or channels for transmitting the messages
- Research to confirm the contours of the audiences (from preferred media to knowledge of the organization or product to language use) and research on previous campaigns and the competitive landscape
- Testing options for early creative (to see if it rings true with audience samples)
- Research before, during and after the campaign to assess effectiveness and possible course corrections

DOI: 10.4324/9781003248330-15

Creating a Campaign

The ultimate goal for communications professionals is a campaign that achieves strategic communications goals for an organization. Campaigns operate across the full spectrum of disciplines, from direct mail to social media to broadcast media to skywriting.

Campaigns are infinitely variable. They can be very short, a week or a month, or last a year or more. They can be local, regional, national or international. In some instances, you will have time to plan. Other times, such as in the event of a disaster, you may have to quickly create and implement a campaign.

The previous chapters are replete with descriptions, examples, suggestions, tips and techniques that can be used in today's rapidly changing media environment.

If a collection of those tactics can be seen as layers of a cake, the linking of them, the overall coloration and final design of a campaign, can be thought of as the icing – the final touch.

A communications campaign is a series of actions coordinated by a solid, detailed plan that link together and play out over time to inform, synthesize thinking, or spur audiences and stakeholders to action.

This chapter includes step-by-step tips on how to create a public relations plan with a variety of tactics. It includes examples of award-winning PR campaigns to use as a guide to create your own campaign. Lastly, this chapter provides opportunities to create PR plans in class and as individual and team projects.

Before launching a PR campaign, a written plan must be drafted that describes the purpose of the initiative and how it will be implemented and evaluated. That way, the client, staff or senior management knows exactly what the campaign is designed to accomplish, who is responsible for each part of the campaign, how much it is expected to cost and how long will it take to implement.

Within a campaign, the tactics described elsewhere are honed and refined, put together like a 1,000-piece jigsaw puzzle and, when successful, a marvelous, nuanced, pleasant picture appears.

The picture in this instance is that of an organization that has a mission and a vision and is staffed and energized by people who collaborate daily to perform tasks and polish its good works to make the company known as a positive entity, to engage stakeholders, and to encourage growth and success.

Campaigns can have a wide range of goals, from short and simple to long and complex.

Some examples:

- Introducing a new cookie under an established brand, like Christmas Oreos. A campaign like this will follow tradition and exist within the standards established by years and years of communications and known by consumers far and wide. The campaign will likely be short and limited because it serves a limited period of time and does not have to create understanding or comfort among purchasers.
- An election campaign for a relatively unknown candidate. Such a campaign will have a very steep hill to climb because multiple steps have to be taken

to introduce the candidate to the voters, to build on that introduction and increase knowledge, to have voters become comfortable and appreciate the candidate, and, in the best possible outcome, to move voters to cast ballots for the candidate. Obviously, there are many steps to be taken and decisions to be made between the introduction of the candidate and the election – from writing press releases and speeches to meeting with media representatives to building a set of messages for social media, broadcast, advertisements and a wide range of media options.

- Launching a nonprofit campaign for a charity that supports families that need a hand to find affordable housing, sufficient food and other living necessities. If the nonprofit organization has a history and a following, the job is relatively easy. Past contributors and supporters will be a key target audience; a campaign that needs to find new support may need to find new messaging, new graphic designs and even a new spokesperson or influencers.

Focus on the Client

Even if you are working in a large organization as part of the PR department or a broader communications group, it is valuable to think of the person or persons who are giving you an assignment to fulfill as clients. Clients are the bosses, the ones providing resources ranging from financial to staffing to permissions and access to information and expertise.

Clients have the right and obligation to set expectations for the work you are about to do, to review that work at key stages or at set intervals, to make suggestions and changes, and, finally, to accept the finished products when they are satisfied that they meet their expectations.

Whether you are working for an internal client or for a client of an agency, you need to be attentive to their interests and requirements and to provide counsel and suggestions about the communications aspects. At times, clients may ask for more than you believe is possible or prudent, given your professional knowledge and expertise. At times, clients may not accept your "creative" approaches and want to be more traditional or repeat earlier approaches.

Those are situations in which there needs to be a reasoned, detailed explanation and discussion so that all sides understand and agree on the approach, methods and especially language. One of the benefits of having a written plan is that is that it helps everyone involved to understand the activities to be done, the sequencing and the timeline, as well as who is in charge.

At times, there is such a wide gap in points of view that it is not possible to come together. At those times – which are not frequent but do happen – it is best to part company or bring in other resources and people to see if there can be an agreement to accept an approach and move forward.

Such discomfort may be avoided by hard work at the beginning of creating a campaign, especially when working with a client for the first time. It is better to spend time looking at examples of campaigns in the same industry or product area and having a roundtable discussion about strengths, weaknesses, graphical approaches, media choices, spokespeople and tone. Such topics can be seen as subjective, but if there is not a consensus for an approach, these topics can be roadblocks.

One highly effective approach, in the experience of the authors, is creating a presentation of competitive work and showing it to the client with time to discuss and dissect all the elements mentioned previously. Such a presentation also has the benefit of establishing a competitive benchmark and understanding of the environment in which the campaign will be introduced.

Along with a thorough analysis of the client, it is highly recommended that baseline research be conducted to determine the state of opinion about the client, the industry, the competitors and specifically the topic, product or service that is going to be promoted.

Such research can help determine targeted messages for specific audiences and the best channels – social media, broadcast, print or any of the many other choices. The campaign may use different channels for different stages or for different times of the year. For example, television is often reduced in value during summer months when people are out of doors more than during colder months.

Baseline measurements can be useful in determining the effectiveness of the campaign over time because they give a starting point on which to measure progress of attitude or behavior changes in tandem with the campaign. It is important to remember that a number of factors can influence target audiences and that changes, or lack of changes, may or may not be the result of campaign activity.

Strategic Campaign Elements

All campaigns for an organization should have certain elements in common. All of them should support and extend the overall goals and objectives of the organization. It is essential that the vision, mission and stated objectives of the organization be respected even if they are not stated explicitly. To include elements that do not fit with current communications and branding will make an organization seem inconsistent or uncertain of its own direction.

All strategic communications start with research. And a public relations campaign is no exception. The plan itself will include a description of the problem or opportunity to be addressed. This is generally referred to as a situation analysis. The plan will also include measurable goals and/or objectives, a strategy to implement these goals/objectives, target audiences, key messages, the tactics to be implemented, a timetable, a budget and a way to evaluate the success of the campaign.

A strategic element of the public relations plan is deciding which tactics to create. The decision of which tactic or tactics to use is not about simply using the latest PR tool or using what has been done in the past simply because "it has always been done that way." As Marshall McLuhan wrote, "The medium is the message." In other words, deciding which tactic to implement is a key part of the strategy. A tactic needs to be appropriate for the audience, the message, the goal and the overall image of the organization.

Here is a list of the key elements of a communications campaign:

1. Situation analysis: description of the problem or opportunity to be addressed; should include what research may need to be done before or after the campaign
2. Measurable goals or objectives: number of impressions, views, or changes in audience opinions, attitudes or actions – buying the product, for example
3. Strategy to implement the goal or goals: messages, media, timing, research
4. Target audiences
5. Key messages
6. Tactics to be implemented
7. Timetable
8. Method to evaluate the success of the campaign

Sample Detailed Strategic Plan for Nonprofit Rebranding Campaign

Authors' note: This case was provided by the chief communications officer of a non-profit that prefers to remain anonymous; therefore, here, the nonprofit and the illness it combats are identified as ABC Org and ABC malady. The case has been reviewed for accuracy and is a real case.

The following case contains decisions about changing the messaging platform of an organization based on detailed research. Each of four categories of donors or potential donors is defined with specific messages, refined approaches and desired outcomes. The case provides important insights into the processes and decisions that communications professionals make as they develop detailed, strategic campaigns.

This case also includes specific instructions to communicators on how to approach and communicate with different classes of donors as well as partners and fundraisers – all key audiences for communications from this nonprofit.

You might conclude that some messages are repeated. Remember that there are a number of different audience segments and that it is important to recognize the subtle differences in messaging among them. Remember also that messages need to be heard more than a few times to be remembered and to result in action.

Background and Situation Analysis

A nonprofit organization – ABC Org – based in New York City with an annual revenue of between $50 million and $75 million seeks to expand its donor and supporter base. The singular mission of this nonprofit is funding medical research to end a specific disease – ABC malady. The nonprofit is the largest private organization of its kind in the world; however, without the benefit of mass-market events such as walkathons, it has significantly lower name recognition than its peers and, therefore, relies heavily on elevating the impact of its reputation through its public relations strategy and content strategy, which are primarily executed across its digital channels: website (blog, news and general website content related to mission and impact), social media, podcasts, videos and PSAs for all formats.

To evaluate and build the organization's brand and to engage new and current constituents in its mission and drive fundraising revenue, the organization conducted a brand and marketing study from December 2017 to May 2018 with an external partner that specializes in the nonprofit industry.

The brand and marketing study included these key deliverables:

- A positioning statement: the single idea of which was to own in the minds of target audiences
- A statement of positioning for tone and style: the feelings the organization wants people to associate with the organization

The study summarized the following guiding strategies for the organization's brand and marketing efforts:

- Expand the brand through a content strategy and lead-generation activities.
- Put the return in "return on investment" by more aggressively and frequently highlighting impact and outcomes.
- Deepen relationships with constituents by more consistently sharing mission content.
- Raise visibility by targeting people earlier in their understanding of the disease and research and the impact it has on their outcomes.

Among the recommendations from the study was to craft compelling organizational and persuasive messaging that tells the organization's story and that is a catalyst for action among all constituents:

- People impacted by the disease
- Donors
- Corporate partners
- Social media followers
- The general public

As a result, the organization decided to launch an impact messaging project with the same external partner in September 2019.

Goals Achieved Through the Messaging Project

Messaging

The impact messaging project had two goals:

- Revise organizational key messages regarding impact, including, among others:
  - Proposed boilerplate(s) to be used in all "about us" moments (end of news releases, etc.)

- Elevator pitches
- Social media bio copy

- Produce tools for the communications team to use to train across the organization, including, among others:

  - A "train the trainers" session for communications staff
  - A messaging guide
  - Persuasive messaging according to a set of personas/segments

Scope

The messaging project kicked off with a review of existing messaging tools, positioning and personality and included deliverables for each of the two areas: organizational messaging and persuasive messaging.

Organizational Messaging Elements

- Developing organizational key messages (a document that outlines the most critical messages staff and board members should communicate when writing or talking about the organization, including mission impact)
- Developing a boilerplate set of paragraphs and an elevator pitch (developed based on approved key messages and review of existing copy)
- Suggesting social media bio copy for organizational pages and any organizational hashtags to use based on the final messaging platform
- Writing a messaging guide with an overview of the final brand strategy, organizational messaging and persuasive messaging and how to use them
- Conducting a two-hour training on how to use the messaging and how to be a brand ambassador, including scenarios and tools that the communications team can use to train staff and board members

Persuasive Messaging Process

- A discussion about which audiences to focus on, based on segmenting capabilities, to effectively apply the persuasive messaging approaches based on existing resources and tools
- Audience research in the form of ten 30-minute phone interviews with people representing key personas to fill in any gaps from the brand and marketing study
- Building on the new research and existing research, created donor personas or mindsets
- More persuasive messaging (generally a workflow or messaging map) for different segments that staff and board at all levels could use to speak or write to, based on the personas that were developed, that defines the key ideas and messages to emphasize with each segment
- Developed language to make the case for audiences to support the organization

Research Findings: Survey and Interviews with Key Audiences

Audiences Included in Research and How Data Was Gathered

- Prospects and small-level donors ($0–$2,499): survey shared via email
- Mid-level donors ($2,500–$24,999): four interviews
- Major donors ($25,000+): five interviews
- Independent fundraisers: eight interviews
- Corporate partners: two interviews

Following the research phase, detailed personas for each of the aforementioned audience groups were created, as was a persuasive messaging guide for how to speak to each group, which included three elements for all communications to ensure that they engage, position and reassure.

Persuasive Messaging Guide

The organization developed five donor profiles, a persuasive framework and messaging to inspire giving. Use these personas and messages as inspiration, as language to copy and paste, and as a reference point when writing fundraising appeals to specific donor audience segments.

Prospects and Small-Level Donors

Who they are	• Individuals who haven't given yet or who have given $2,499 or less • People who are likely to be impacted by the disease (living with, survivor, immediate family, close friend)
What they value	• Research – because they believe that it is the best, most effective way to end the disease • A long-term vision – because they've seen the impact of the disease firsthand and are motivated by a picture of the future without it • Research leadership and excellence – because they want to know they're giving to a powerful and effective organization
Why they choose our organization	• We're a research powerhouse. • Our singular commitment to research means that every dollar goes to breakthroughs. • Our approach to funding and collaboration makes us highly effective. • We are one of the most fiscally responsible nonprofits in the nation.

Communicating with Prospects and Small-Level Donors

Our communications should do three things:

1. **Engage** their values and motivations.
2. **Position** the organization as a way to act on their values and motivations.
3. **Reassure** them that they're making a good investment.

As you craft communications, look for opportunities to reinforce the ideas that follow.

Thread these key ideas throughout all communications:	Use these points to support and reinforce the key idea:
1. Engage We want donors to believe that research is the only way to end the disease now and for future generations.	• Every xx minutes, someone is diagnosed. • The diagnosis disrupts every facet of a person's life and the lives of their loved ones. • Research supports treatment for individuals today and more lives saved tomorrow. • There are more than xx thousand survivors in the United States. • Research will lead to discoveries that we can't imagine today – discoveries that will change lives.
2. Position We want them to see the organization as a research powerhouse.	• We lead breakthroughs because we are the largest private funder of this research. • Research is our only focus. • Our scientific advancements fuel the most important outcomes – more survivors, fewer deaths and improved quality of life for those with the disease.
3. Reassure We want donors to know that their dollars are used efficiently and effectively.	• Our focus on research means that your dollars go directly to accelerating discoveries. • We have a high fundraising efficiency and we're one of the most fiscally responsible nonprofits in the nation.

Example Messaging for Prospects and Small-Level Donors

Draw from the following messaging in communications. You can use these messages as inspiration with light editing or copy and paste them directly into your piece (if it works in context). You won't need to use every message in every context.

1. Engage

Every [time: day/hour/minute], someone in the United States is diagnosed with ABC malady – and without research, there is no cure. Research is the only way we'll be able to discover lifesaving treatments for every person with ABC malady today – and ensure that future generations don't have to face this disease tomorrow.

Research fuels the most important outcomes – more survivors, fewer deaths and improved quality of life for those with ABC malady.

Call to action: Support ABC Org to make the single best investment in ending ABC malady.

2. Position

We are a leader in the ABC malady research field. We know that research is the best path forward to find cures, and that's why we're the largest private funder of ABC malady research in the world.

Over nearly XX decades, ABC Org has changed the trajectory of ABC malady. We can't stop now. The field is moving faster than ever, and we're leading the charge.

Call to action: Donate to ABC Org to advance lifesaving discoveries for every single person impacted by ABC malady.

3. Reassure

We have one focus: research. Our singular commitment to ending ABC malady through research gives us the dedicated attention needed to excel. It also means you know exactly where your dollars are going – toward breakthroughs for every patient.

Call to action: Give to ABC Org. Your investment will directly accelerate the science behind the next breakthrough and move us closer to eradicating ABC malady.

Mid-Level Donors

Who they are	• Individuals who have given between $2,500 and $24,999 • People who are likely to be very close to ABC malady (living with, survivor, immediate family)
What they value	• Any initiative with the potential to end ABC malady • A long-term vision – because they've seen the impact of ABC malady firsthand and are motivated by a picture of the future without it • Research – because they believe that it is the best, most effective way to end ABC malady
Why they choose the organization	• Our focus on research • Because we fund the scientists that have been behind every breakthrough • The scope and scale of our work – the number of dollars invested in research and our worldwide network of scientists

Communicating With Mid-Level Donors

Mid-level donor communications should do three things:

1. **Engage** their values and motivations.
2. **Position** the organization as a way to act on their values and motivations.
3. **Reassure** them that they're making a good investment.

As you craft communications, look for opportunities to reinforce the ideas that follow.

Thread these key ideas throughout all communications:	Use these points to support and reinforce the key idea:
1. Engage We want mid-level donors to believe that research is the only way to end the disease now and for future generations.	• Every two minutes, someone in the United States is diagnosed with the disease. • The diagnosis disrupts every facet of a person's life and the lives of their loved ones. • Research supports treatment for individuals today and more lives saved tomorrow. • Research will lead to discoveries we can't fathom today – discoveries that will change the lives of people affected by the disease.
2. Position We want mid-level donors to see the organization as the leader in research for this disease and therefore a donation as the best investment in ending it.	• Research is our singular focus. • We fund and convene the best minds in science; this model has been proven to accelerate progress. • We've been behind every major breakthrough in research for this disease.
3. Reassure We want mid-level donors to feel encouraged to give because they are confident that their dollars are used effectively.	• Your dollars go directly to accelerating discoveries. • We're one of the most fiscally responsible nonprofits in the nation.

Example Messaging for Mid-Level Donors

Draw from the following messaging in communications. You can use these messages as inspiration with light editing or copy and paste them directly into your piece (if it works in context). You won't need to use every message in every context.

1. Engage

Without research, there is no cure. Research is the only way we'll be able to discover lifesaving treatments for people living with the disease today – and ensure that future generations don't have to face this disease tomorrow. Research fuels the most important outcomes – more survivors, fewer deaths and improved quality of life for those with the disease.

2. Position

ABC Org is the largest funder of this research in the world. We know that research is the best path forward to stop the disease in its tracks.

Our unique approach combines investment and collaboration. We fund and convene the world's leading scientists, accelerating new discoveries and pushing the entire field forward. In fact, our researchers have been part of every major breakthrough.

Over nearly XX (years/decades), we have changed the trajectory of the disease. We can't stop now. The field is moving faster than ever, and we're leading the charge.

Call to action: Donate to ABC Org to advance lifesaving discoveries we can't even fathom today.

3. Reassure

We have one focus: research. Our commitment to ending the disease through research gives us the dedicated attention needed to excel. It also means you know exactly where your dollars are going – toward breakthroughs.

Our scientific expertise combined with our team's smart stewardship of funds ensures that every dollar you give goes as far as possible.

Call to action: Give to ABC Org. Your investment will directly accelerate the science behind the next life-changing discovery and move us closer to stopping the disease in its tracks.

Major Donors

Who they are	• People who give $25,000 or more
What they value	• Research – because they believe that it is the best, most effective way to end the disease • Strong leadership (in individuals and organizations) • Impact and excellence
Why they choose ABC Org	• They like that our focus is on research. • They view us a leader in the disease research space. • They are motivated by our reputation for excellence and trustworthiness. • They trust the founders and current leaders and the direction they're taking the organization.

Communicating with Major Donors

Our major donor communications should do three things:

1. **Engage** their values and motivations.
2. **Position** ABC Org as a way to act on their values and motivations.
3. **Reassure** them that they're making a good investment.

As you craft communications, look for opportunities to reinforce the ideas that follow.

Thread these key ideas throughout all communications:	Use these points to support and reinforce the key idea:
1. Engage We want major donors to believe that research is the only way to end the disease.	• There are many ways to support the disease community, but only research will end the disease. • Research supports treatment for individuals today and more lives saved tomorrow. • Since our founding, deaths from the disease have declined by nearly 40%. • Research will lead to discoveries we can't fathom today.
2. Position We want major donors to see ABC Org as the leader in research and therefore the best investment in ending the disease.	• Our founders were dedicated to research – and that's never wavered. • Our investigators have been behind every major breakthrough.
3. Reassure We want major donors to feel encouraged to give because they trust us and have confidence in the organization.	• Your dollars go to the best minds in science. • We have a lean and experienced team that ensures smart stewardship of funds. • We're one of the most fiscally responsible nonprofits in the nation.

1. Engage

Without research, there is no cure. Research is the only way we'll be able to discover lifesaving treatments for people living with the disease today – and ensure that future generations don't have to face this disease tomorrow.

Research fuels the most important outcomes – more survivors, fewer deaths and improved quality of life for those with the disease.

Call to action: Support ABC Org to make the single best investment in ending the disease.

2. Position

ABC Org was established with a single idea: that research is the best path forward to stop the disease in its tracks. Since our founding, our focus has never wavered.

Over nearly XX (years/decades), ABC Org has changed the trajectory of the disease. We have been behind every major breakthrough. The field is moving faster than ever, and we're leading the charge.

Call to action: Donate to ABC Org to advance lifesaving discoveries we can't even fathom today.

3. Reassure

We fund the best minds in science who are pioneers in their fields and who propel us toward new breakthroughs.

This leading scientific expertise combined with our lean team's smart stewardship of funds ensures that every dollar you give goes as far as possible. We are one of the most fiscally responsible nonprofits in the nation.

Call to action: Give to ABC Org. Your investment will directly accelerate the science behind the next breakthrough and move us closer to eradicating the disease.

Partners

Who they are	• Organizations that share your vision of a world without the disease
What they value	• A feeling that this disease connects us all and a desire to be part of the solution • An opportunity to authentically give customers and employees a way to make an impact on a cause that is important to them and that affects so many people • Having an impact on an individual level • Initially, our high ratings and scale of funding; eventually, a belief that research is key to stopping the disease
Why they choose ABC Org	• We have been behind every major breakthrough in research. • Our expertise and stewardship of funds ensures that dollars go as far as possible. • Each dollar supports progress and makes life better for people with the disease.

Communicating With Partners

Your partner communications should do three things:

1. **Engage** their values and motivations.
2. **Position** ABC Org as a way to act on their values and motivations.
3. **Reassure** them that they're making a good investment.

As you craft communications, look for opportunities to reinforce the ideas that follow.

Thread these key ideas throughout all communications:	*Use these points to support and reinforce the key idea:*
1. Engage We want partners to believe that ABC Org is the best investment.	• Every two minutes, someone in the United States is diagnosed with the disease. • The diagnosis disrupts every facet of a person's life and the lives of their loved ones. • Research will lead to discoveries we can't fathom today – discoveries that will change the lives of every single person affected by the disease.
2. Position We want them to see ABC Org as the leader in research and therefore the most effective partner.	• We have a singular commitment to research. • We fund and convene the best minds in science and this model has been proven to accelerate progress. • We have been behind every major breakthrough.
3. Reassure We want partners to feel assured that their dollars are used effectively and that they have a direct impact on people.	• Our sole focus on research means that your dollars go directly to accelerating discoveries. • Our scientific advancements fuel the most important outcomes – fewer deaths and improved quality of life for those with the disease. • Deaths from the disease have declined by nearly 40% since our founding. • We're one of the most fiscally responsible nonprofits in the nation.

Example Messaging for Partners

Draw from the following messaging in communications. You can use these messages as inspiration with light editing or copy and paste them directly into your piece (if it works in context). You won't need to use every message in every context.

1. Engage

A single diagnosis disrupts every facet of a person's life and impacts their loved ones as well. It's a complex disease that unfortunately connects many of us.

Without research, there is no cure. Research is the only way we'll be able to discover lifesaving treatments for every person living with the disease today – and ensure that future generations don't have to face it tomorrow.

Research fuels the most important outcomes – more survivors, fewer deaths and improved quality of life for those with the disease.

Call to action: Support ABC Org to make the single best investment in ending this disease.

2. Position

We know that research is the best path forward to end this disease.

We fund and convene scientists from around the world so they can accelerate new discoveries and pursue research with the potential for rapid clinical applications so that patients don't have to wait.

Over nearly XX (years/decades), ABC Org has changed the trajectory of the disease. We can't stop now. The field is moving faster than ever, and we're leading the charge.

Call to action: Donate to ABC Org to advance lifesaving discoveries for every single person impacted by the disease.

3. Reassure

Our commitment to ending the disease through research gives us the dedicated attention needed to excel. It also means you know exactly where your dollars are going – toward breakthroughs for every patient.

Our scientific expertise combined with our lean team's smart stewardship of funds ensures that every dollar you give goes as far as possible. We are one of the most fiscally responsible nonprofits in the nation.

Call to action: Give to ABC Org. Your investment will directly accelerate the science behind the next breakthrough and move us closer to eradicating the disease.

Fundraisers

Who they are	• Individuals who raise funds on our behalf • People who are likely to be close to the disease (living with, survivor, immediate family, close friend)
What they value	• Any initiative with the potential to end the disease • A long-term vision – because they've seen the impact of the disease firsthand and are motivated by a picture of the future without it • Research – because they believe that it is the best, most effective way to end the disease • A trustworthy and highly ranked organization • Feeling appreciated and being thanked for their time and energy

Why they choose ABC Org	• Our commitment to research means that we're highly effective and that every dollar goes a long way. • We fund the scientists that have been behind every breakthrough. • We are a highly ranked organization on giving websites, which signals a strong reputation.

Communicating With Fundraisers

Your partner communications should do three things:

1. **Engage** their values and motivations.
2. **Position** ABC Org as a way to act on their values and motivations.
3. **Reassure** them that they're making a good investment.

As you craft communications, look for opportunities to reinforce the ideas that follow.

Thread these key ideas throughout all communications:	*Use these points to support and reinforce the key idea:*
1. Engage We want fundraisers to believe that research is the only way to end the disease now and for future generations.	• The diagnosis disrupts every facet of a person's life and the lives of their loved ones. • Research offers answers that transform lives. The more we know about the disease, the better doctors are able to detect it, prevent it and treat it in individual patients.
2. Position We want fundraisers to see ABC Org as the leader in research and therefore a trustworthy investment of their time and their network's donations.	• This year, ABC Org has invested $XXX in research. • Our researchers have been behind every breakthrough.
3. Reassure We want fundraisers to trust ABC Org and to feel confident that the money they raise from their networks is used effectively.	• Your dollars go directly to accelerating discoveries. • We're one of the most fiscally responsible nonprofits in the nation.

Example Messaging for Fundraisers

Draw from the following messaging in communications. You can use these messages as inspiration with light editing or copy and paste them directly into your piece (if it works in context). You won't need to use every message in every context.

1. Engage

This is a complex disease that affects too many of us – and we can all be a part of the solution. Research is the only way we'll be able to discover lifesaving treatments for every person with the disease today – and ensure that future generations don't have to face it tomorrow.

Research fuels the most important outcomes – more survivors, fewer deaths and improved quality of life for those with the disease. Without it, there is no cure.

Call to action: Support ABC Org to drive vital research and bring the end of the disease into focus.

2. Position

This year alone, ABC Org has invested $XXX in research. That's more than any other nonprofit in the country.

Over nearly XX (years/decades), ABC Org has changed the trajectory of the disease. We can't stop now. The field is moving faster than ever, and we're leading the charge.

Call to action: Support ABC Org to be behind breakthroughs in research.

3. Reassure

Our commitment to ending the disease through research gives us the dedicated attention and momentum needed to excel. It also means you know exactly where your dollars are going – toward breakthroughs for every patient.

Our scientific expertise combined with our team's smart stewardship of funds ensures that every dollar you give goes as far as possible. We are one of the most fiscally responsible nonprofits in the nation.

Call to action: Give to ABC Org. Your investment will directly accelerate the science behind the next breakthrough and move us closer to eradicating the disease.

Here is a checklist for the key elements of a PR campaign:

- Who are the audiences? How do they differ? What are the defining characteristics of each demographic grouping?
- What are the specific communications goals for each?
- What are the messages and how does each set of messages (if the messages are different) complement the overall branding and personality of the organization?
- Is this tactic the right one for this audience? Does it fit the audience's information acquisition patterns?

- Do these tactics complement each other to reach strategic objectives?
- Does this PR campaign contain all of the key elements for its success?
- What baseline measurements have been taken to determine knowledge base of the audience and important attitudes or perceptions about the organization?
- How will the campaign or promotion be measured and at what points (only at the end or at the end of certain phases)?

Chapter Summary

Campaigns are the ultimate combination of PR tactics or combination of tactics from various communications disciplines, from PR to advertising to promotions to investor relations to internal (employee) communications.

Campaigns are infinitely variable. They can be very short, a week or a month, or last a year or more. They can be local, regional, national or international.

A defining and critical element of a campaign is its integration and linkage with the organization's established brand and public-facing communications stance. In other words, a campaign should not break away from the way an organization has publicized itself unless there is an overriding rationale. These might include:

- The organization being purchased or merging
- A new, dramatically different strategic direction for the organization
- The need for a new branding message because of changes in the core industry where a company competes

Serious, important campaigns need to be supported and defined by research into audience preferences and segments, the competitive environment, current perceptions and attitudes toward the product, new policies, and persons being promoted.

Exercises

1. Review campaigns at the Ad Council website (www.adcouncil.org/). Pick one with multiple tactics and analyze it for the following:

   a. What are the key messages? Do they flow through all of the tactics?
   b. Who is the apparent target audience? Is there more than one? Be sure to define as completely as possible.
   c. Analyze and comment on each element for effectiveness. Can you tell if some are meant for different targets? What makes them different?
   d. Write an overall summary of the campaign. See if you can find any analytics about its impact in terms of people reached, numbers of impressions, financial value and whether it met the original goals.

2. Analyze the long case about a nonprofit battling a disease. Answer the following questions:

   a. Why did the organization define the key targets as it did? What were the defining characteristics?

    b. Would you have changed the messaging strategy in any way? How? Why?

    c. Reviewing the accomplishments of the campaign, do you think it was effective? Were there other measurements that would have been valuable? What would they have been?

3. Based on your experience in the course, your reading and research, what elements of a campaign are most critical – cannot be disregarded or left out? Explain your thinking and give examples.

4. Create a very brief campaign plan for a local business that you might like to work with. Write down the critical elements, those that you would work on first. Explain why you made those choices.

5. How does a PR specialist make sure that a campaign and the elements within it meet the goals, the branding promise and the personality of the organization?

6. If a client asked you to promote a product or policy that you personally disagree with, how would you handle the situation? Write up at least two possible scenarios that would support your personal beliefs.

Glossary

Client – the person or persons who are asking for a project to be created. Clients can be internal (within the organization where you work) or external (where you and your firm, usually an agency, are hired for specific work).

APPENDIX
STRATEGIC COMMUNICATIONS
CAMPAIGN PLANNER

To accompany *Strategic Public Relations Writing: Proven Tactics and Techniques*

Authors: Jim Eggensperger and Jeanne Salvatore

A step-by-step process for a strategic public relations product campaign

Authors' note: This sample of the planning and process and creativity for a communications campaign has been developed as a teaching instrument for upper-level undergraduate students or graduate students. It is designed as a capstone project guide for such courses as integrated marketing communications, public relations campaign or other multielement communications projects.

It can be used as a series of discrete assignments or in parallel with teaching specifics of communications tactics, providing a central nervous system that connects various elements.

The defining principles include:

- The need for a coherent set of central messages that establish a foundation for any given campaign
- The construction of a series elements – also called tactics – that together will coalesce into a powerful, focused campaign that achieves the goals of the communications assignment
- Communications processes and approaches that will enable communications students or professionals to gather information about competition, audience, the marketing environment and the most effective communications channels for the messages
- Practice in developing messages and crafting the messages to meet the requirements and desires of audiences and communications channels, ranging from newspapers to social media and influencers

This campaign template was developed by authors who are both seasoned communications professionals and experienced educators. It was developed to meet a need that the authors encountered in texts and other support materials that have not been readily available.

It contains the unique feature of italicized "insights" to explain or give context to the assignments and discrete elements. In a course, those may be maintained or revised to fit the standards and approach of individual instructors.

Building a Strategic PR Campaign

Campaign Planner for Strategic Public Relations

This campaign planner was created to provide students with a realistic view into the variety and plethora of elements that may be included in a PR campaign.

The goal of this guide is to demonstrate to communications students how a retained public relations firm or an in-house public relations professional might take a PR assignment and create a program that would help a company distinguish a new product, attract consumers, and successfully compete against established brands and competitors.

The diary/campaign planning is divided into phases just like an actual program. Each phase builds on the one or ones before it.

The objective of this campaign planning guide is to provide an opportunity to apply the theories and concepts of public relations as presented in class, in your text and in case studies. It focuses in particular on writing with a strategic, long-term point of view in mind. In other words, it is designed to help you think on a broad spectrum of issues, potential problems, business strategies, audiences and communications channels.

Each phase provides specific tasks that build on previous material that has been developed. When the project is finished, you will have prepared a complete public relations campaign. In reality, such a program may take weeks, months and even years to develop. It would include performing basic research on audiences, competitors, strategic issues, technological trends and social awareness.

To simplify the tasks to fit into a collegiate schedule, some items have been simplified or reduced in scope from what they would look like at a major corporation or nonprofit or a leading PR firm.

As part of that editing, the key focuses for the campaign will be these three:

- Primary customers. In other words, if you choose to do a retail chain, the target would be consumers for the chain or the channels that those specific consumers use for gathering information, from websites to magazines to broadcast and social media.
- The appropriate media or distribution channels, which is closely aligned with the audience choice. For example, if you choose a business-to-business organization, the media choices for end users – the people who will purchase your products or services – will be different from end users who are primarily retail customers. The media choices may include business publications or websites, trade association publications and even large meetings of people from the industry where the business operates.
- The deliverables that you will create as a PR professional writing for your organization or client both strategically (maintaining the image and marketplace

promise of the organization) and tactically (creating compelling information that is designed to move a reader or listener to act in some way, from learning more about the company and its products to making a purchase or signing a contract).

Insight: A final note of caution: Be careful not to try to "boil the ocean" – not to take on a project that will be too big and too detailed and time consuming for the time available in the course. For example, it might be tempting to create a campaign for Apple, but that would involve the company itself; its philanthropic works; its non-U.S. communications; and all product communications, including those to retailers carrying Apple products (from Walmart to Joe's computers) as well as Apple-certified service organizations and individuals.

Phase 1

The Assignment for the PR Agency or PR Department

You are being assigned to create a multifaceted strategic PR campaign for a new product: **Sam's Hard Seltzer**. It will be a sub-brand for a major beverage company called, for this exercise, **Distinguished Brewing Inc**. It will be competing with other hard seltzers that have been on the market for years.

Your tasks, basically, will be to raise awareness of the new product, to generate good media notice, to encourage positive online discussions and notices, and to try to entice unpaid influencers to mention, if not rave, about the new brand of seltzer.

It is important to start any communications program with plans to measure the effectiveness of the program. The best plans are measurable and specific. Clients and bosses will demand solid evidence of impact and measurements toward goals. The advantages of the new product include:

- Lower calorie count than most of the competition
- Guaranteed healthy by being certified vegan and not using GMO ingredients
- Lower price point per six pack
- National distribution network, so it would be available wherever beer and spirits are sold
- An agreement with NASCAR for sponsorship and a sponsorship agreement with minor league baseball teams

The Outline

This outline is designed to take you step-by-step through development of a strategic public relations project or campaign.

It provides suggested assignments as you would receive in a work environment along with commentary *(in italics)* that provides insights into the thinking that may have gone into such an assignment and suggestions about where you might find information to include in your written plan as well as insights into desired outcomes and questions that can help you make decisions about organization and language. It is worth noting that creating an outline is a proven tactic to create communications plans of all sorts and is not just an instrument to be used in class.

> **Insight:** The commentaries are in italics for your edification and not to be used in the strategy.

You will see that you are being moved along a progression of activity designed to create the elements of the three segments outlined earlier.

The segments are designed to come together in a seamless strategic communication plan and set of deliverables – such as news releases, video scripts, informational graphics, speech scripts, social media postings, influencer and media pitches, and others described in your textbook.

Executive Summary

It is often said that nothing happens until something is written down.

Developing an executive summary has two major values:

First, it creates the initial plan for the overall PR program – what the goals are, the audiences, the key messages, potential media targets and measurements. The assignment originated somewhere, and whoever generated the idea had some outcome in mind.

Outcomes can include such results as:

- Selling more products
- Increasing donations for a nonprofit
- Answering questions about a product or service
- Generally improving perception or opinions about an organization in the minds of key audiences
- Responding to a crisis

The executive summary can be used to confirm agreement on a specific outcome and other details, including, very specifically, who is responsible and who makes final decisions on critical details like budget, timetable, key messages and measures of success.

Here are some more types of PR programs and where they might originate:

- Announcing a new product or service or organization is a natural reason for an announcement of some weight.
- A major change in the management of an organization calls for a PR plan and set of deliverables because many stakeholders will have an interest in who is running or having a major influence on the running of an organization.
- A crisis of some sort generates questions and requires a PR response. Many organizations have templates in place for various situations that might befall them, from natural disasters to product recalls.

- Brand support – a campaign to reinforce an organization's brand – can be generated by a sense or other information that the brand is not as well regarded as it previously had been or because competitors are enjoying a higher profile than in the past.
- Declining profits or revenues or donations (in the case of nonprofits) can call for a change in communications strategy involving public relations and related communications disciplines.

Insight: The summary narrows or eliminates options so that you and the team know that you are headed north and not south or west. In that light, it saves time.

The second value: putting goals and direction on paper will give you and any other members of the team something concrete to discuss. And the executive summary certain can – and almost certainly will – change over time.

The executive summary will be finalized to reflect the finished strategic PR plan or campaign. It will provide executives and/or clients a quick view of the project, which may be all they want to read. It should summarize the key points of your plan.

Assignment

Write a two-page draft of a program you think might work to promote the new seltzer. Do some preliminary research about similar products and about trends in beverage consumption – hard seltzers in particular. See if you can find out who the consumers for these products are currently and make some suggestions about what media might appeal to them.

Phase 2

Corporate Image Analysis and Definition

Specific communications must reflect the organization's fundamental strategy and direction as exhibited in its mission statement, vision, executive speeches and formal documents like the annual report. Strategy underlies virtually every decision of well-run organizations, from charitable foundations to industrial or digital behemoths. Strategy serves as a long-term plan and map as well as the structure of the organization's personality or brand.

Brands are names generally associated with a product or a group of products or an organization. If you have only one product, your company name may be your brand name. Your brand name should communicate your products' attributes, benefits, values, culture and even personality.

Since you are working for an imaginary company in this planner, you have the chance to define its branding and corporate personality. Write a paragraph or two on what the organization stands for – its goals, values, mission and vision. Discuss how the brand name will be incorporated into a logo. Keep in mind that customers are more likely to remember the brand and its attributes if the product's brand name and logo are meaningful and relevant to them.

For your strategic PR plan, the corporate strategy is critical. When a public pro-nouncement or action contradicts the actions of an organization, friends and critics both will take notice and the organization will look disorganized and inept. This seg-ment of the strategy summarizes the organization strategy, emphasizing its intentions and behaviors and giving examples of how it operates.

Assignment

For this section, you will need to define the corporate image strategy. Look at two or three companies in the Fortune 100 (*Fortune* magazine publishes a list of the top 500 corporations in America each year, based on revenues). In general, the companies at the top of that list do strategic PR and branding very well. Look at their PR work and then create a four-page document that describes your company in ways similar to ones that you find being used by professional and effective in top companies. Be sure to answer these questions and others you come up with.

If you are focusing on the hard seltzer case, you may want to choose beverage com-panies. However, if you are focusing on another industry or type of organization, use these questions as a guide:

Some questions this section should answer are:

- What does your company "stand for"?
- What do you want your customers and other stakeholders to believe about your company?
- What is the image you want to project?
- What makes your company special?

Phase 3

Competitive Analysis

It is critical in most situations to understand what the competition looks like and how it behaves. For example, some competitors are defined by major promotions and making a big splash – think of Red Bull and the competitions the company sponsors. Others are more reserved and like to advertise the good works that they sponsor. Think of Coca-Cola.

Understanding the approaches of the competition will influence the types of mes-saging, the media chosen and perhaps the messages. If there is a large issue affecting the area where your organization operates, most competitors may create messaging on that topic. If the PR campaign is focusing on a special capability of your organization, that could be the focus.

Once you have figured out your major competitors, be careful to define your company's position in relation to them. For example, if you are working with a rel-atively new company or organization and the main competitors have been around for quite a while, you may want to focus on being fresh and new and imbued with new ideas.

Insight: It is sometimes helpful to do a SWOT analysis of the competition. The exercise can point to areas where they might be vulnerable to your expertise and competence. If you want a detailed explanation of SWOT (strengths, weaknesses, threats and opportunities), look online or in business strategy books.

Assignment

Based on your research and observations about the competition, develop a matrix similar to the one that follows, to define the messages among the top competitors. You may need to create several matrices if you find that the competition is sending messages through numerous channels.

	Message 1	Message 2	Message 3
Competitor A	High emphasis	Not used	Low emphasis
Competitor B			
Competitor C			

Assignment

Based on the research you did for the executive summary, start looking at competitive brands. Identify the brands and the parent companies. Look at their marketing efforts, from video or print ads to social media postings to anything else you can find – sponsorships, billboards, celebrity endorsements and, in particular, PR output. Look for press releases and media kits.

Analyze the ones you think are the best – the most formidable competitors.

Answer these questions:

- What do they do well? What not so well?
- What is the key selling point of each brand?
- What are the PR efforts like? What kinds of tactics (such as news releases, social media, infographics and video) do they use?
- How often do they put out new information?
- Who are the apparent audiences for each brand?
- What do you think is the image each company is promoting?

Insight: From this analysis, you should be able to find gaps in coverage and discover opportunities for different messages, different media and unique approaches that are not being used by the competition.

Phase 4

Audience Identification

Audience analysis and identification are vital steps in creating a campaign or project.

Insight: After all, the whole point of the project is to encourage or entice people to change behaviors or attitudes or mindsets. Even if an organization has been in business for long time and managers believe they know their audience or audiences very well, a check can be valuable. Audiences shift; generations get replaced. New competitors arise. Many companies were caught flat-footed when the cell phone was introduced; they thought wires would last forever and so would their businesses. Same was true for digital photography.

And think of bookstores who said that Amazon would never be a problem. Or travel agents who could not have envisioned that people would be able to research and book their own trips.

One issue to think about: the new seltzer appears to be in danger of cannibalizing some of its parent company's other products; for example, it is not clear that people will drink both beer and alcoholic seltzer at one sitting or even on the same day. For this part of the exercise on hard seltzer, you should write a page or two about Distinguished Brewing Inc. Base your thinking on a major beverage company.

In that light, you should describe the characteristics of your existing customer, including their purchasing behavior – how, when and why people buy specific alcoholic drinks. And where they buy them. Based on research or personal experience, you can project when and why they purchase beverages This customer analysis should also discuss the communications now being directed at customers and potential communication avenues that are not being used.

Focus on the consumer decision-making process as it relates to your product. External information search is especially important here because this information will be used in developing the media plan.

One of the most common approaches to understanding consumer behavior is a stair-step approach where succeeding steps build on the previous ones.

As a basic example, a new product needs to be introduced to the target audience. That process is one of introduction or providing knowledge about the product or service or personality.

After research or experience would lead the communications team to believe that the product or service or personality is known by a significant portion of the key audience, more detail and other information could be provided. This might be accomplished by pitching interviews or appearances on late-night TV. For products, the phase could include sampling. For example, the product could be introduced at a music festival or coupons could be distributed to encourage consumers to try the product.

In the next phase or step up the stairs, audiences are energetically encouraged to change behavior: to buy the product or service; to purchase songs or albums by a new artist; to change brands of a product type.

Factors that affect the purchase decision – situations, pricing, ready availability of the product – should be identified as well as current trends that may have an impact. Identifying these factors will help in developing the tactical portion of the PR campaign.

You can find some of this information by visiting stores that sell products similar to the one you are promoting. And by analyzing advertising, promotions and publicly available information from the competitors you have identified. There may also be articles about new promotions or ad campaigns in marketing and advertising publications available through most college libraries. Look at *Ad Age* and *Adweek* and online at newsletters like "Marketing Daily" on the mediapost.com website. Searches like this are kind of like being a detective – or a researcher.

Also: check with research services (pew.org, Gallup, Nielsen, IRI) for articles or insights into consumer behavior.

For example, an article in the *Wall Street Journal* talks about the competition between craft beers and hard seltzers. It carries a graph and data from the research firm IRI. The full article is available online at wsj.com and downloadable from a database in most college libraries.

Figure A1.1 Hard seltzer sales
Source: IRI via *Wall Street Journal*

Ad Age published the following about a campaign by the Johannes Leonardo agency, which was assigned to handle the brand.

"There is a real truth in our message," says Boston Beer Co. Chief Marketing Officer Lesya Lysyj. "It is actually what people are saying and what they are doing; they are switching from their old drink."

Hard seltzer has emerged as the biggest alcohol category disruptor in years, stealing share from long-established brands in other categories. Hard seltzer sales in stores soared by 187 percent to nearly $900 million in the 52 weeks ending July 13, according to Nielsen, which projects alcoholic seltzer sales to eclipse the $1 billion mark by the end of 2019.

Notably, seltzers have emerged as a party go-to for young adult men, an occasion that light beer once dominated. "In some respects hard seltzers are a stake in the heart of beer," says Benj Steinman, publisher of industry trade publication *Beer Marketer's Insights*, adding that "its popularity with guys is the curveball that no one really saw coming. It's a big phenomenon."

Within that article, there were a number of interesting strings to follow as well as good sources of more information:

- The name of the ad agency
- The name and title of a company that's in the industry and has launched its own hard seltzer
- Figures from a Nielsen study
- The name and title of an executive from the trade publication *Beer Marketer's Insights*

Assignment

Based on your research and analysis of the competition, define who you think is the best audience or audiences for your company and its new product.

Who do you think they are in terms of age group, gender, household income, geographic placement and relationship status (married, single, living with someone, widowed, etc.)?

Then do some research on the company and industry. Look at sites like nielsen. com and pew.org to see if there are studies about your industry and the desires of people for your kind of products or services. Summarize your paper by comparing your impression and the results of your research. For most industries, there are associations and specialized publications that collect information that can be valuable in planning a campaign.

For example, in the beverage business, there is an association called the Brewers Association. And there are publications like the *Beverage Journal* and *Beer Marketer's Insights*. You should search for others, as well as blogs, podcasts and general news stories in the business press.

The federal government has data on most industries and segments. You can find information about companies on their websites and on sites like marketwatch.com, cnbc.com or motleyfool.com.

Phase 5

Competitive Analysis

The competitive analysis defines the environment where the PR project will be launched. In other words, what factors and competitive products or company will the product and the PR campaign face? What are the major competitors, based on industry analysis of cases sold or dollars earned?

You should also look at the communications of the competition. Review its website and social media sites. Make sure to read the news releases and other announcements. You may also want to take a look at its annual report. It may contain valuable information about upcoming plans for the company. Collect any ads or videos or other materials (including packaging) from the competition to understand where your client's products may fit and to make sure that you are not repeating or coming close to duplicating selling points or language.

Understanding the competitive marketplace will help you define and focus your messaging as well as presentation values, from colors and typefaces to descriptive language. You don't want your product to be known as a follower. Perhaps, we can write. We don't want the product to get lost in media clutter.

You will want to explore these questions or others you think of:

- How do you describe the environment in which this program is being launched? Will you meet a particular need or respond to an event? Does current research show a decline or weakness in competitive positioning?
- Are there current issues, social or technical or consumer, that need to be addressed?
- Can you think of a new threat or opportunity that it might be facing, based on industry trends or news about other companies in the industry?

Insight: Such indicators might be, but are not limited to, financial growth, number of customers, market share, innovativeness.

When Netflix was just barely founded, the executives went to see the chief executive of Blockbuster Video – a nationwide chain of stores that rented video tapes – looking to be bought. Blockbuster said, "No, thanks." Five years later, Blockbuster was out of business and Netflix was on the way to being a huge success. It was known as a disruptor company that didn't play by the rules Blockbuster and cable networks were following.

Assignment

For the seltzer product, try to find current ads and news releases about other competing products. After gathering as many as you can find, analyze them. Create a report for a potential client about what you find and how your client might create images, language and messages that work in areas not covered by the competition or that appeal to audiences in different ways. By way of example, a competitor may focus on sporting events. Your client may decide to focus on music festivals or events like Fourth of July parades. Be sure to look at the media used by the competition and seek areas not being occupied or where you can make a splash. Your report should include **charts that demonstrate the data you have gathered and should use very specific language and graphics to define the competition**.

Phase 6

Opportunity Analysis

Based on the competitive analysis, discuss what opportunities exist in your market or the environment in which your company is operating. Part of this opportunity analysis is examining the attractive factors that represent the reason for your business. These opportunities should reflect the potential you can realize in the marketplace through implementing this communication strategy you are developing.

Opportunities may be the result of market growth, lifestyle changes, solving specific customer problems, positive market perceptions about your business or your company's ability to offer greater value that will create a demand for your products.

Look at what industry experts and consultants are saying about the industry and primary companies.

To find data on your company and its competitors, look at sites like these:

http://hoovers.com

http://fortune.com

http://cnbc.com

And search through the library databases for industry magazines like *Aviation Week* or *Beverage Digest* or *Progressive Grocer*. They provide industry overviews and environmental analyses.

Assignment

Based on your searches and online material, develop an annotated outline for finding audience information. Describe the demographic information you encounter and any studies that have discovered information on the attitudes, purchase decision bases, demographic categories and information on specific products linked to demographic groups. Explain how the information may help you define messages and channels for the campaign you are developing. Keep in mind specifics that can inform message language and positioning.

Phase 7

Finalizing the Public Relations Strategy

This is where all of the previous work comes together. And where you show off your strategic public relations skills and thinking.

First, define the goals of the PR strategy. It can be as simple as increasing visibility for the brand by increasing publicity and other observable actions. The goals may be accomplished through various PR tactics, including press releases, interviews with executives, establishing a vibrant social media presence or any of the tactics in your text that your research has shown would be valuable and competitively astute and effective.

It can have multiple dimensions and be spread over many months.

You will need to give consideration to how to maintain a good image in your community and with your various publics.

- How will you generate positive publicity about your company and products?
- How will you approach your various audiences? What media and messages?

- How will you distinguish your company from its competition?
- How will you measure your current image and any changes that occur during the period of the campaign? If we talk about measurement, we need to explain how to do that.

Assignments

Part 1

Develop a plan that contains messages for each segment of the audience and includes specific taglines (identifying slogans like Nike's "Just Do It") and key phrases for the entire campaign. All messages should fit within the corporate image that you have created and in the branding approach you have defined.

Part 2

Choose the media you will use for each audience. There may be overlap – social media may work for multiple segments but print news stories may reach only certain demographic groups.

Part 3

Create a first flight of messages for each audience and each medium. Write them so they are consistent and support the overall branding and image of the company and the product but are tailored for each audience as much as possible.

Phase 8

Evaluation

Measuring the effectiveness of a PR campaign is not easy, but spending a large amount of time and resources on a campaign without trying to determine its effectiveness does not make sense. In this section, discuss the following questions and any others you can think of:

- How you will evaluate the overall effectiveness of the campaign? Be as specific as possible, whether you will employ quantitative or qualitative tools and what kinds of questions you may ask to obtain valuable, useable information.
- In general, quantitative tools are ones that result in numerical responses such as the level of interest in a topic – answers that range from very positive to very negative and are given different values. Those values are then tabulated and statistically compared.
- Qualitative tools ask more contextual questions to provide answers that are more impressionistic than surveys provide. Each has its place, depending on situations, time available and budget, among other factors.

- On what levels will you evaluate effectiveness: short term, long term, product specific or brand specific?
- It is important to remember that evaluation is directly related to the objectives and goals of your PR campaign. In other words, be sure to ask specific questions related to messages expected to be in the campaign or that have been used.

Assignment

Develop a three- to four-page measurement plan that will describe what information you will seek and from what audience segments. Be sure to include channels, any season implications, keywords and links to the brand of the sponsor company. Write a set of questions that could be used in a survey or in focus groups where you will have people sample the product and view early drafts of messages and graphics.

Phase 9

Creating the Campaign

To finalize the project, create tactics that will use the insights and materials you have developed and created so far.

Deliverables can include:

- A series of tweets that carry the key messages and are aimed at specific audience segments. Write them to be played out over time, perhaps one a week for three months.
- Press releases about the product focusing on specific topics, from the flavor to the places it will be sold to what promotions are planned. Create quotes from influencers who might convince consumers to purchase the product. Talk about ingredients and any socially aware ideas such as sourcing, low-carbon-emissions manufacturing.
- Establish a blog for the product and plan the topics which will be covered. Each edition need not be long, but should be newsworthy and interesting.
- Plan a media website where fact sheets, graphics, corporate bios, corporate history and other materials can reside and where they will be available to the press at any time.

GLOSSARY

A

Advertorial – an article, website page, or video programming that is designed to look and read like objective journalistic content but is, in fact, a paid advertisement.

B

B-roll video – supplemental video that is supplied to give options to journalists or other gatekeepers who want to create their own production of a news item or background piece. B-roll can contain establishing video of facilities or common elements from a company or organization as well as video of executives. For example, an auto company might include video of workers on production lines as well as new models of its car.

Blogs – take many forms. In general they are conversations or informational websites created, posted and established on the internet on routine schedules. The tone can range from very serious to humorous. Originally started as online diary-like reflective writing, blogs have changed and expanded in type, topic and importance. Organizations use them to put out information quickly and in their own formats and language. Entries typically show with newest on top.

C

Call to Action – a statement designed to get an immediate response from the person reading or hearing it.

Click-through – the action or facility of following a hypertext link to a particular website.

I

Infographic – graphical display of information that helps the viewer to comprehend a situation or process or provides insight into the workings of a company activity or event. When done well and addressing the needs and knowledge of the chosen audience an infographic can convey complicated information in a simple, engaging and even striking way.

J

Jargon – a technical word or phrase that is used or understood by a specific industry.

M

Media Gatekeepers – the people who decide what information is used or not used in their news outlets.

N

News Hook – newsworthy information presented with the goal of capturing the attention and interest of both the news media and their audiences.

Newsletters – have a long history of production by organizations of all types, from clubs to large, commercial enterprises. They range in production value from copier versions of computer documents to highly designed and professionally printed editions rivaling magazines or catalogs. The concept of collected news articles and informational notices has transitioned from print to online, with organizations both distributing newsletters digitally and making them available for download on websites.

News Release – an official written statement provided to newspapers, magazines, television news programs, online media and radio stations

O

Op-eds – opinion or expert writings that appear in publications or online near the editorial opinion section or site of a news organization. Op-eds originated opposite the editorial page of major newspapers, but have some to mean a wide variety of articles, from responses to a news organization's published opinions to more academic articles that explain and illuminate topics that range from financial to technical to social issues.

S

SMART – acronym of PR planning that stands for Specific, Measurable, Attainable, Relevant and Time-Bound audiences.

Stakeholders – people or organizations that have an interest or responsibility in dealing with an organization. Examples include shareholders of public companies, employees of organizations of all types; government agencies that regulate or oversee operations of organizations, and many other types of people and organizations, depending on the activities and goals of the organization.

T

Talking points – key messages that need to be the focus of a presentation. They should emphasize the strategy of the public relations activity. May include press discussions, speeches or employee meetings.

TED Talks – punchy, concise talks, no more than 18 minutes and focused on a single topic. TED stands for technology, entertainment and design, but the talks have evolved to cover virtually any topic in the human imagination.

Thought leaders – can be an important target audience. The authors of this textbook define thought leaders as the people who have the power and influence to change the opinions of others.

U

User generated content – digital communications such as video which is generated by the end user or an internal company facility. Compare to tactics created by professional production companies hired for specific projects.

V

Vlogs – are short for video blog or video log. They are essentially blogs but done using video, taking advantage of less expensive and accessible video capture and editing tools that have become common. In addition video distribution has become very inexpensive, making YouTube a highly valued platform for vlogs. Vlogs may be enhanced with other forms of digital content, from video links to graphics and interactive images.

VNRs – video news release. Either a release completely on video (usually accompanied by B-roll footage) or a video produced as part of a news release package.

W

Writing style guide – a set of standardized writing practices required for a project, brand, industry, or field of study

INDEX